ATLANTIC OCEAN, 1770

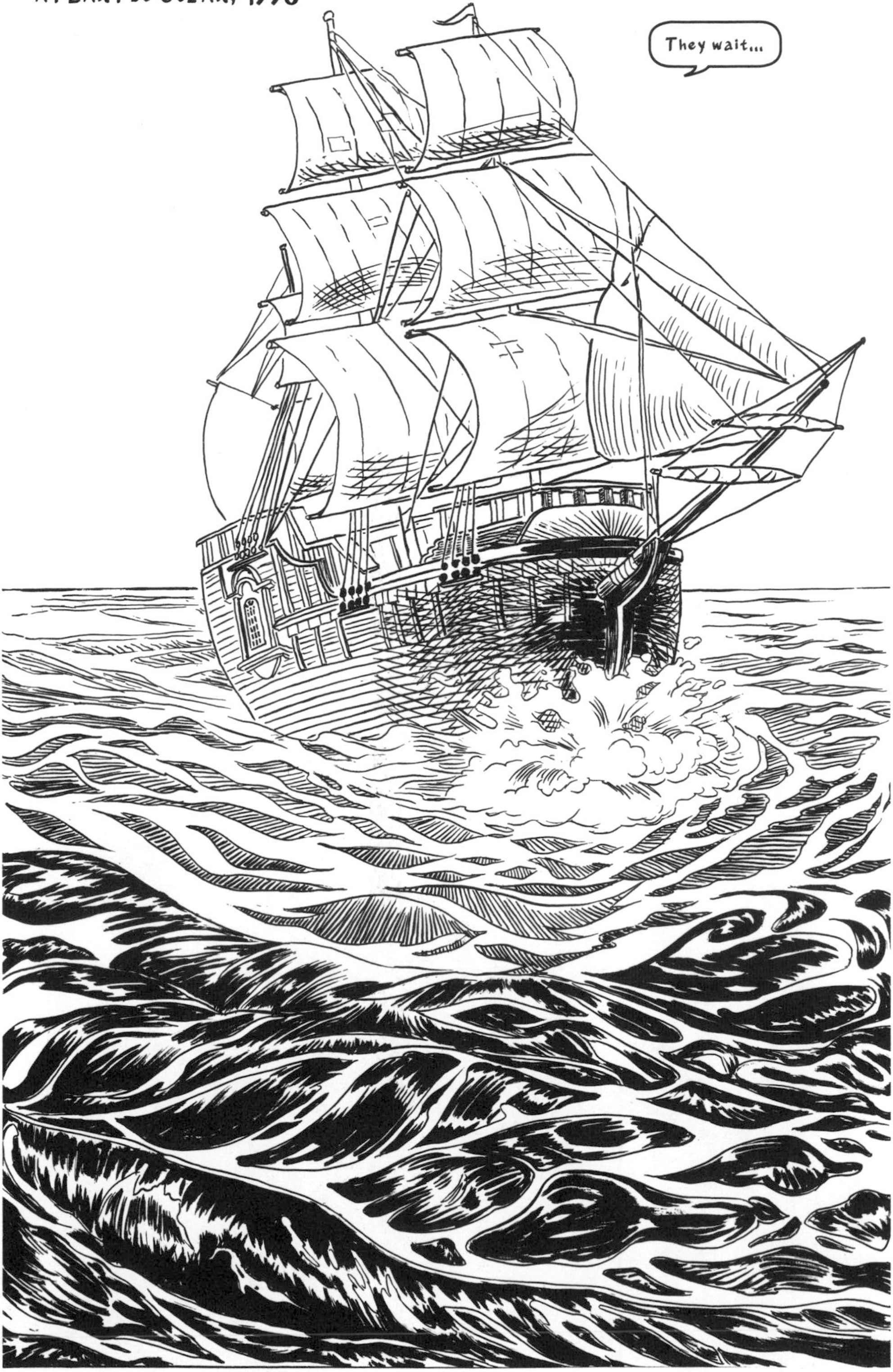
They wait...

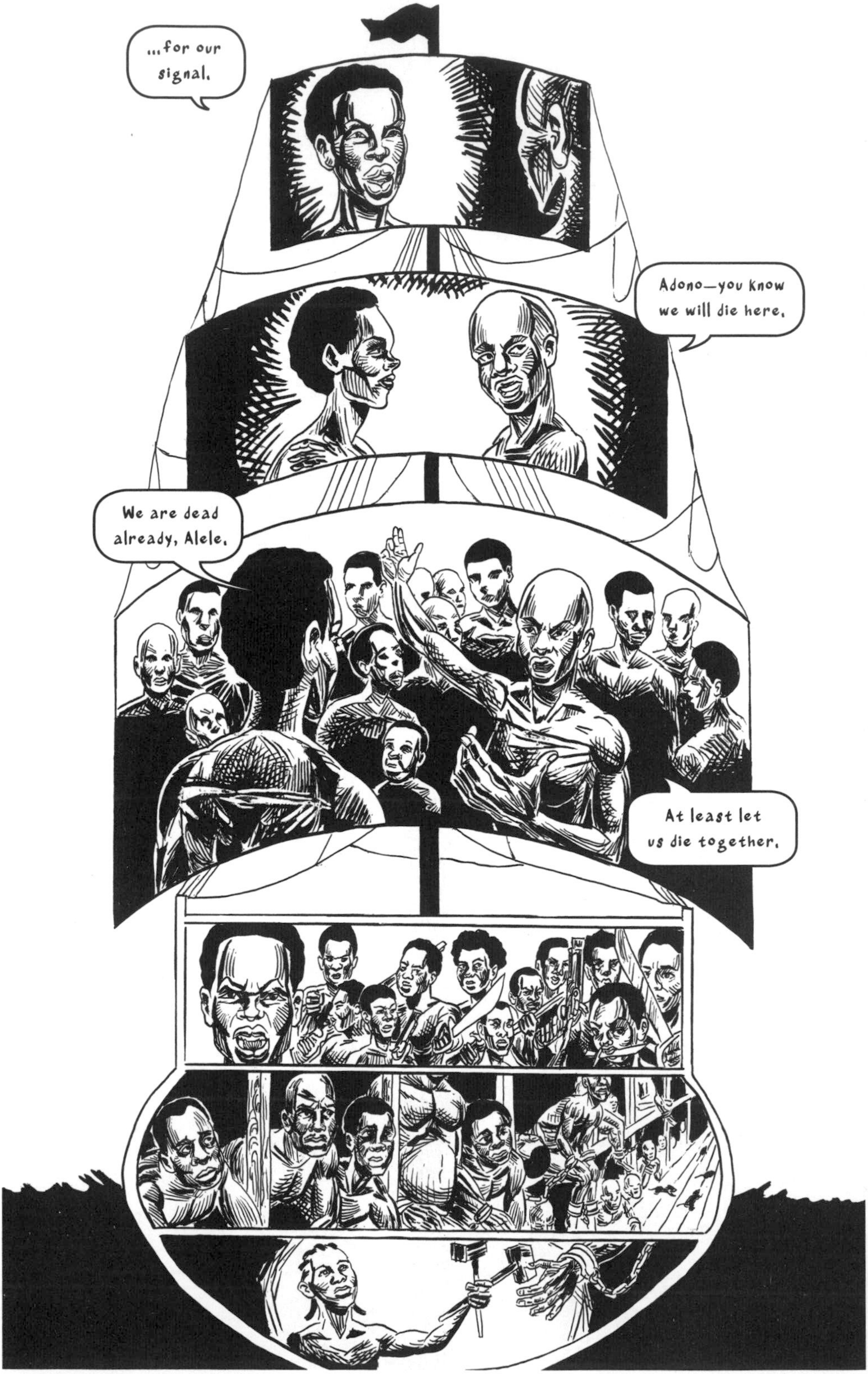
...for our signal.
Adono—you know we will die here.
We are dead already, Alele.
At least let us die together.

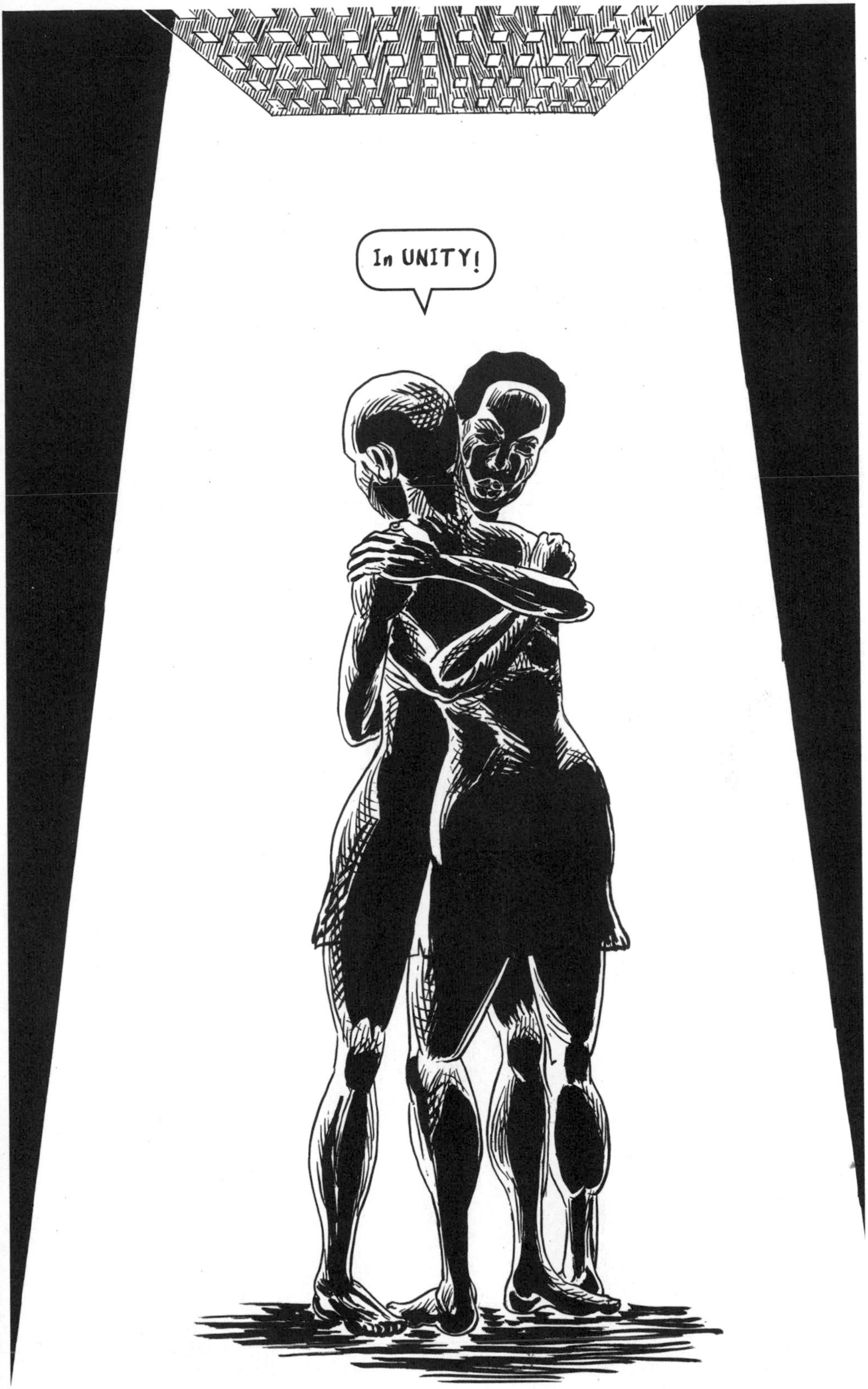
In UNITY!

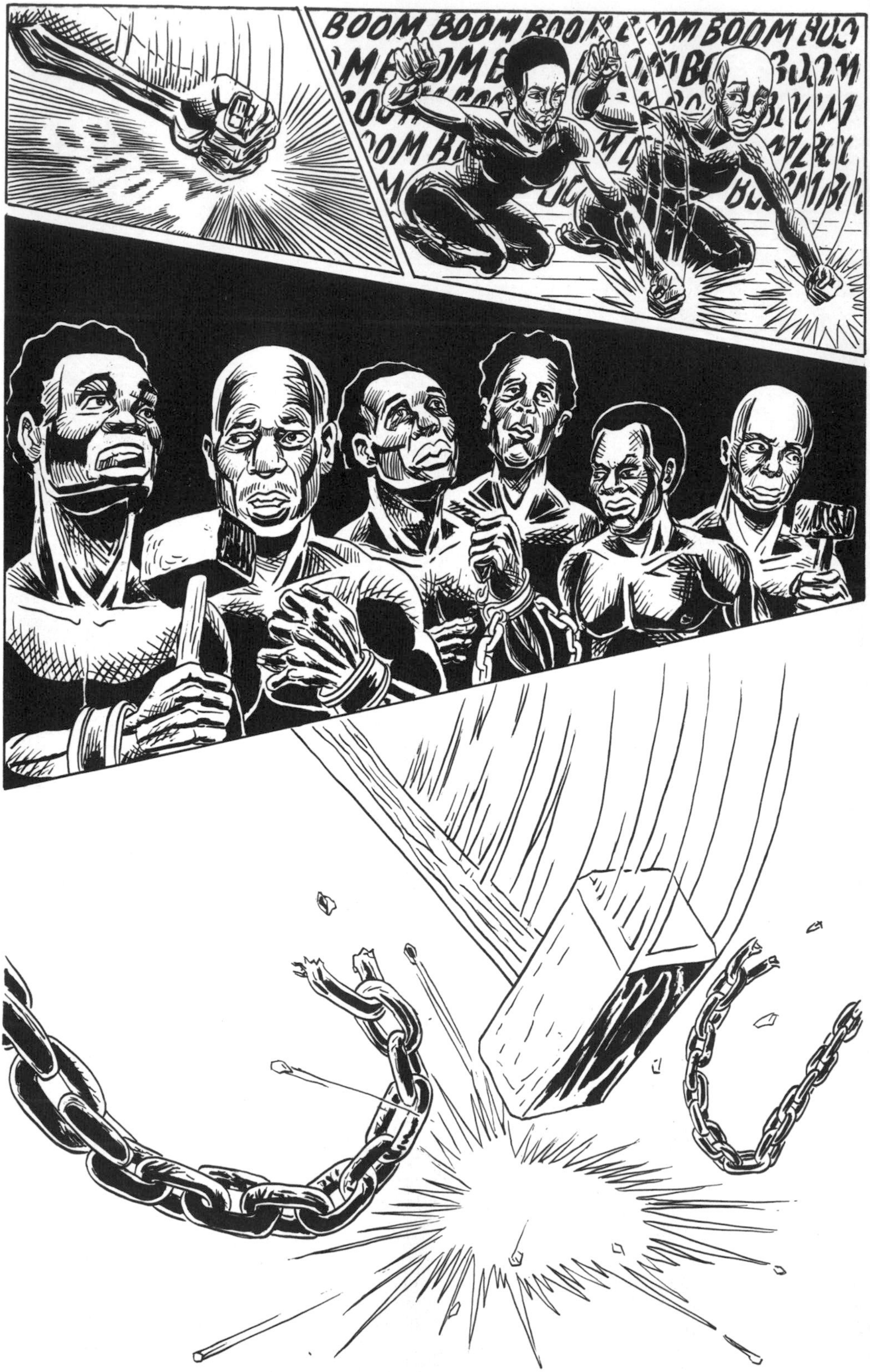
BOOM BOOM BOOM BOOM BOOM

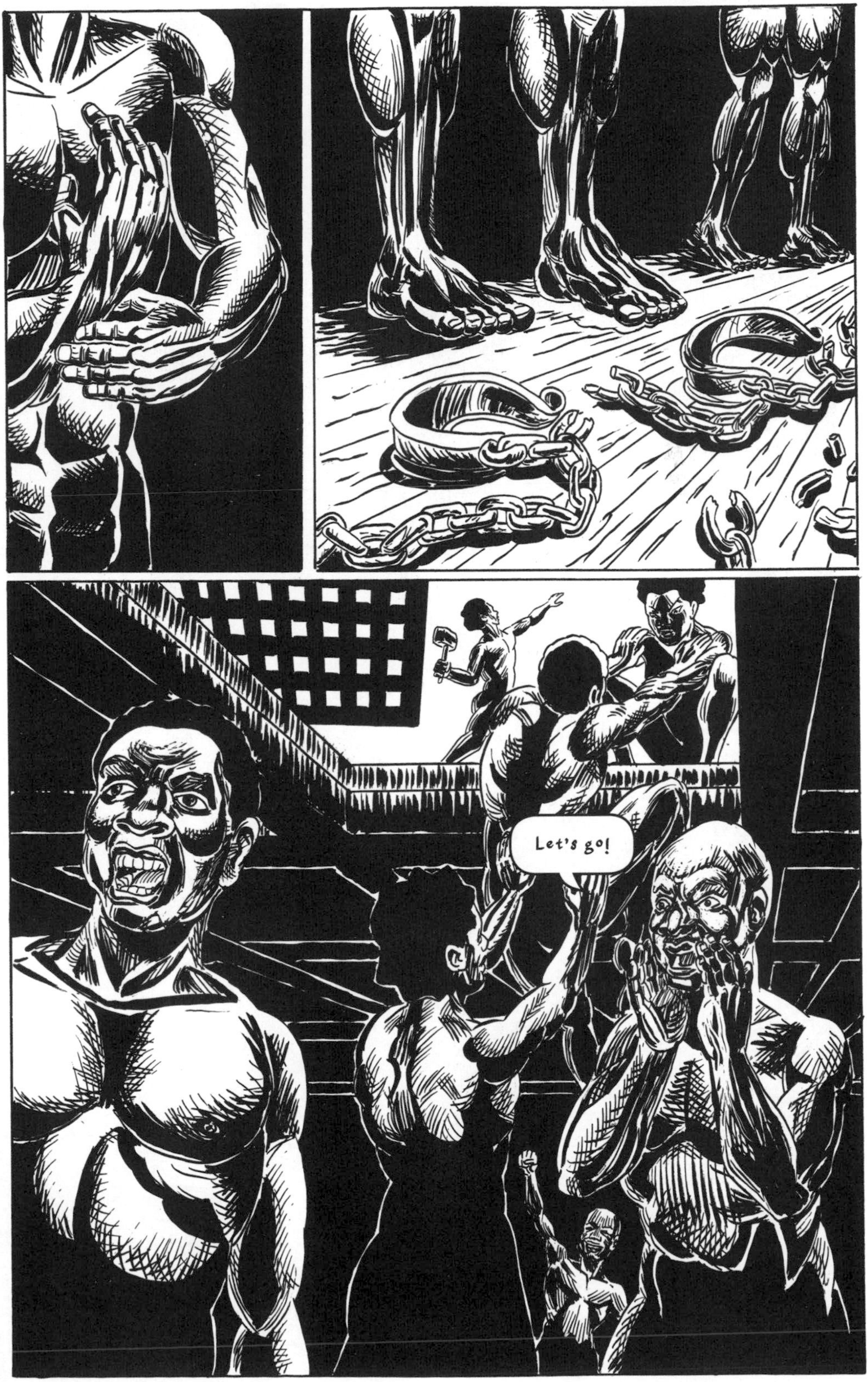
Let's go!

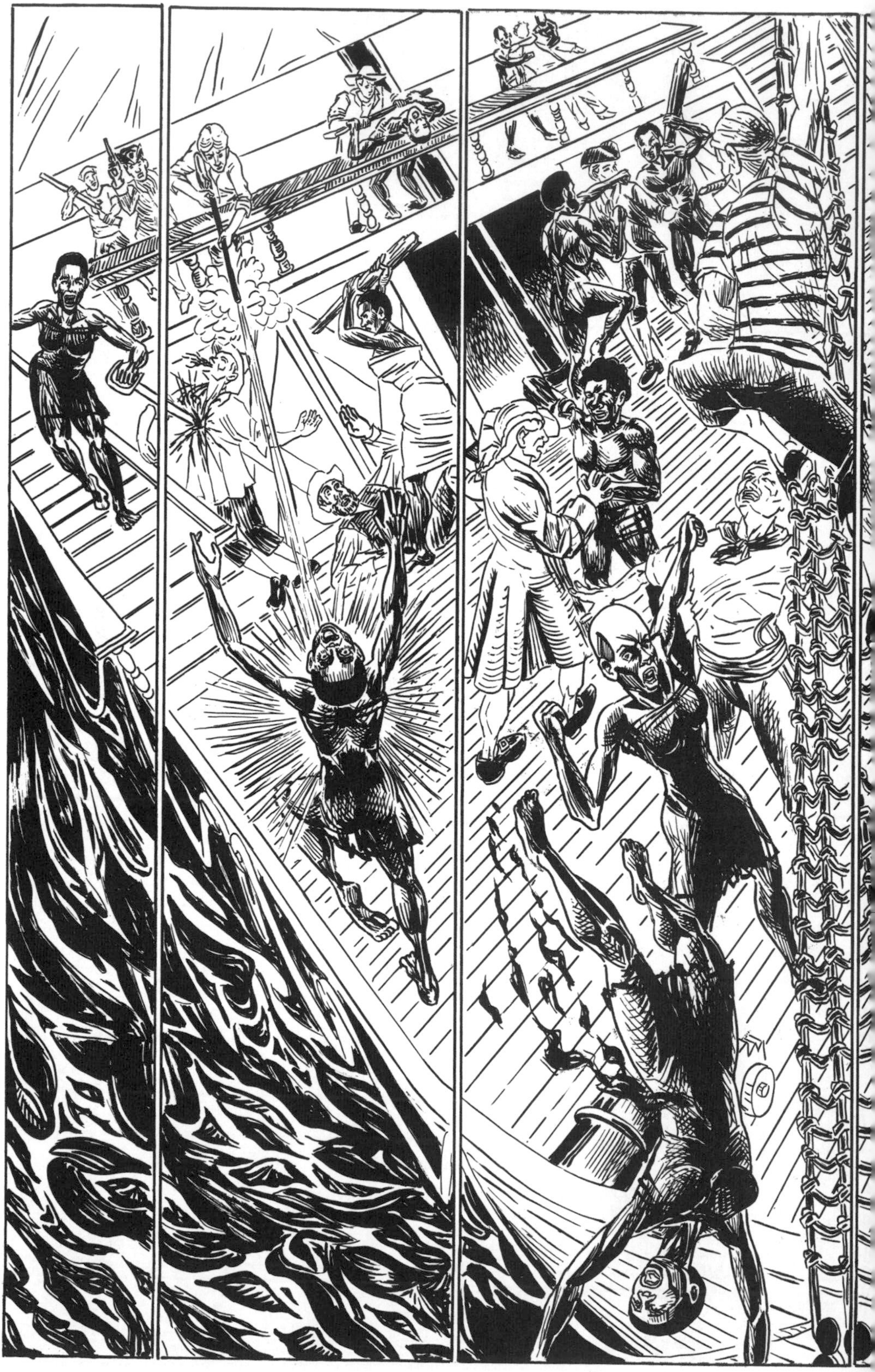

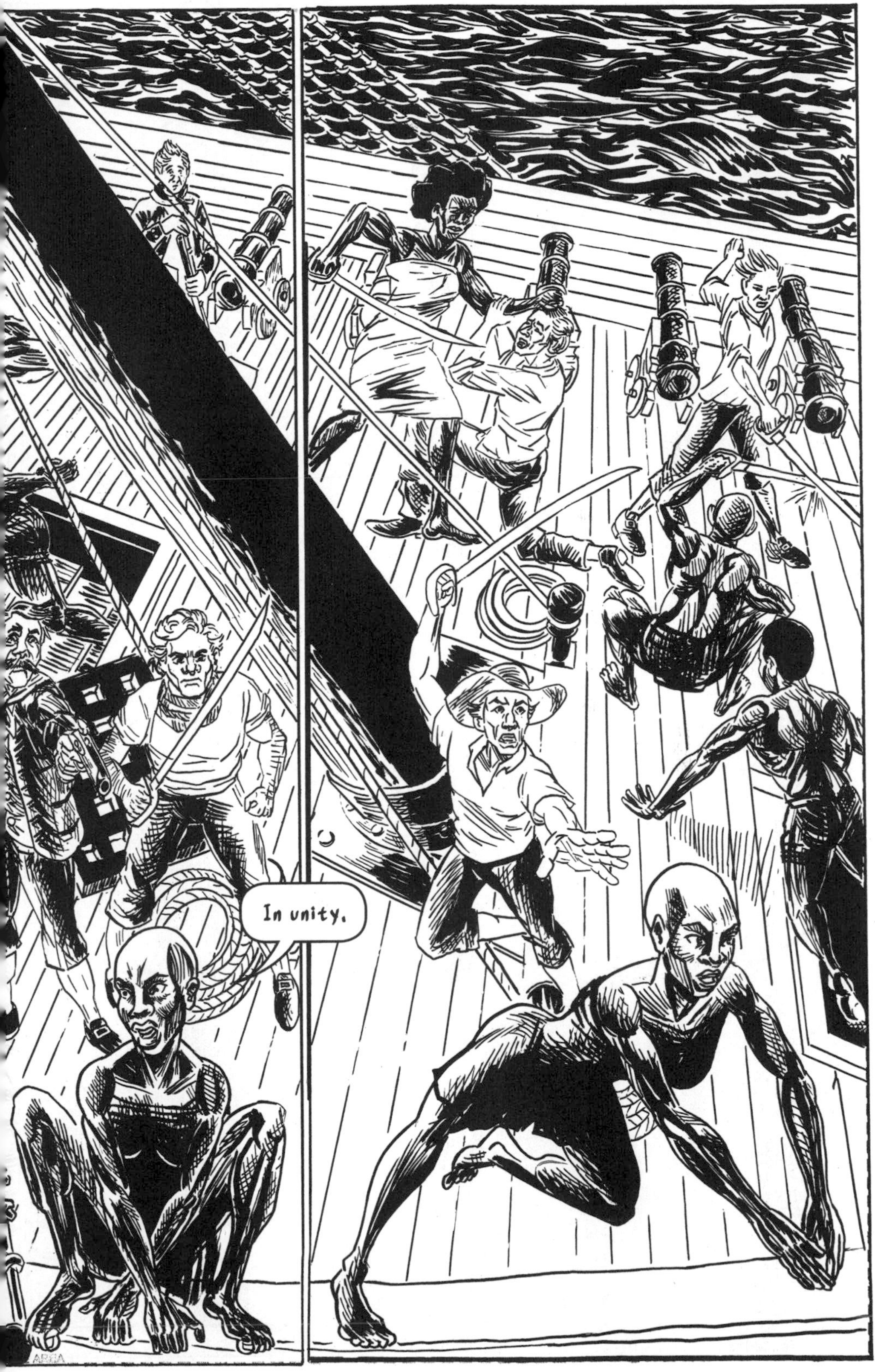
In unity.

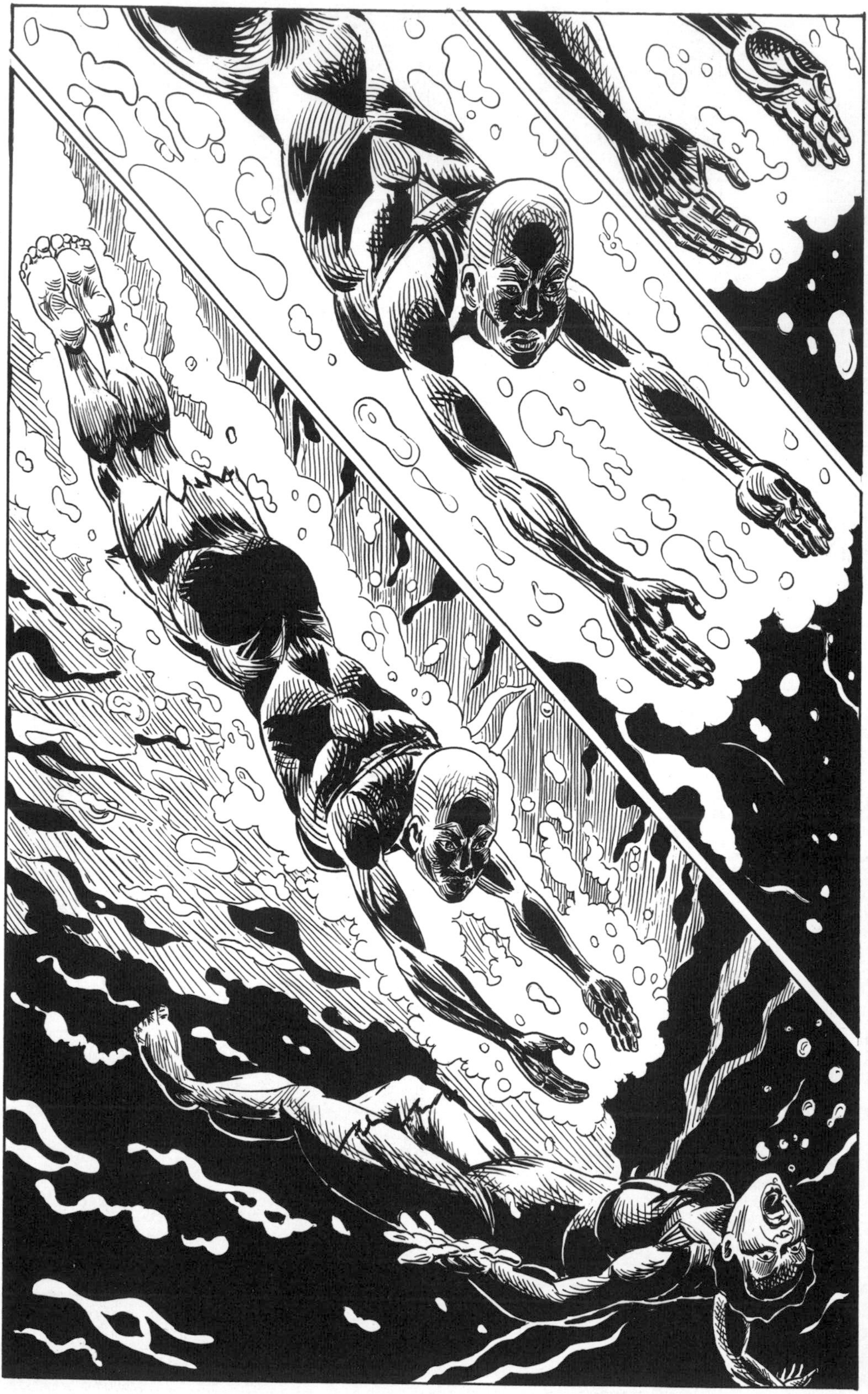

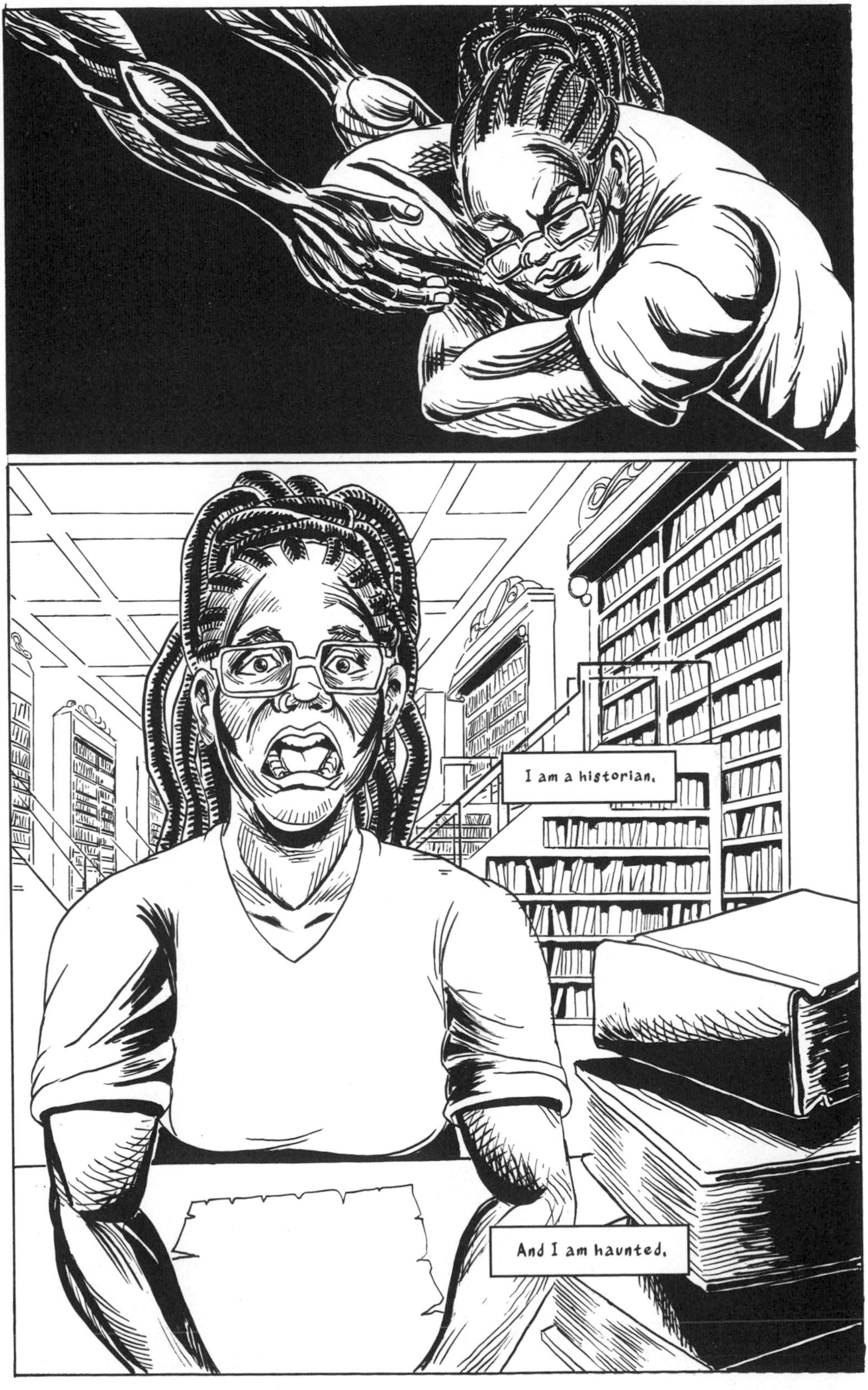
I am a historian.
And I am haunted.

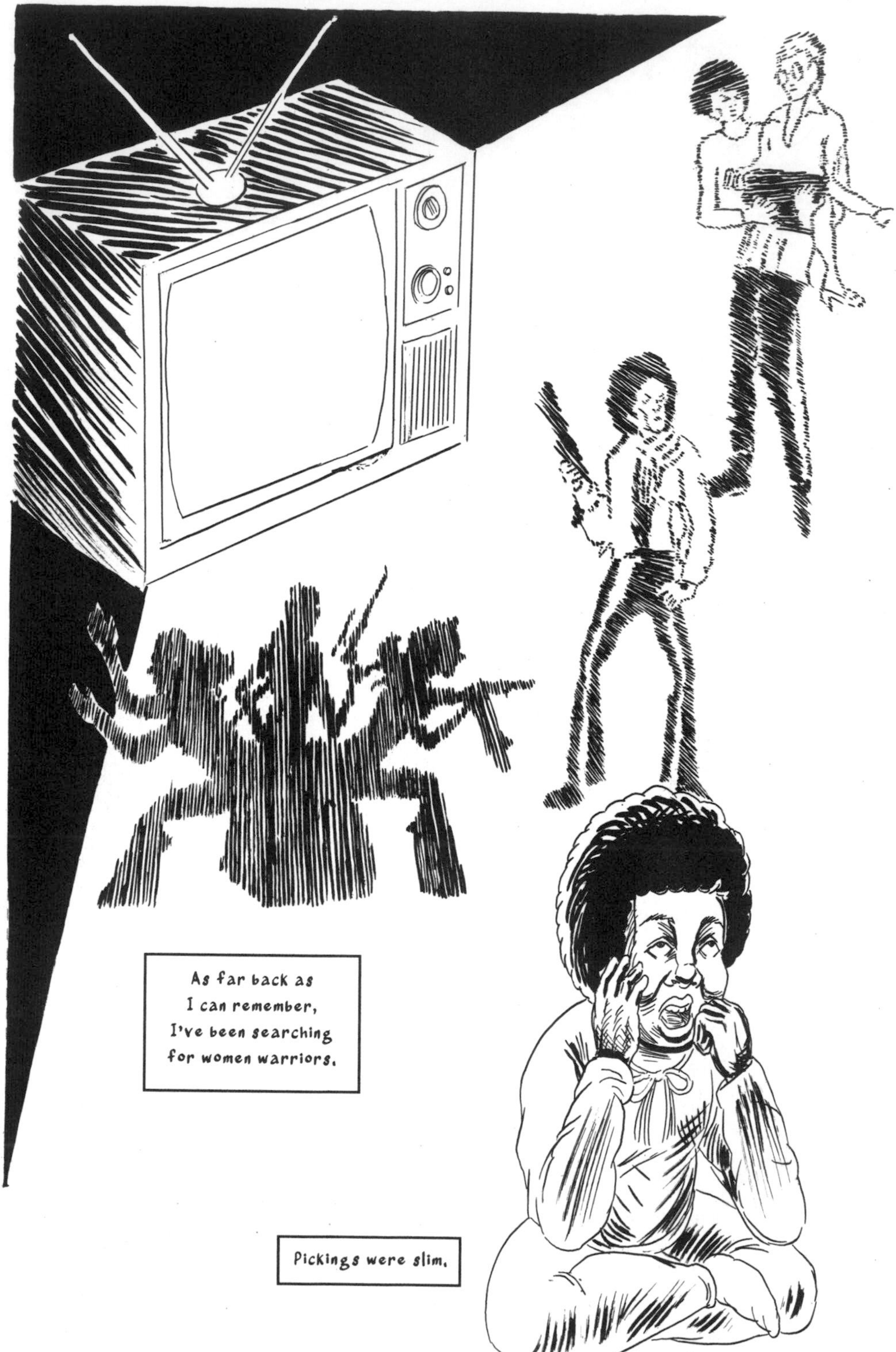
As far back as
I can remember,
I've been searching
for women warriors.
Pickings were slim.

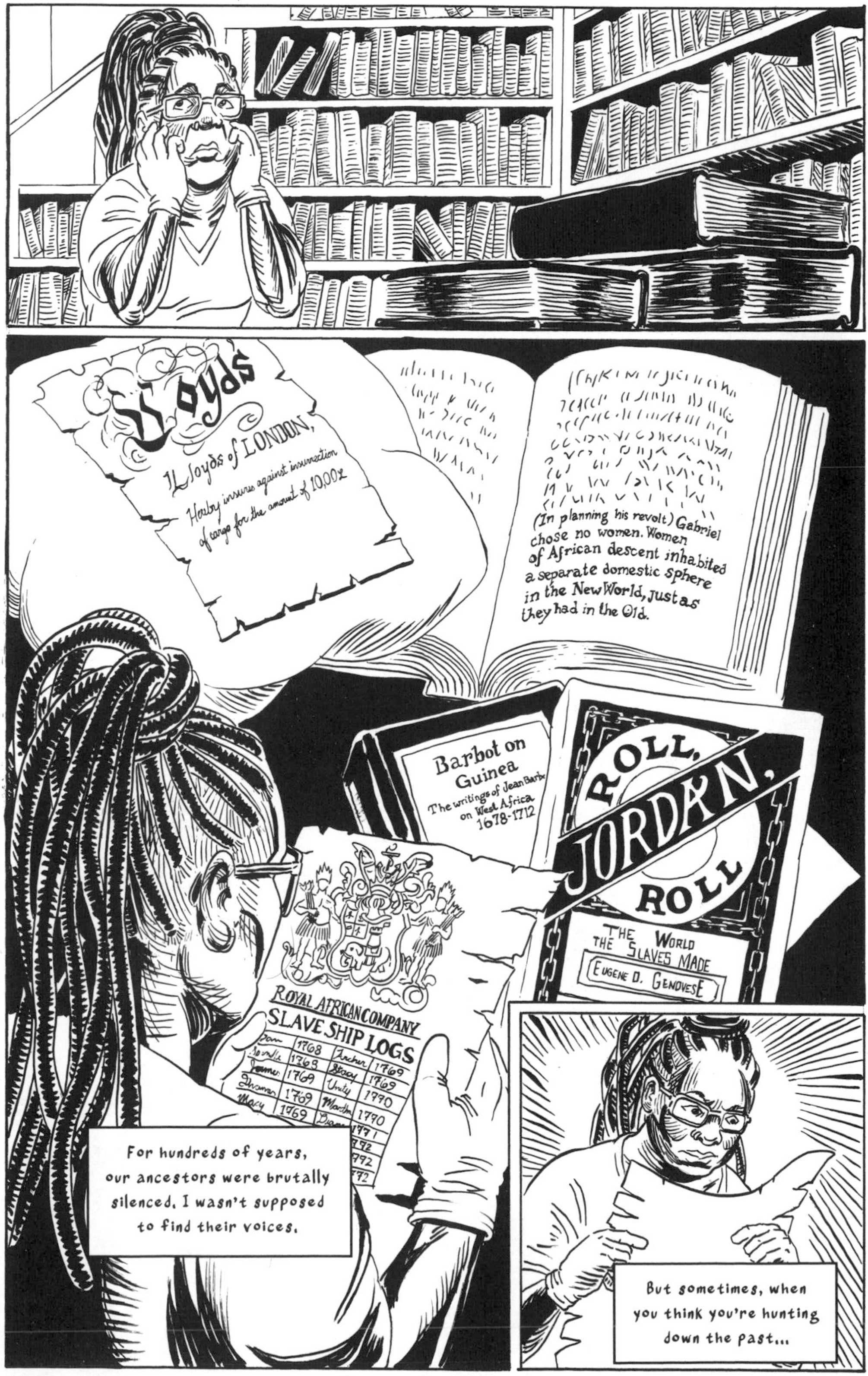
Lloyds
Lloyds of LONDON,
Hereby insures against insurrection of cargo for the amount of 10,00£
(In planning his revolt) Gabriel chose no women. Women of African descent inhabited a separate domestic sphere in the New World, just as they had in the Old.
Barbot on Guinea
The writings of Jean Barb
on West Africa
1678-1712
ROLL, JORDAN, ROLL
THE WORLD THE SLAVES MADE
EUGENE D. GENOVESE
ROYAL AFRICAN COMPANY
SLAVE SHIP LOGS
For hundreds of years, our ancestors were brutally silenced. I wasn't supposed to find their voices.
But sometimes, when you think you're hunting down the past...

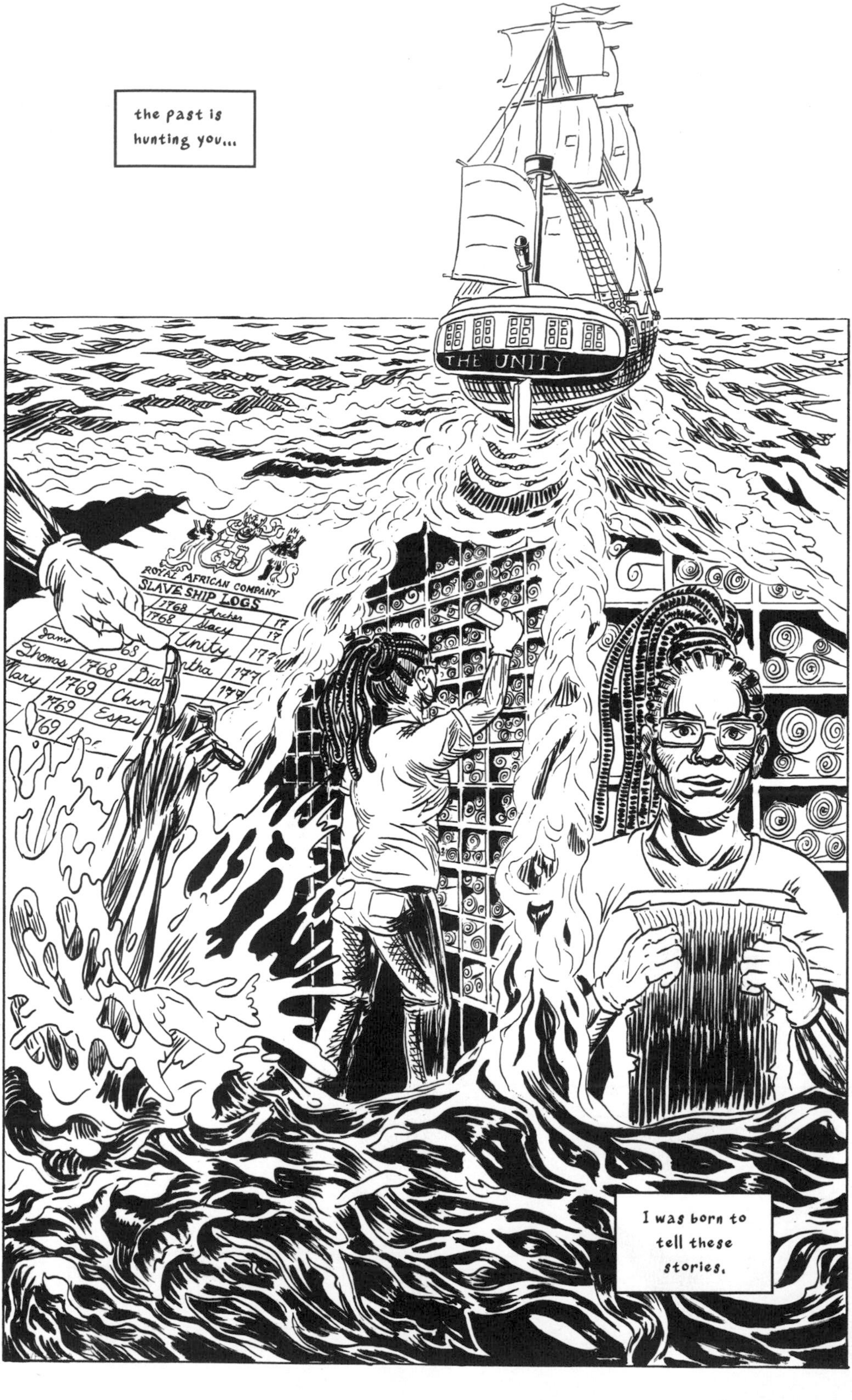

the past is hunting you...
THE UNITY
ROYAL AFRICAN COMPANY
SLAVE SHIP LOGS
I was born to tell these stories.

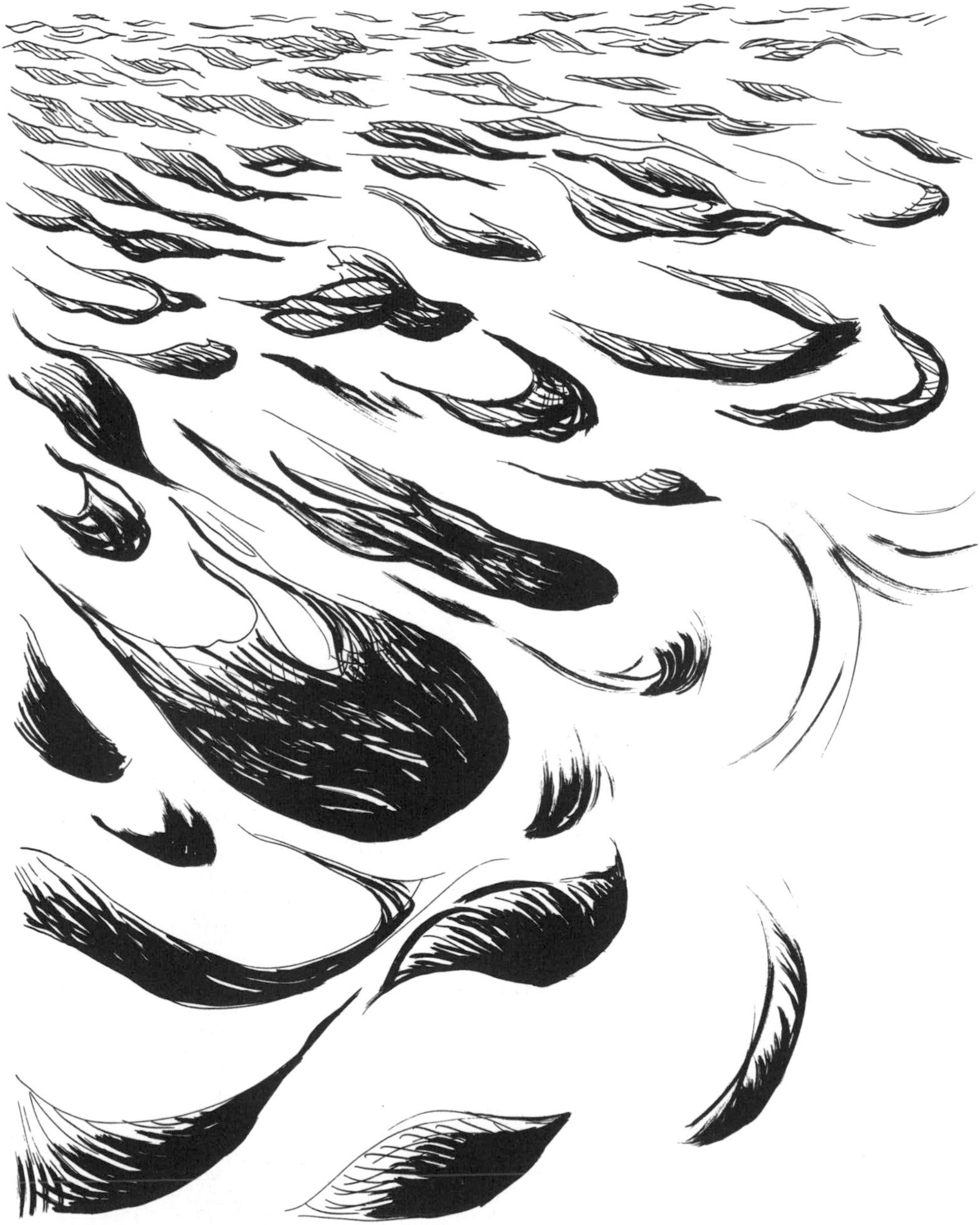

WAKE

The Hidden History of Women-Led Slave Revolts

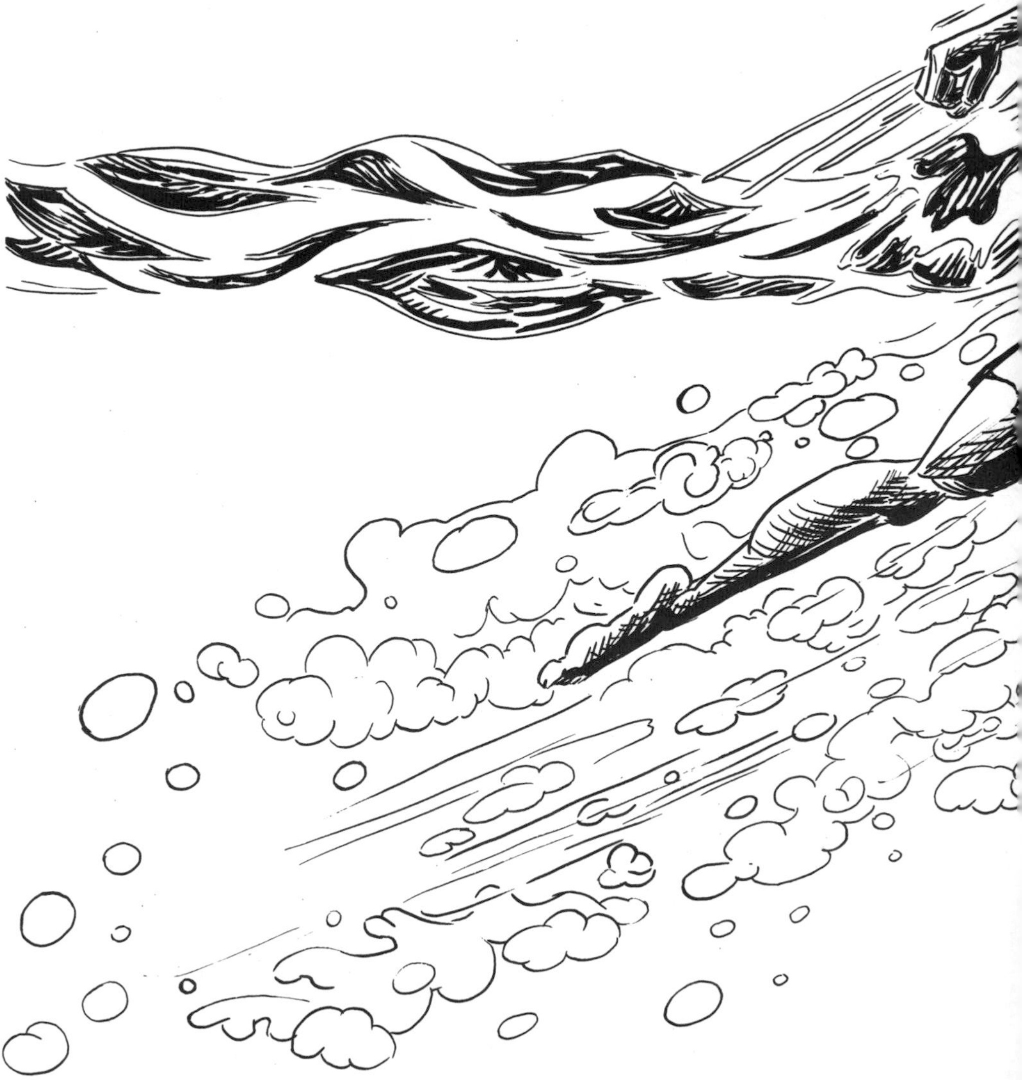

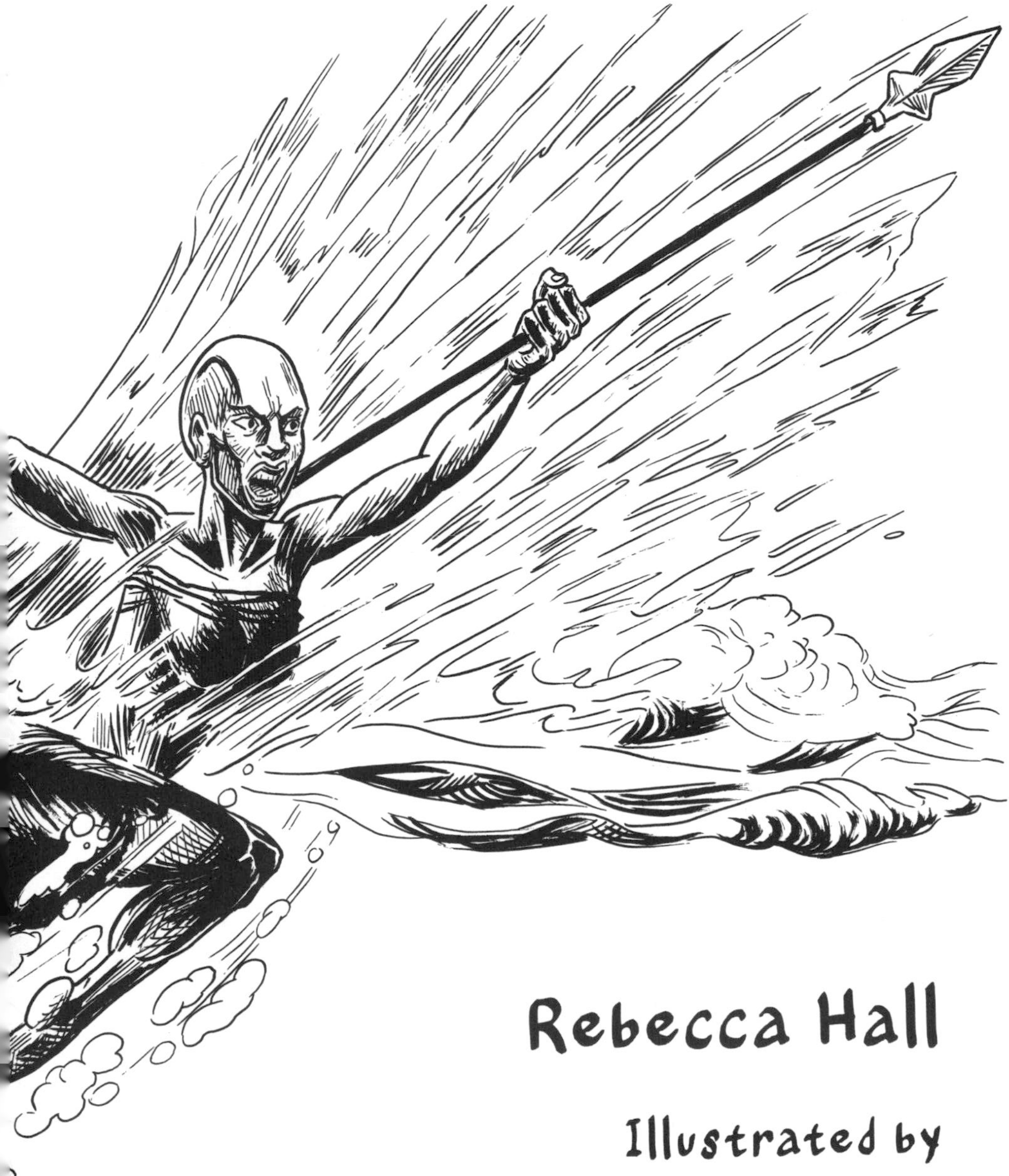

Rebecca Hall

Illustrated by
Hugo Martínez

Lettered by Sarula Bao

Simon & Schuster
NEW YORK LONDON TORONTO SYDNEY NEW DELHI

Simon & Schuster
1230 Avenue of the Americas
New York, NY 10020

First Simon & Schuster hardcover edition June 2021

SIMON & SCHUSTER and colophon are trademarks
of Simon & Schuster, Inc.

For information about special discounts for bulk purchases,
please contact Simon & Schuster Special Sales at 1-866-506-1949
or business@simonandschuster.com.

The Simon & Schuster Speakers Bureau can bring authors to your
live event. For more information or to book an event, contact the
Simon & Schuster Speakers Bureau at 1-866-248-3049
or visit our website at www.simonspeakers.com.

Manufactured in the United States of America

10 9 8 7 6 5 4 3 2 1

Library of Congress Cataloging-in-Publication Data has been applied for.

ISBN 978-1-9821-1518-0
ISBN 978-1-9821-1520-3 (ebook)

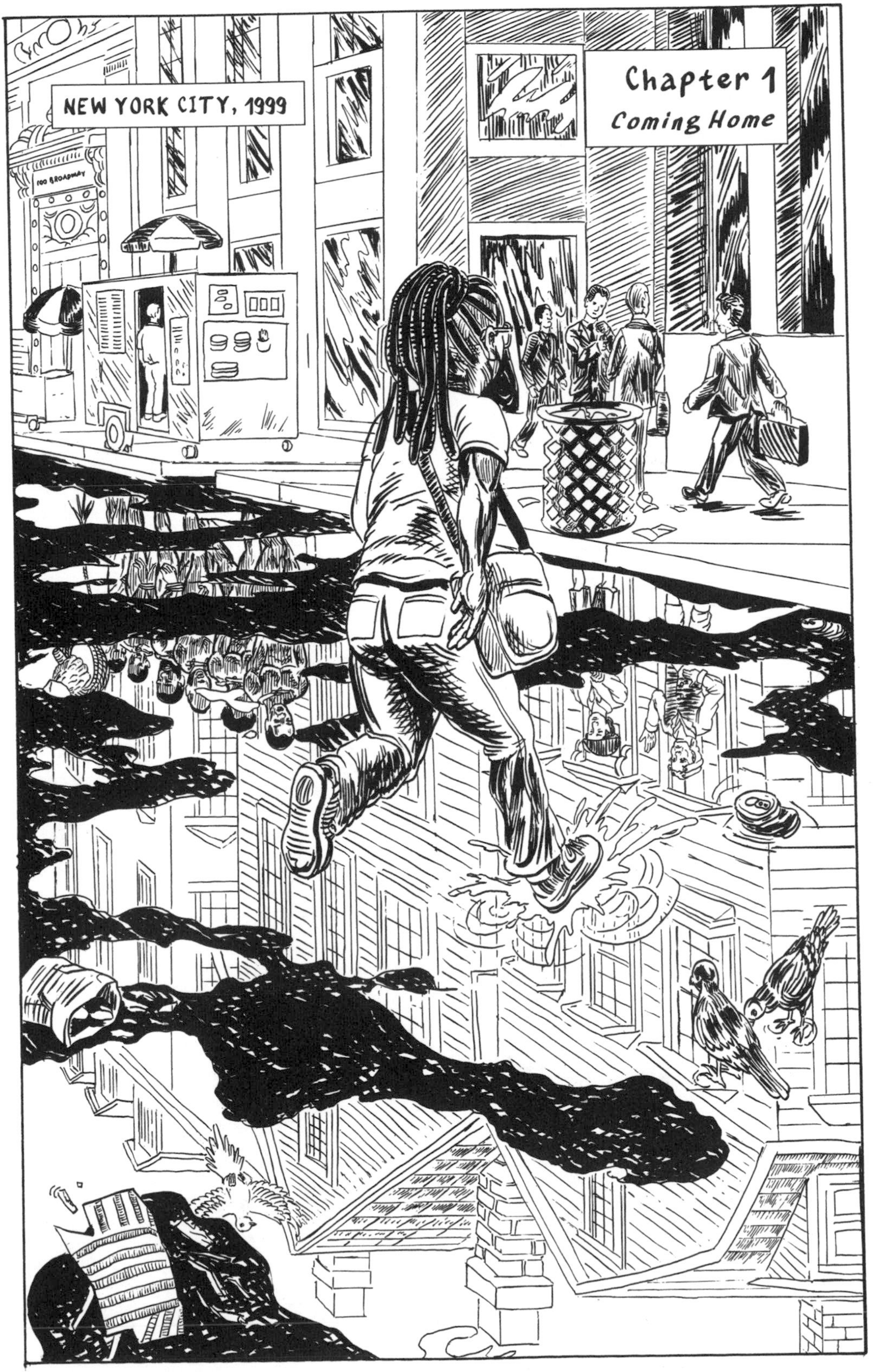
NEW YORK CITY, 1999
Chapter 1
Coming Home
100 BROADWAY

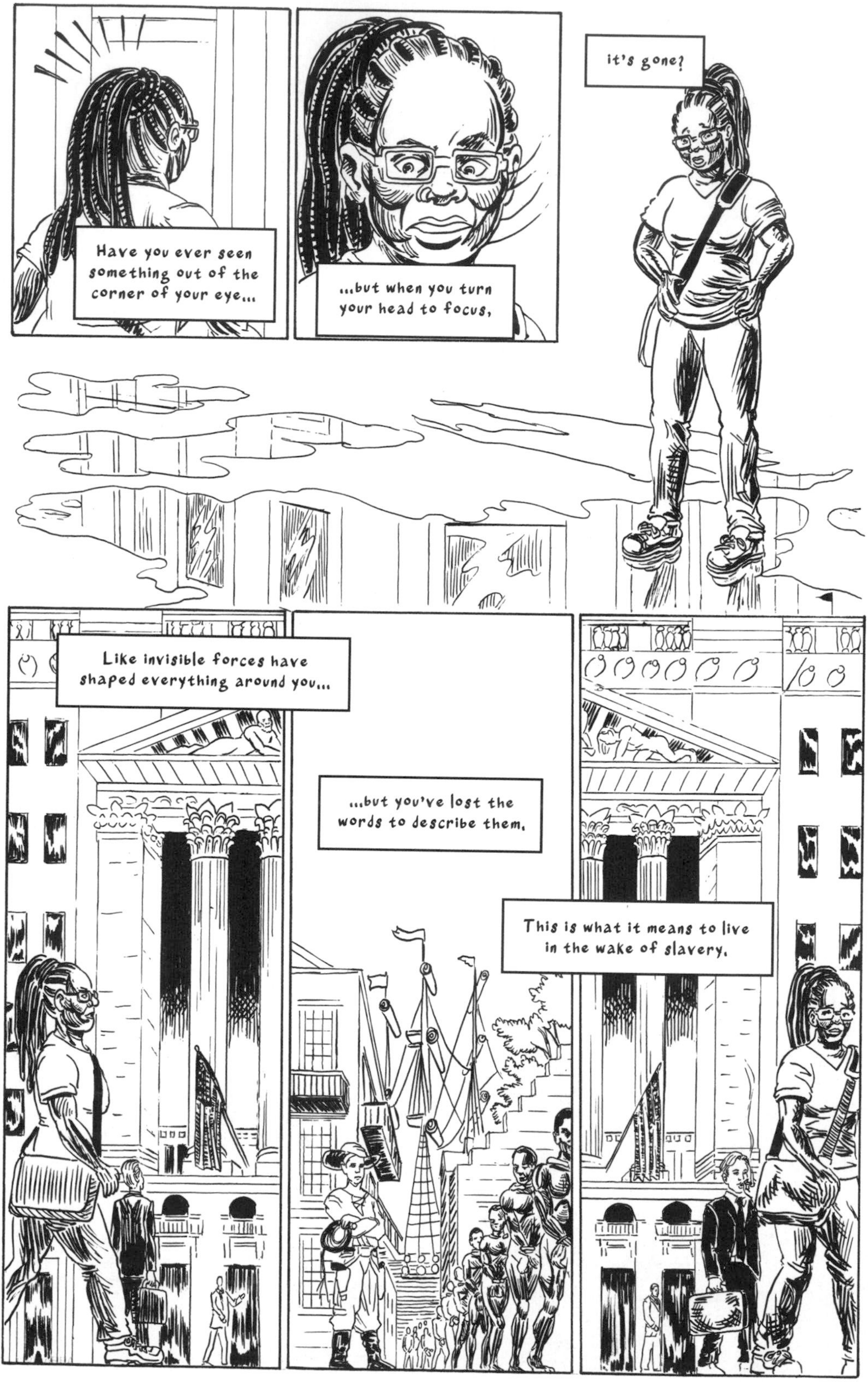
Have you ever seen something out of the corner of your eye...
...but when you turn your head to focus,
it's gone?
Like invisible forces have shaped everything around you...
...but you've lost the words to describe them.
This is what it means to live in the wake of slavery.

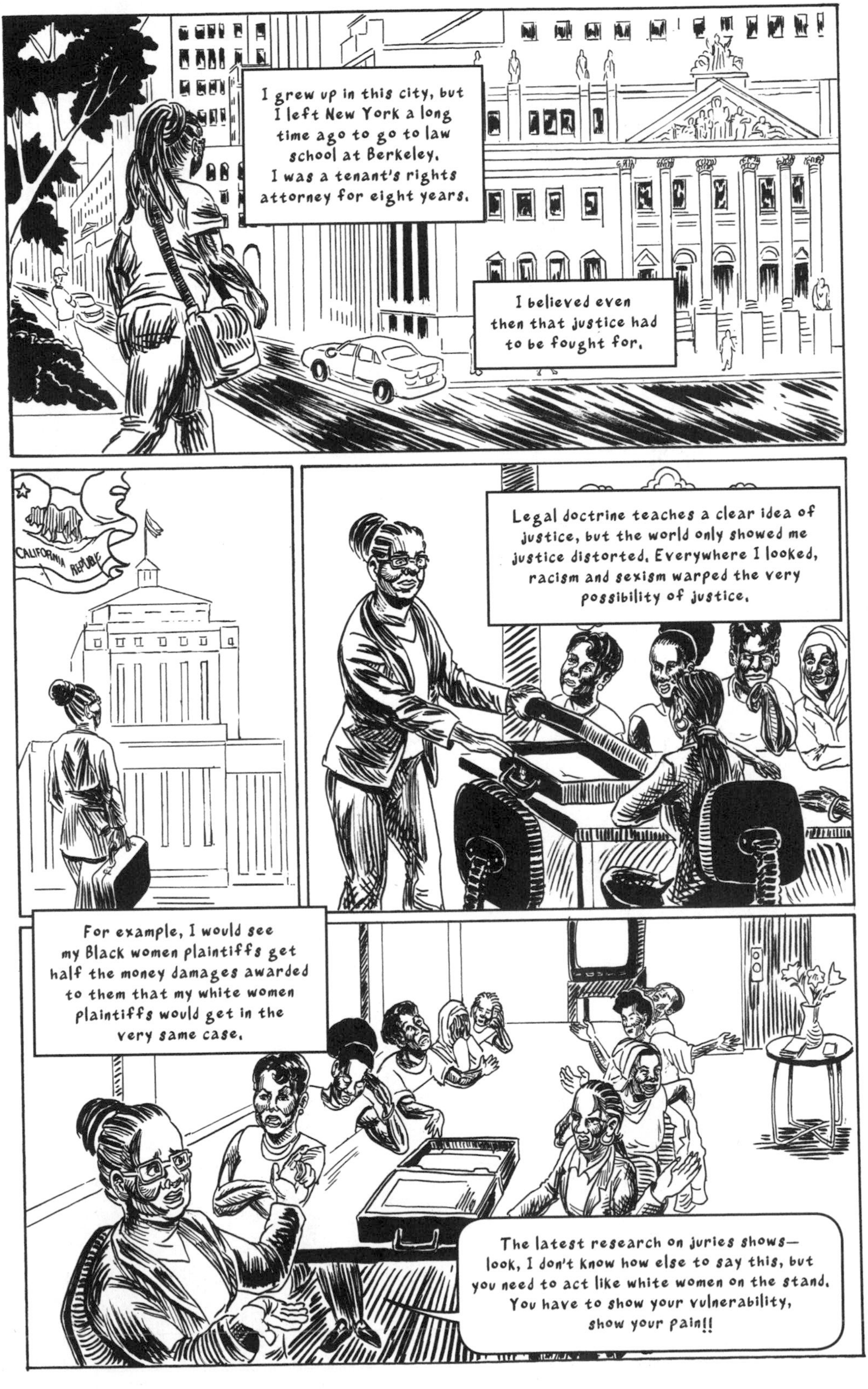
I grew up in this city, but I left New York a long time ago to go to law school at Berkeley. I was a tenant's rights attorney for eight years.
I believed even then that justice had to be fought for.
CALIFORNIA REPUBLIC
Legal doctrine teaches a clear idea of justice, but the world only showed me justice distorted. Everywhere I looked, racism and sexism warped the very possibility of justice.
For example, I would see my Black women plaintiffs get half the money damages awarded to them that my white women plaintiffs would get in the very same case.
The latest research on juries shows— look, I don't know how else to say this, but you need to act like white women on the stand. You have to show your vulnerability, show your pain!!

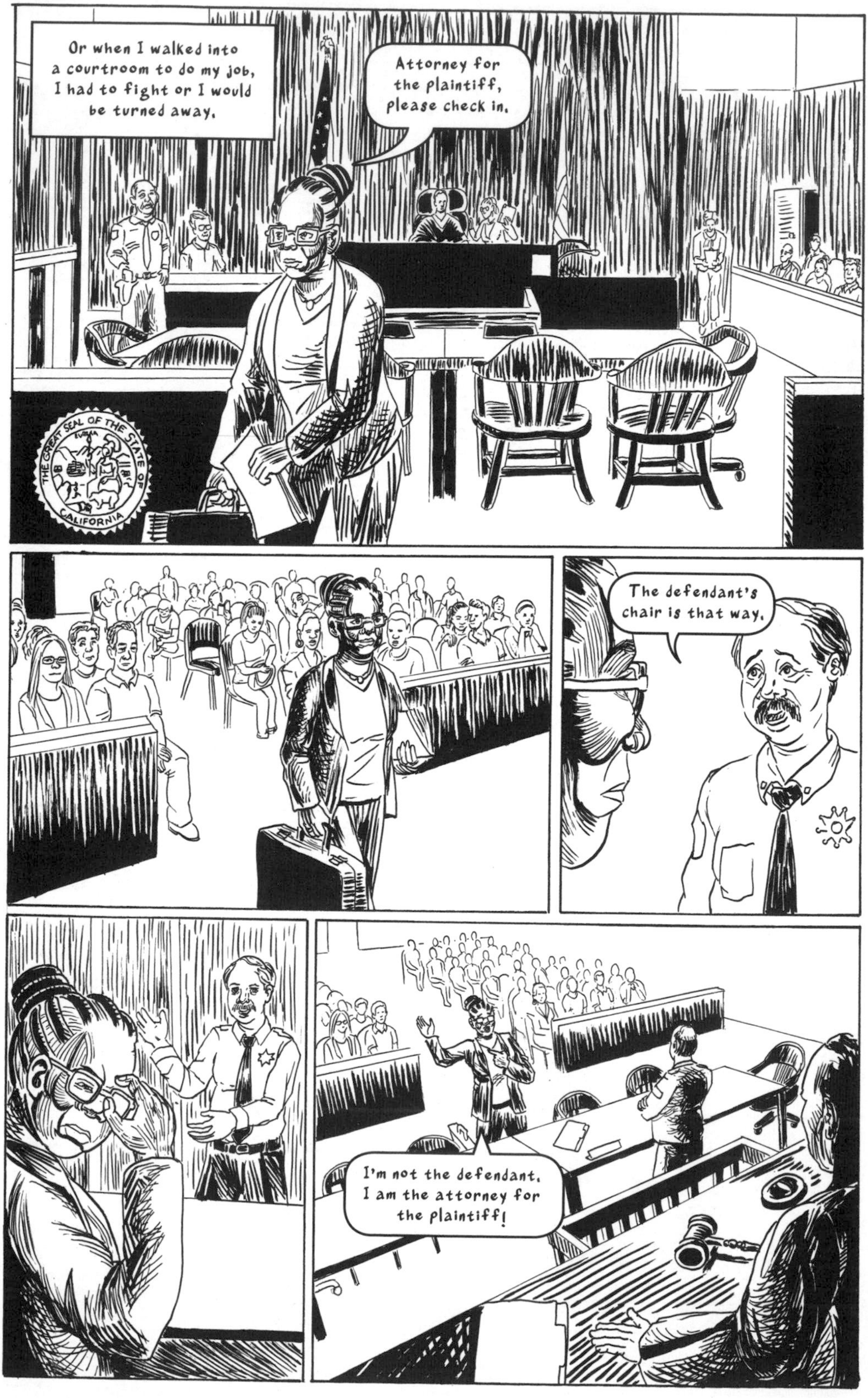
Or when I walked into a courtroom to do my job, I had to fight or I would be turned away.
Attorney for the plaintiff, please check in.
THE GREAT SEAL OF THE STATE OF CALIFORNIA
The defendant's chair is that way.
I'm not the defendant. I am the attorney for the plaintiff!

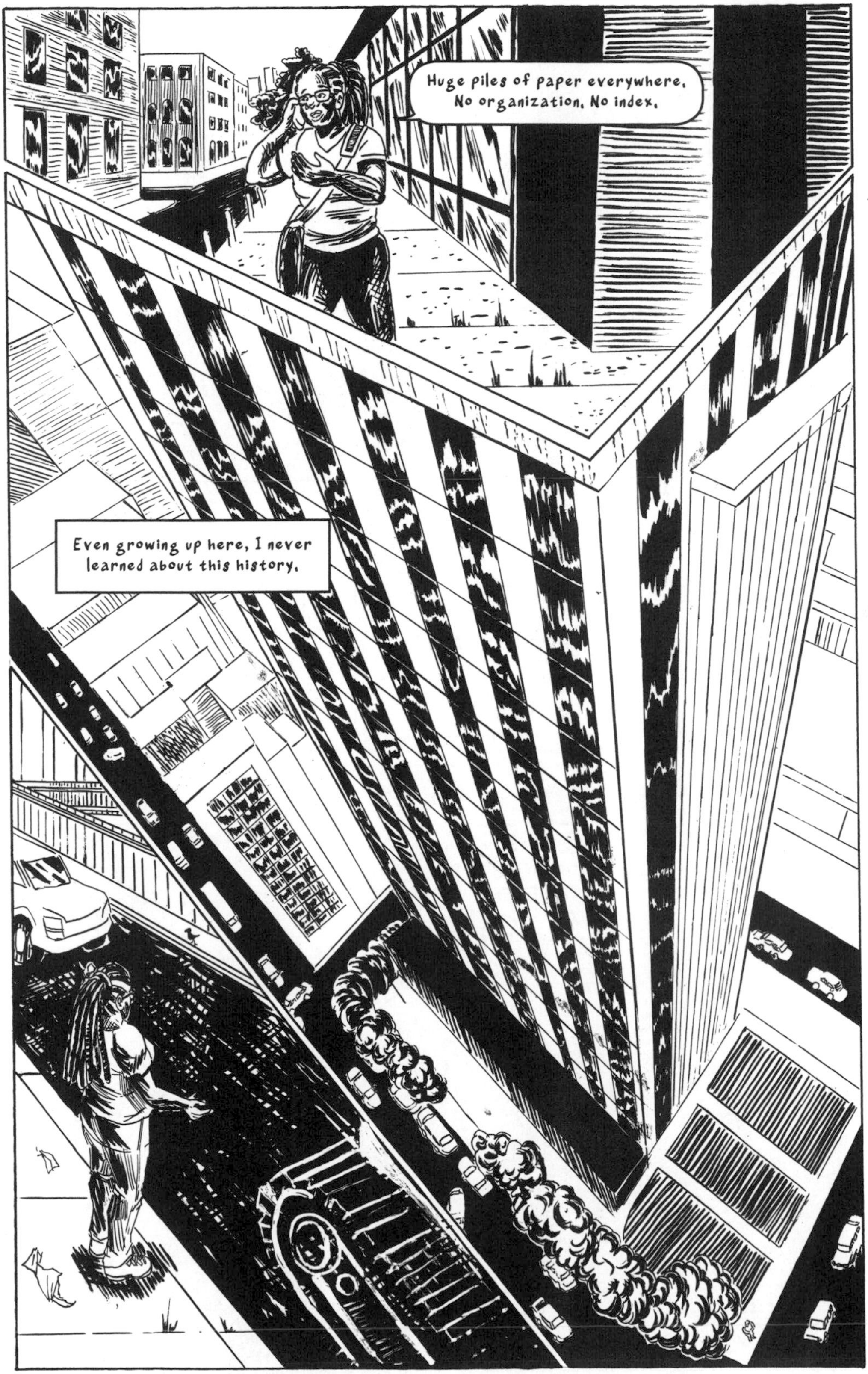
Huge piles of paper everywhere. No organization. No index.
Even growing up here, I never learned about this history.

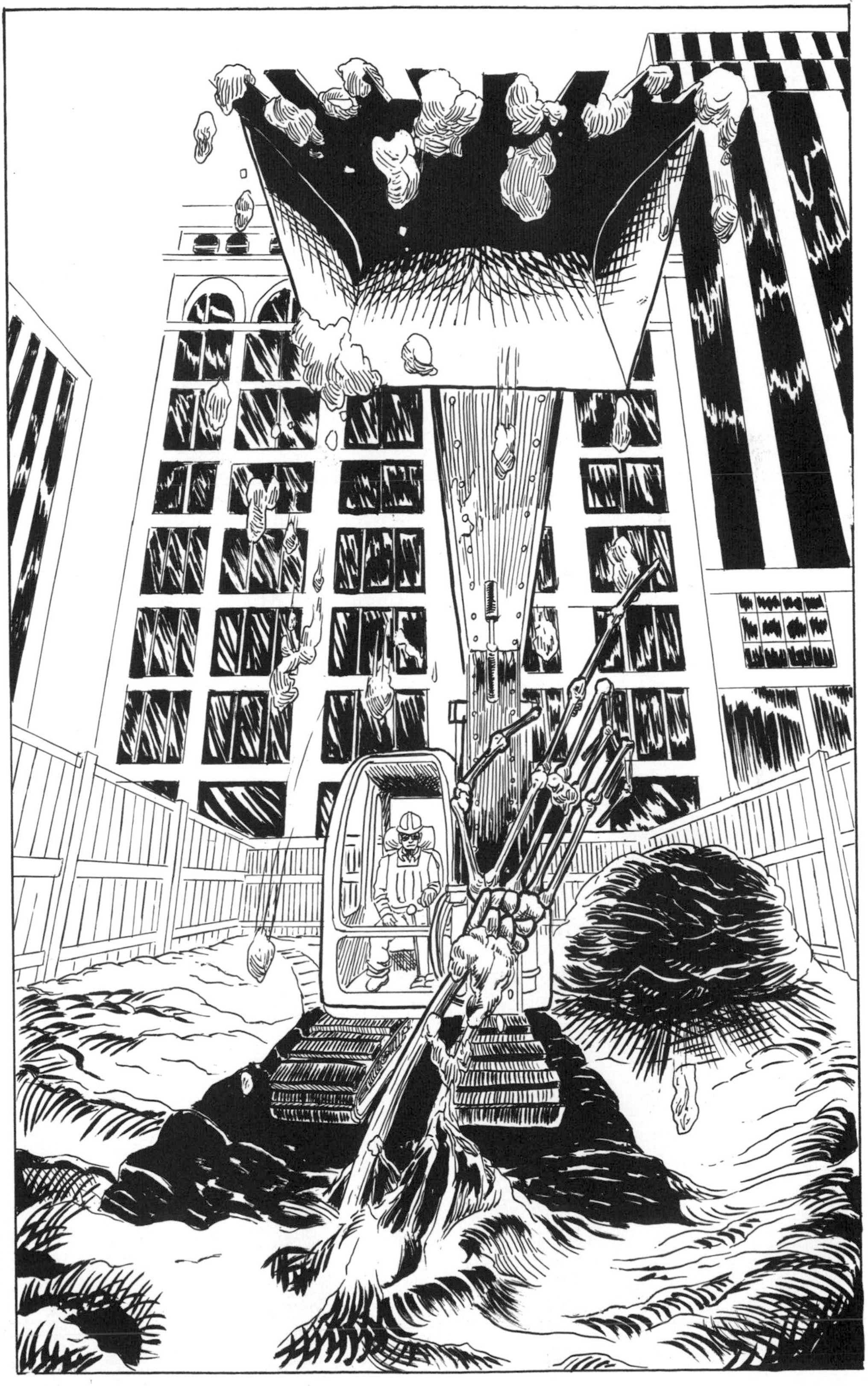

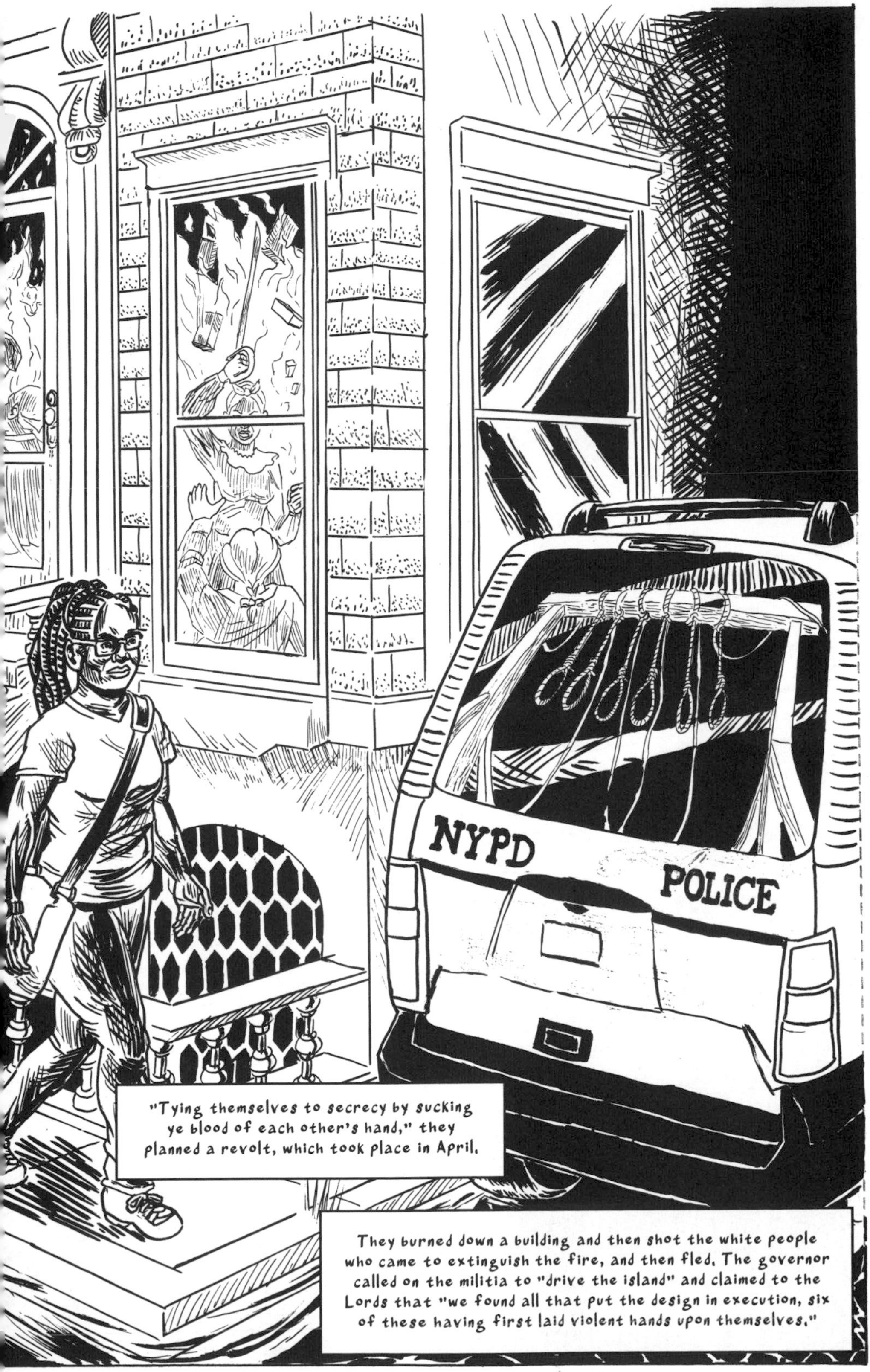
"Tying themselves to secrecy by sucking ye blood of each other's hand," they planned a revolt, which took place in April.
They burned down a building and then shot the white people who came to extinguish the fire, and then fled. The governor called on the militia to "drive the island" and claimed to the Lords that "we found all that put the design in execution, six of these having first laid violent hands upon themselves."
NYPD
POLICE

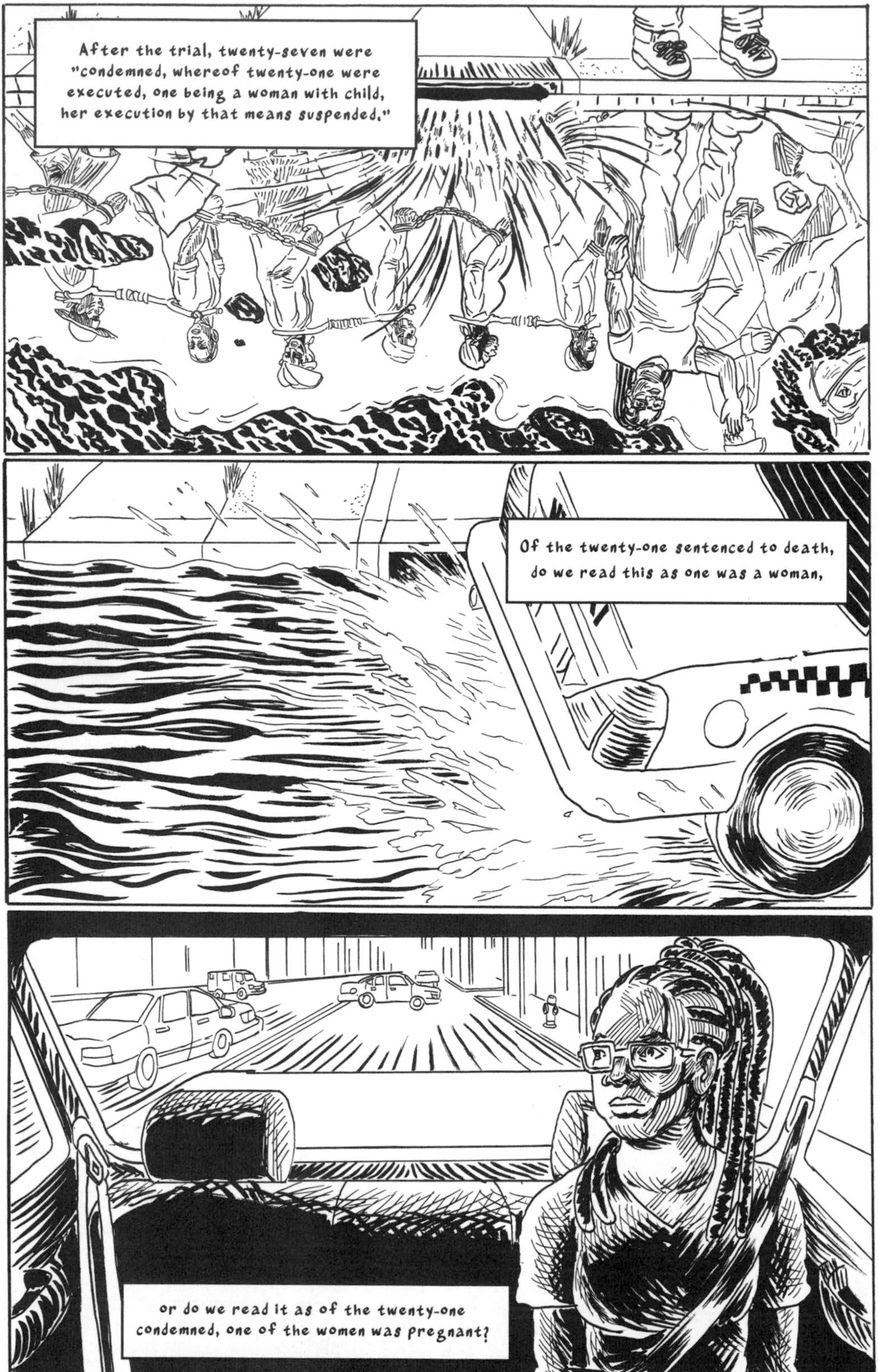
After the trial, twenty-seven were "condemned, whereof twenty-one were executed, one being a woman with child, her execution by that means suspended."
Of the twenty-one sentenced to death, do we read this as one was a woman,
or do we read it as of the twenty-one condemned, one of the women was pregnant?

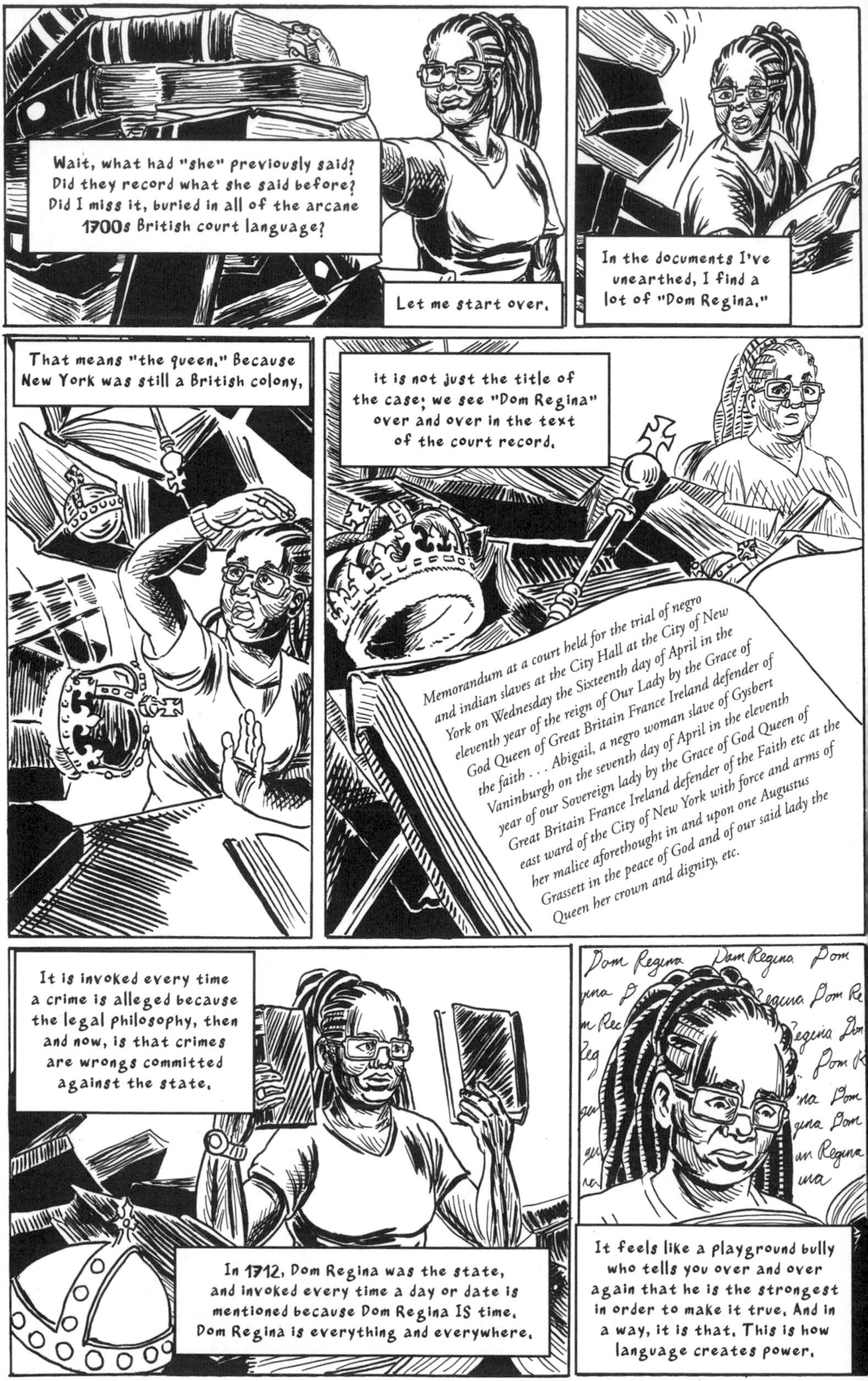
Wait, what had "she" previously said? Did they record what she said before? Did I miss it, buried in all of the arcane 1700s British court language?
Let me start over.
In the documents I've unearthed, I find a lot of "Dom Regina."
That means "the queen." Because New York was still a British colony,
it is not just the title of the case; we see "Dom Regina" over and over in the text of the court record.
Memorandum at a court held for the trial of negro and indian slaves at the City Hall at the City of New York on Wednesday the Sixteenth day of April in the eleventh year of the reign of Our Lady by the Grace of God Queen of Great Britain France Ireland defender of the faith . . . Abigail, a negro woman slave of Gysbert Vaninburgh on the seventh day of April in the eleventh year of our Sovereign lady by the Grace of God Queen of Great Britain France Ireland defender of the Faith etc at the east ward of the City of New York with force and arms of her malice aforethought in and upon one Augustus Grassett in the peace of God and of our said lady the Queen her crown and dignity, etc.
It is invoked every time a crime is alleged because the legal philosophy, then and now, is that crimes are wrongs committed against the state.
In 1712, Dom Regina was the state, and invoked every time a day or date is mentioned because Dom Regina IS time. Dom Regina is everything and everywhere.
Dom Regina Dom Regina
It feels like a playground bully who tells you over and over again that he is the strongest in order to make it true. And in a way, it is that. This is how language creates power.

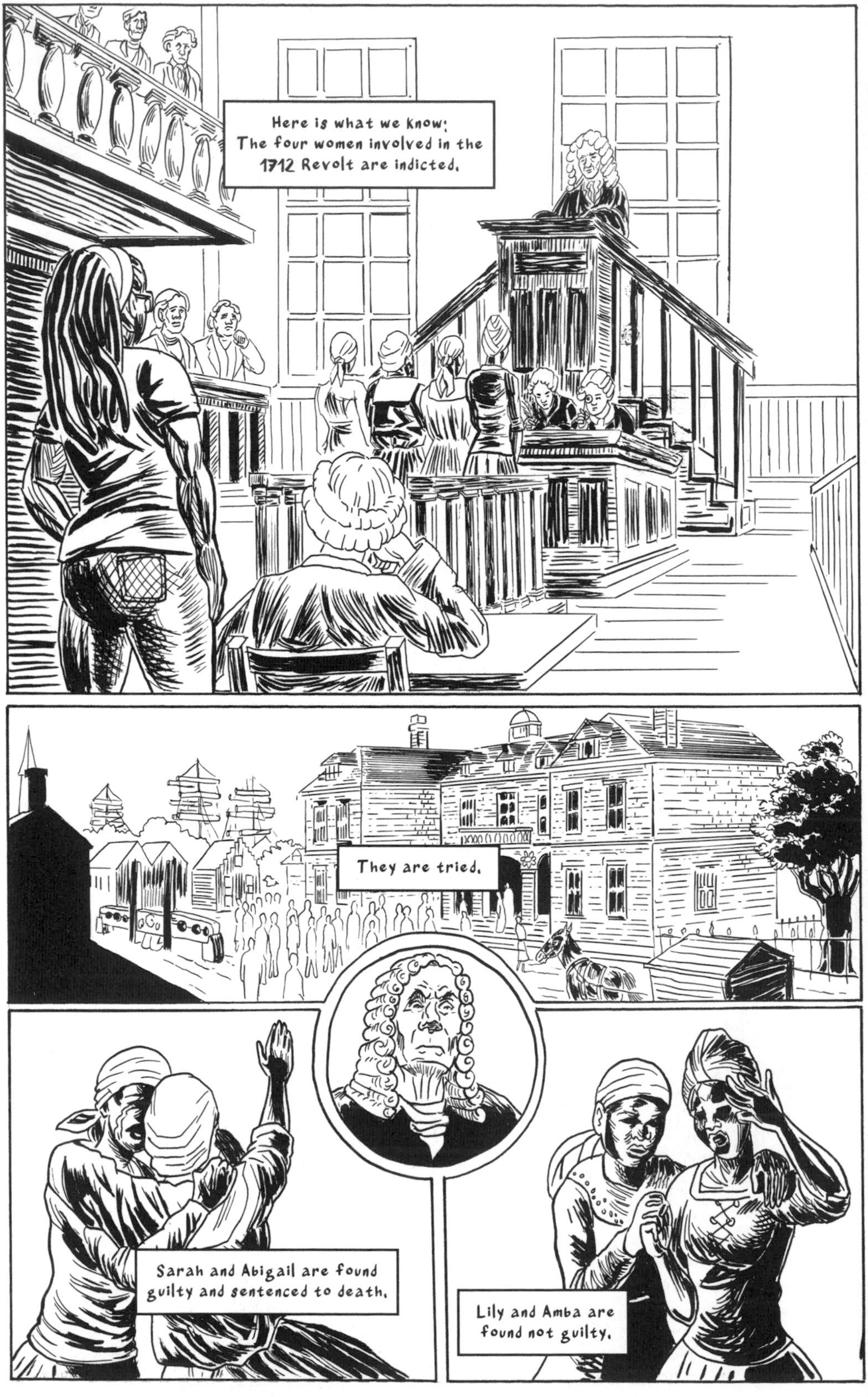
Here is what we know:
The four women involved in the 1712 Revolt are indicted.
They are tried.
Sarah and Abigail are found guilty and sentenced to death.
Lily and Amba are found not guilty.

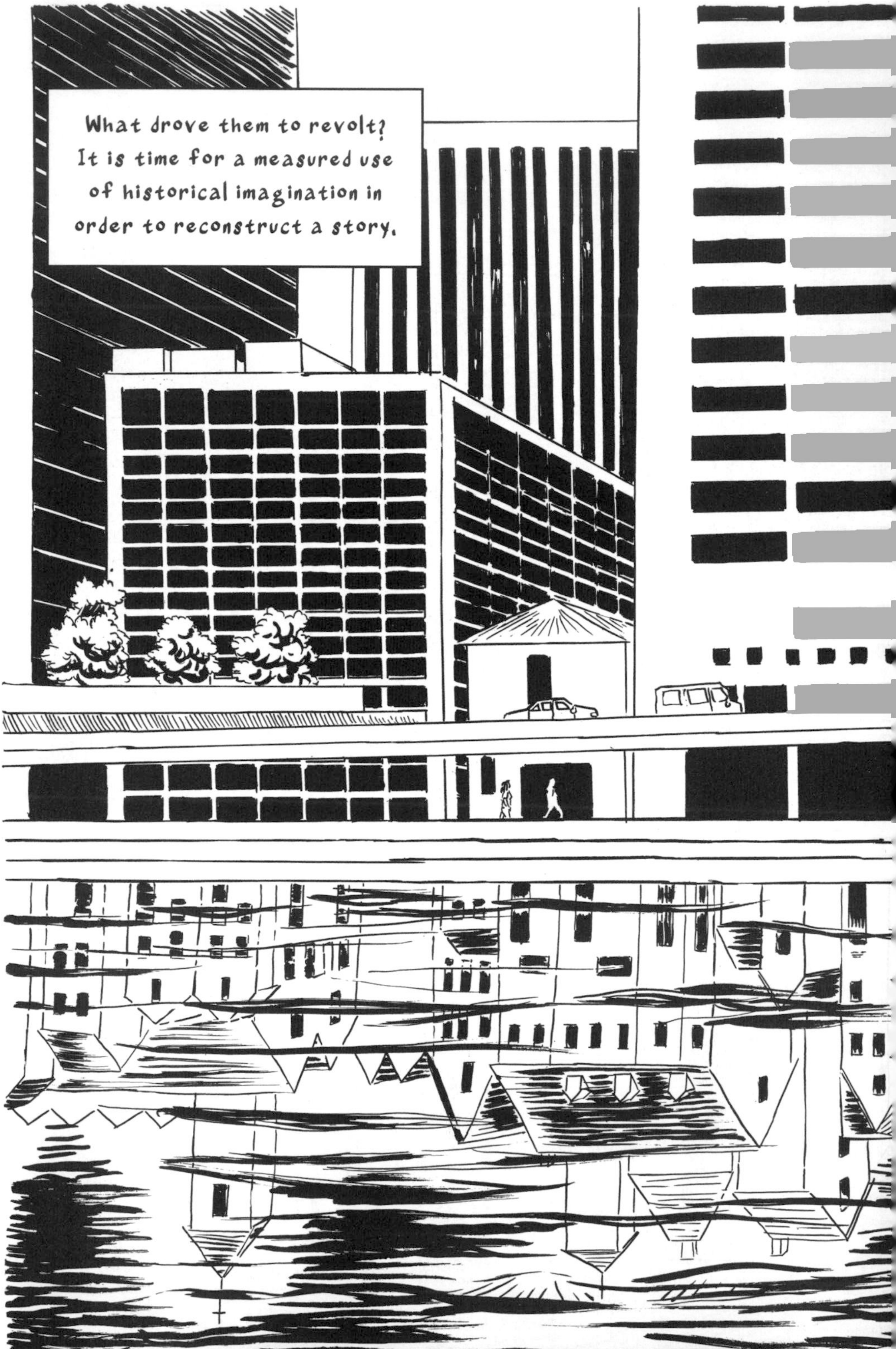
What drove them to revolt? It is time for a measured use of historical imagination in order to reconstruct a story.

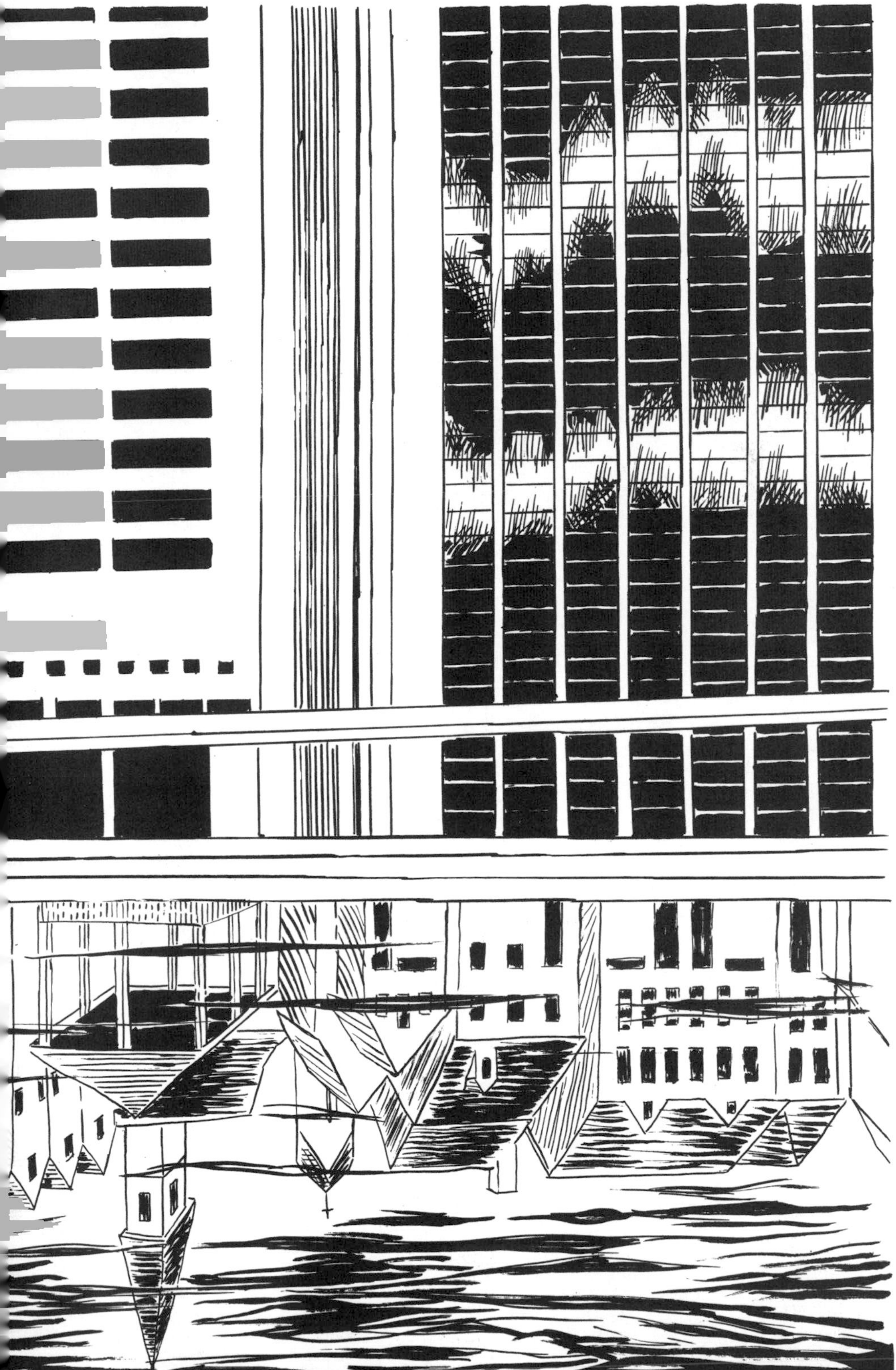

Chapter 3
Some Hard Usage

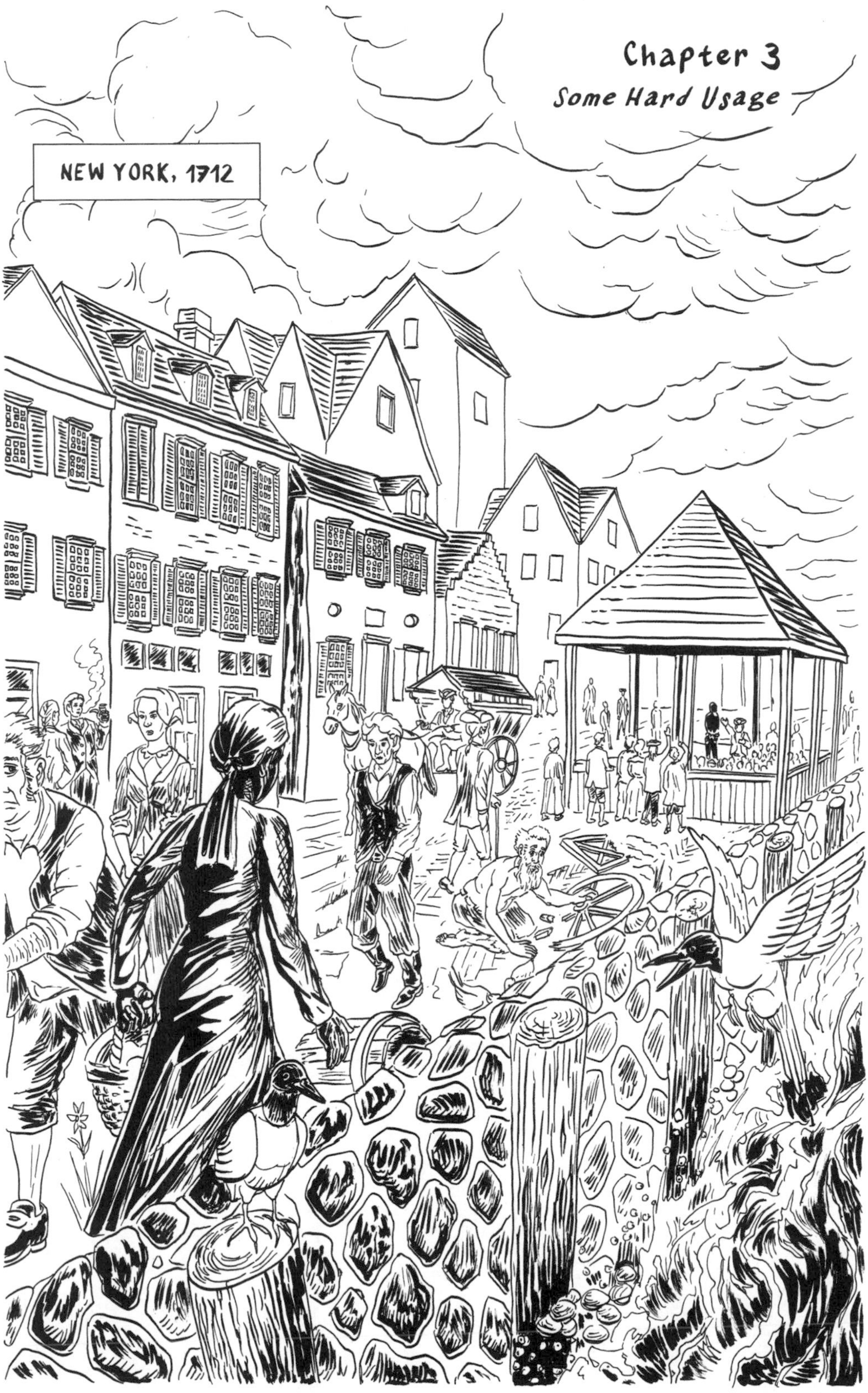
NEW YORK, 1712

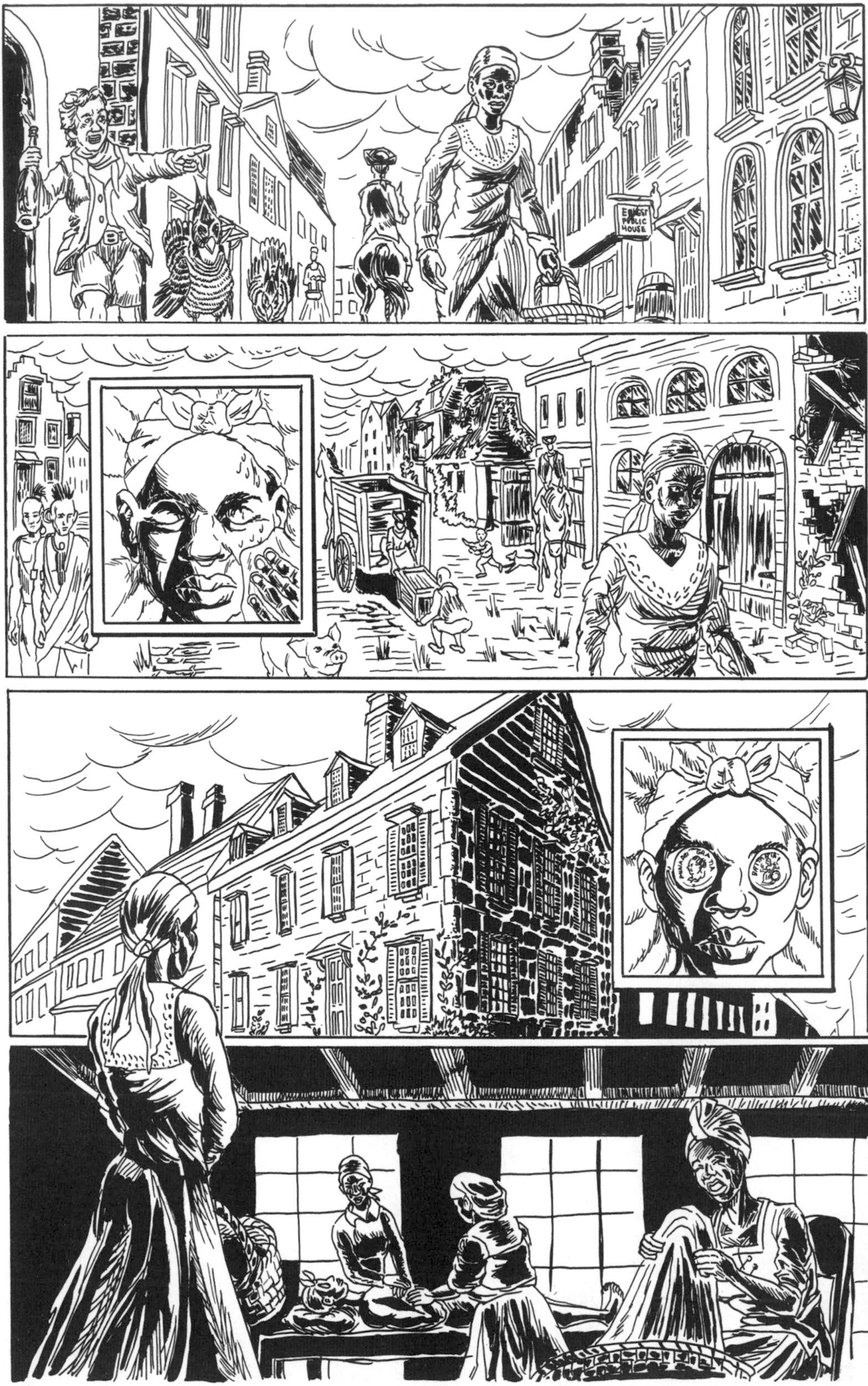
PUBLIC HOUSE
GRATIA

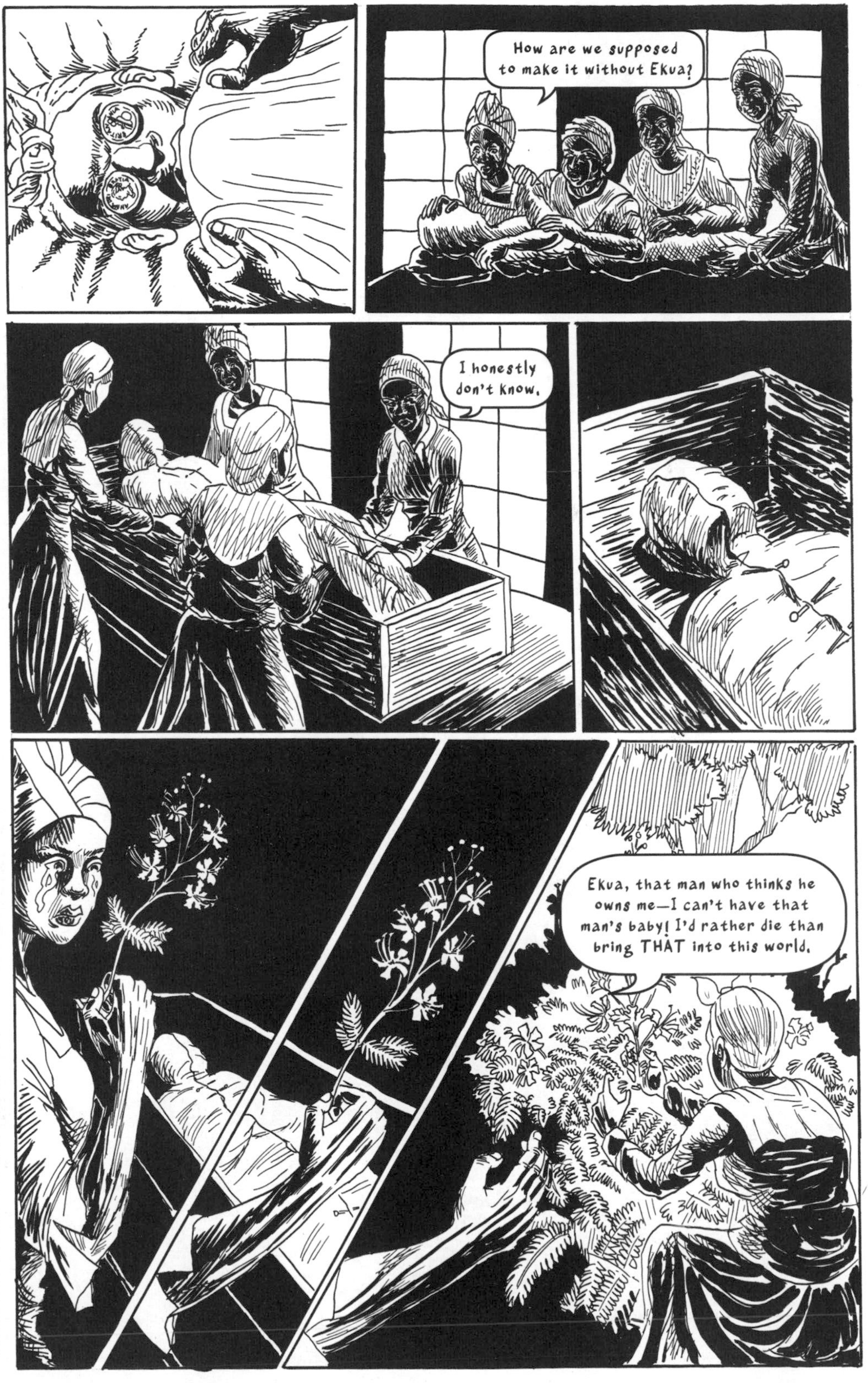
How are we supposed to make it without Ekua?
I honestly don't know.
Ekua, that man who thinks he owns me—I can't have that man's baby! I'd rather die than bring THAT into this world.

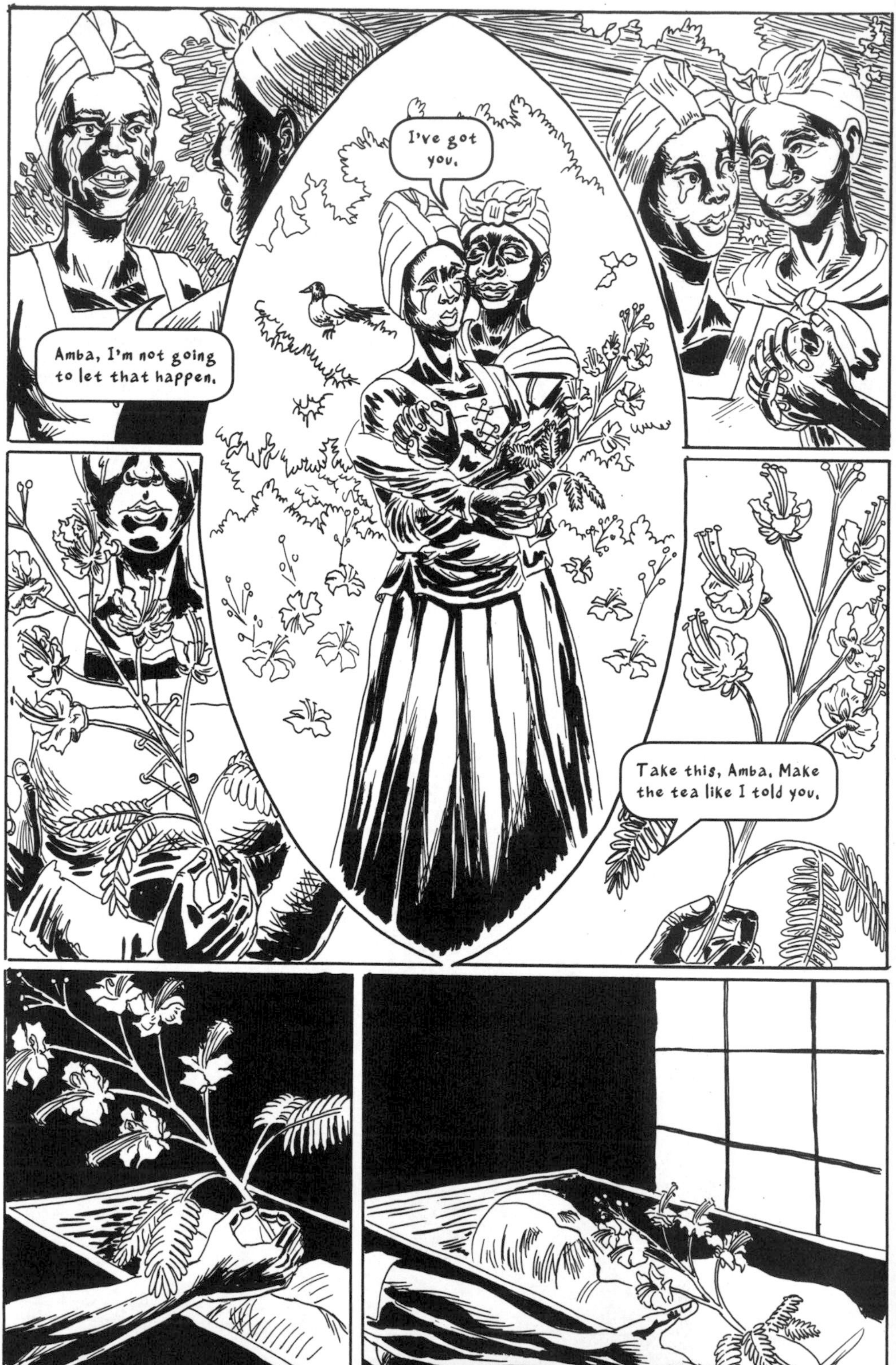
Amba, I'm not going to let that happen.
I've got you.
Take this, Amba. Make the tea like I told you.

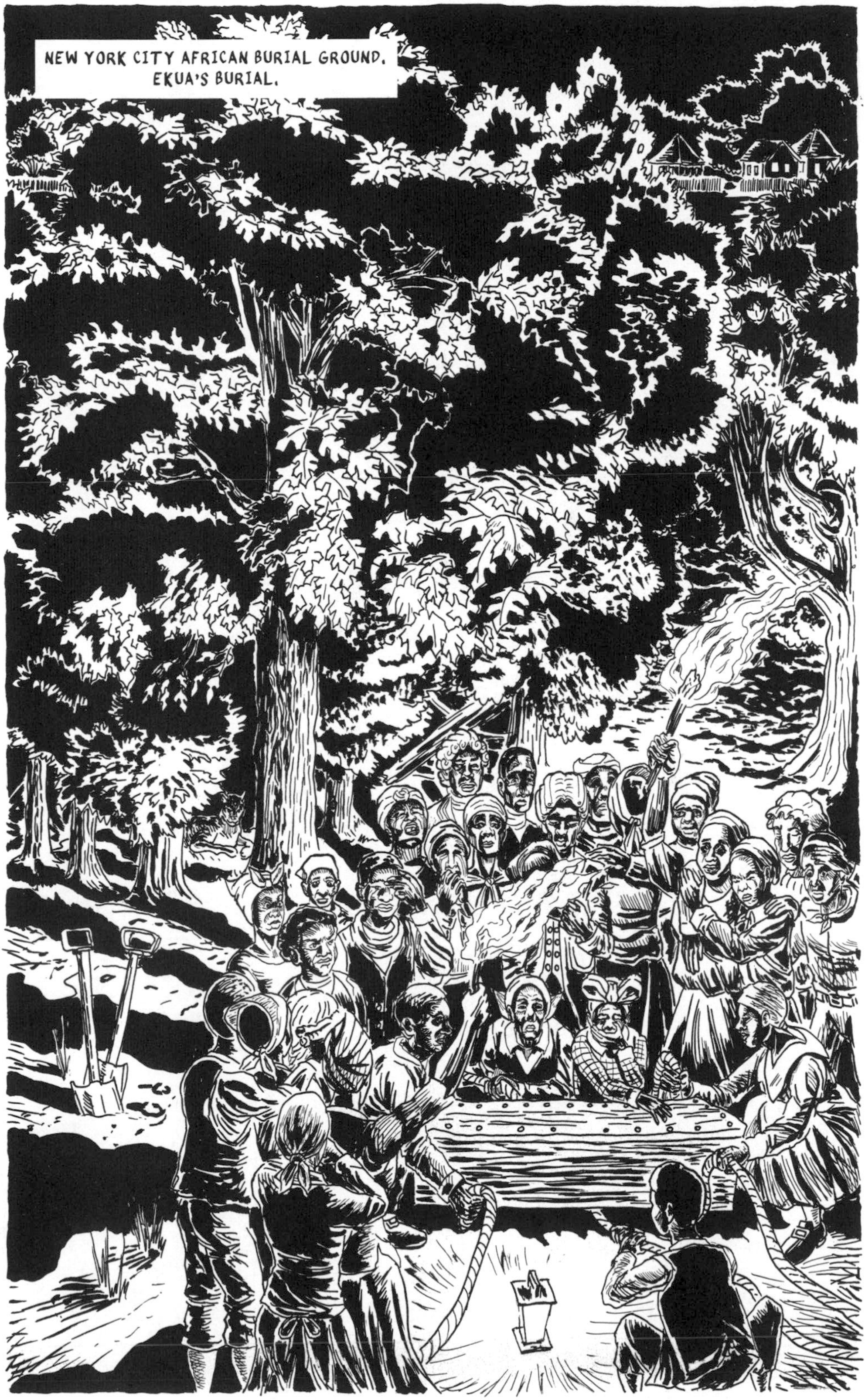
NEW YORK CITY AFRICAN BURIAL GROUND.
EKUA'S BURIAL.

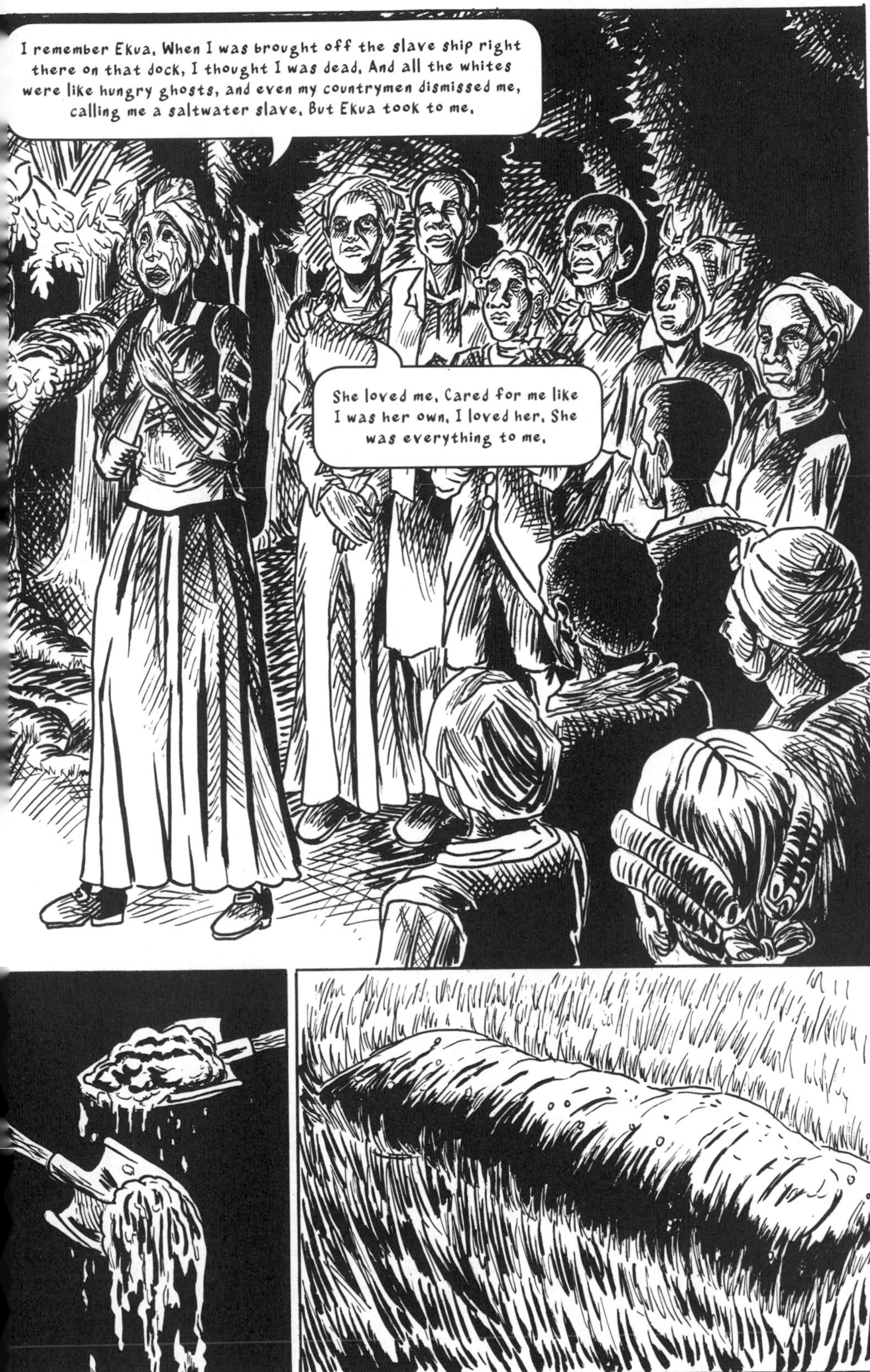
I remember Ekua. When I was brought off the slave ship right there on that dock, I thought I was dead. And all the whites were like hungry ghosts, and even my countrymen dismissed me, calling me a saltwater slave. But Ekua took to me.
She loved me. Cared for me like I was her own. I loved her. She was everything to me.

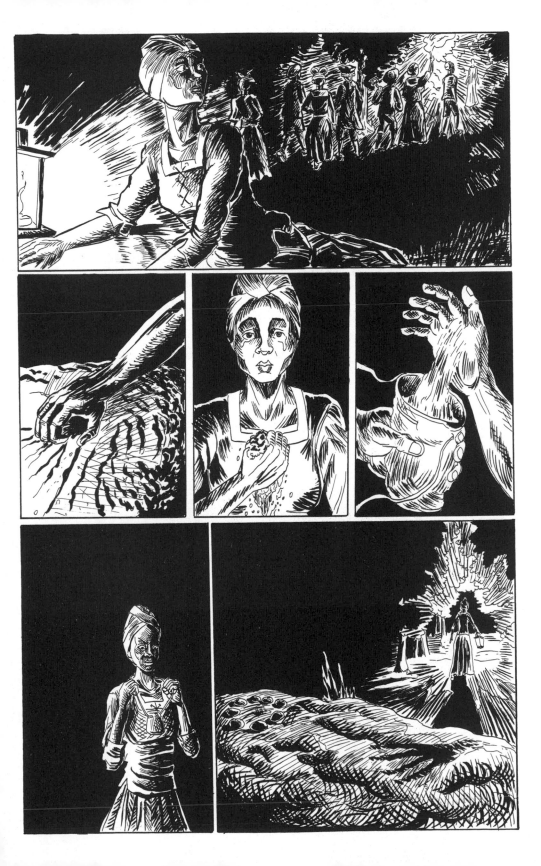

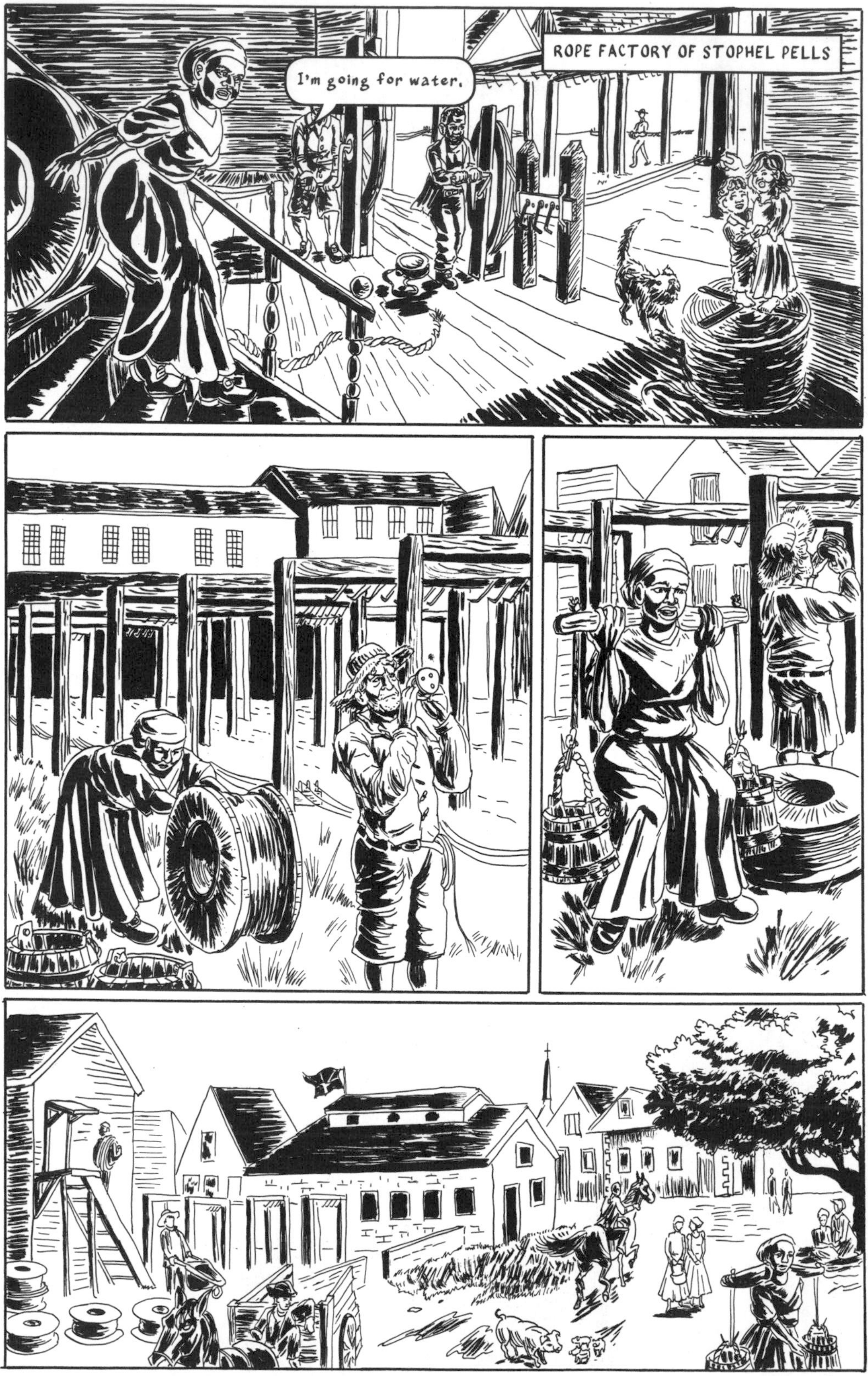
ROPE FACTORY OF STOPHEL PELLS
I'm going for water.

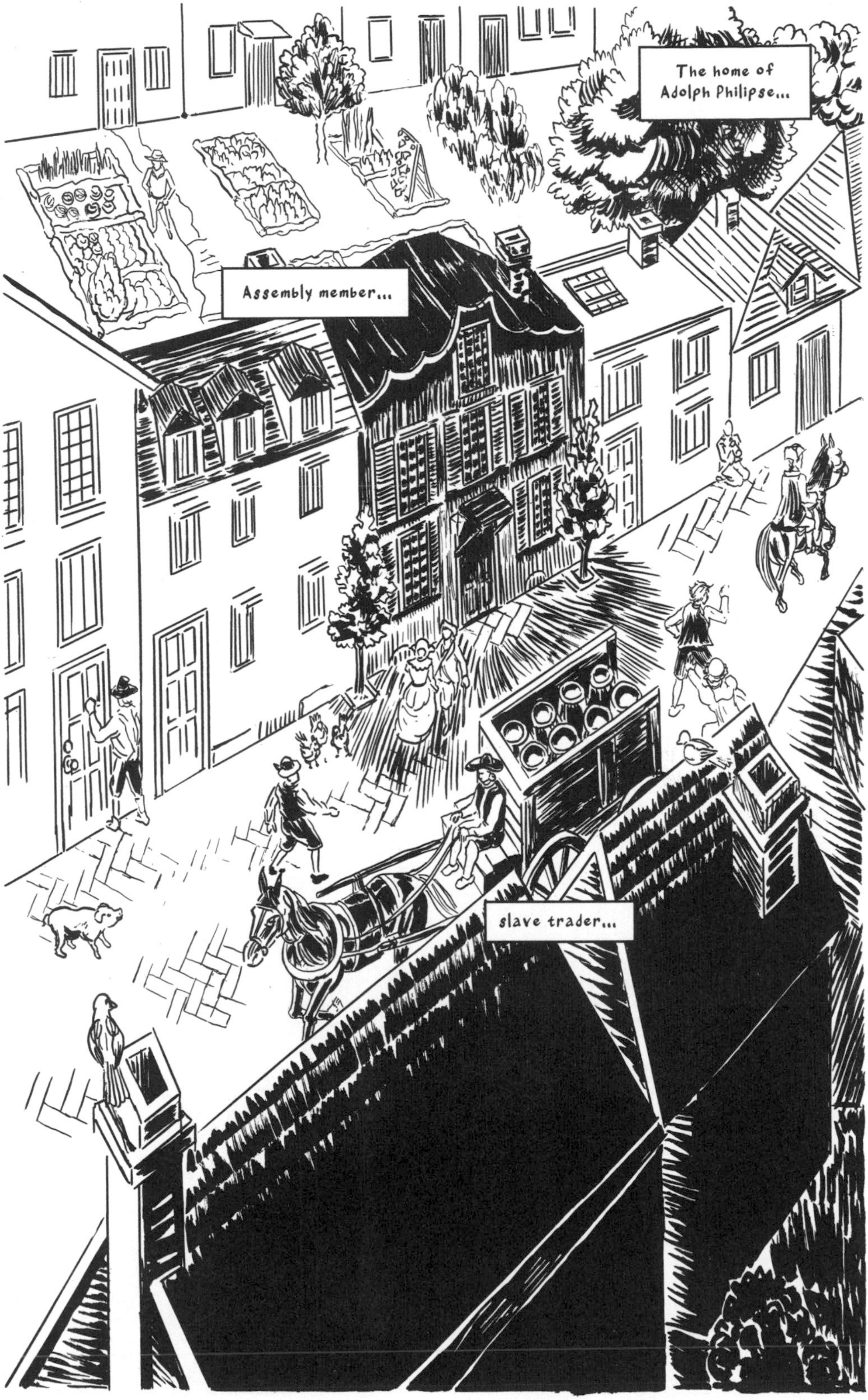
The home of Adolph Philipse...
Assembly member...
slave trader...

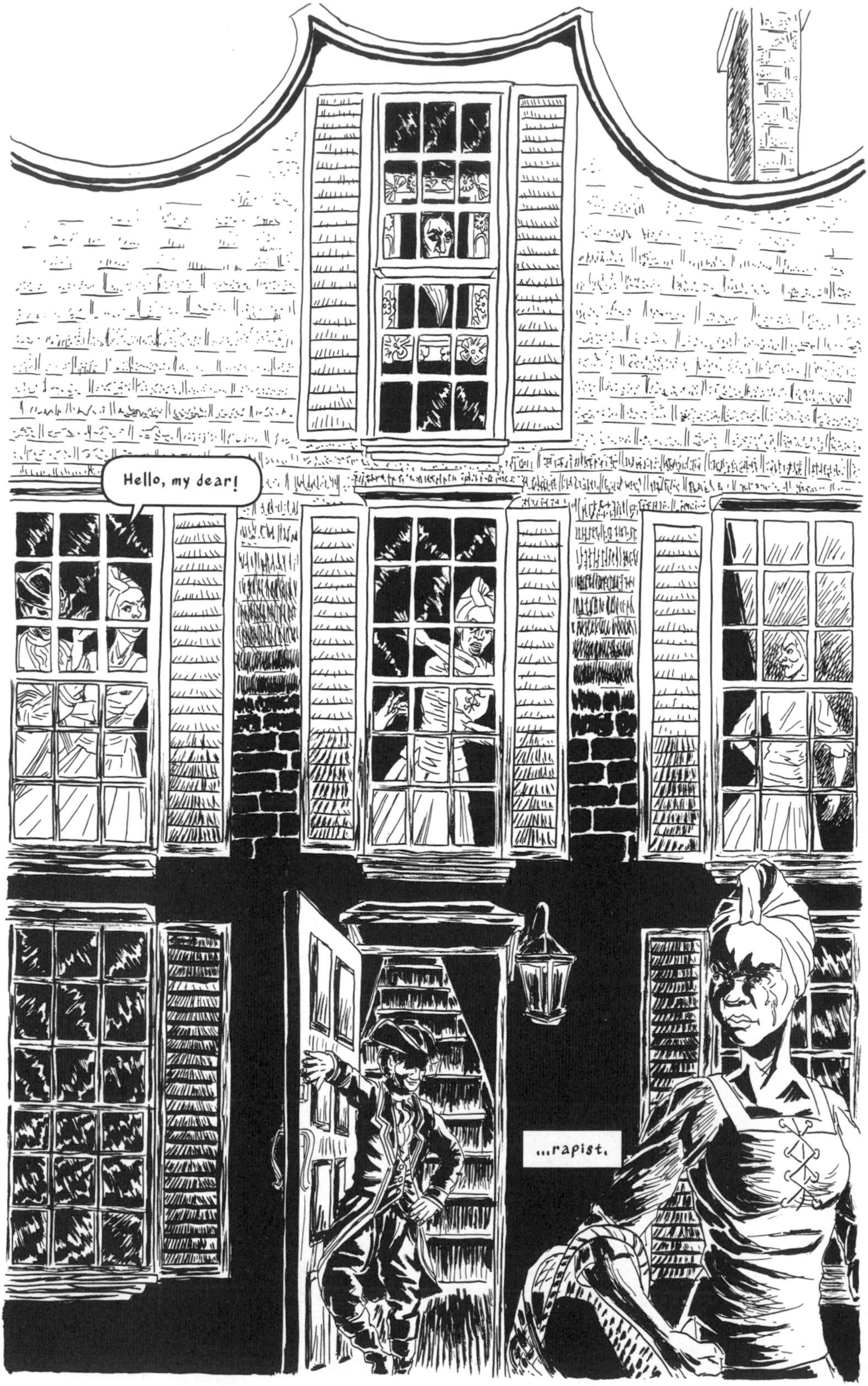
Hello, my dear!
...rapist.

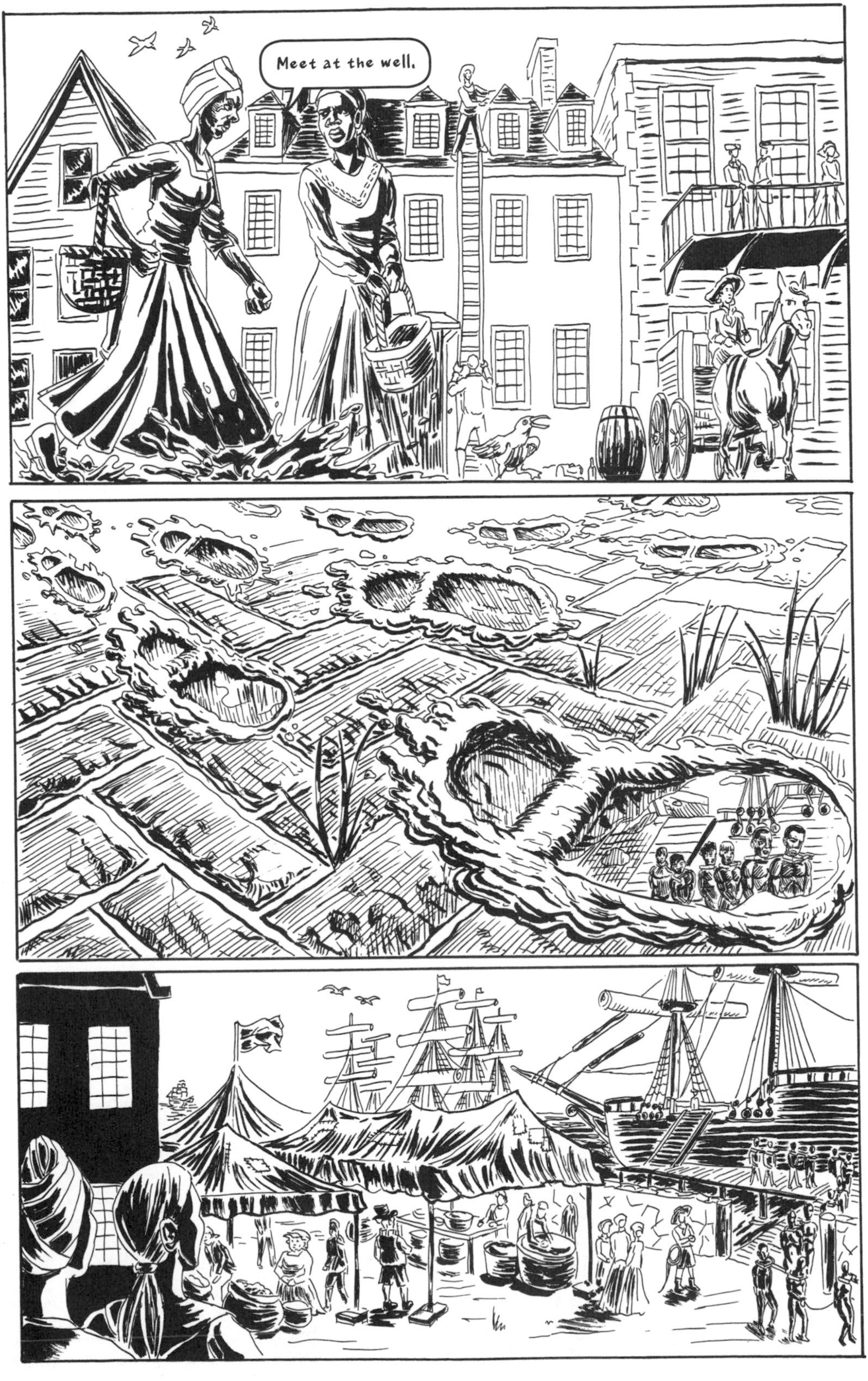
Meet at the well.

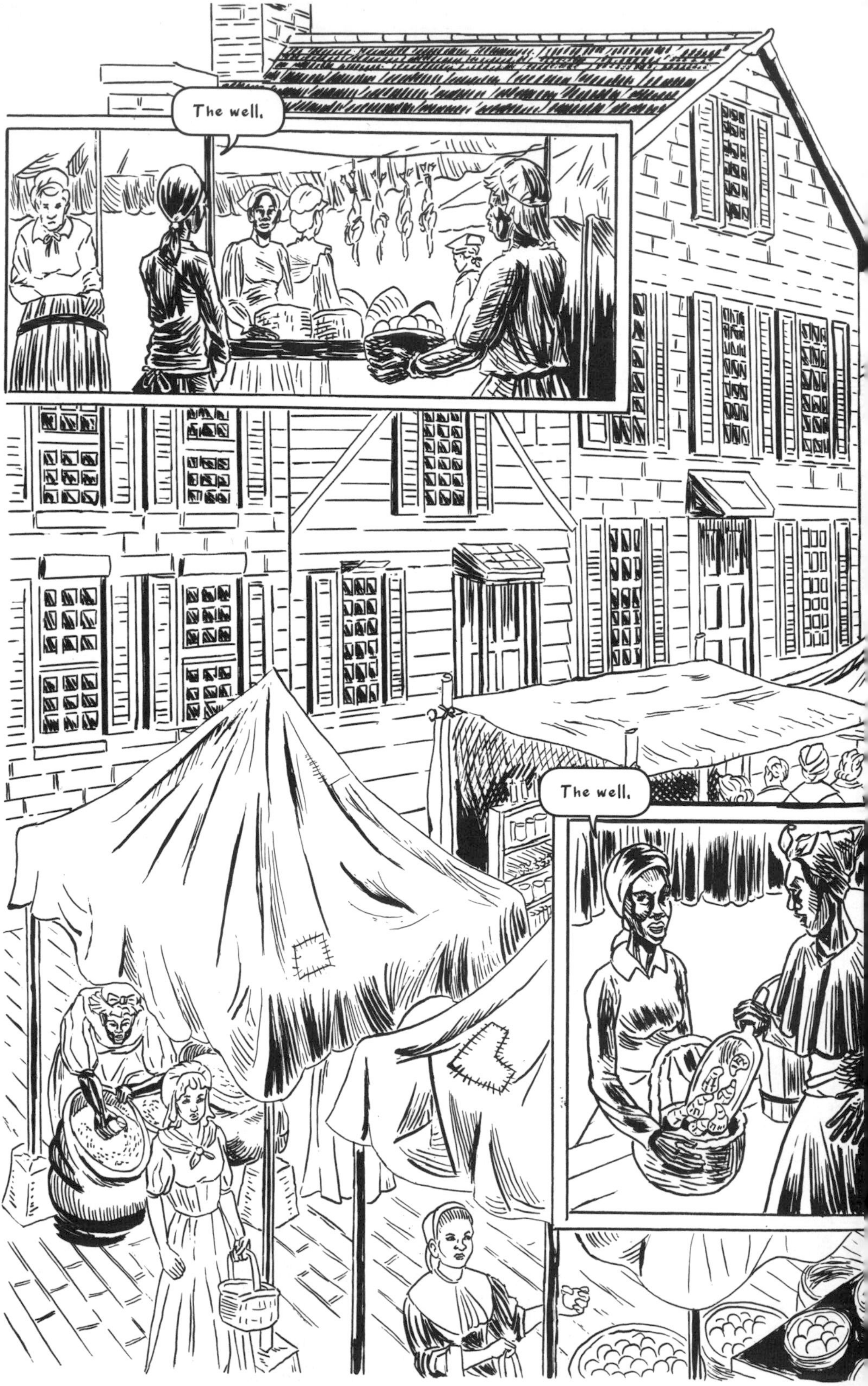
The well.
The well.

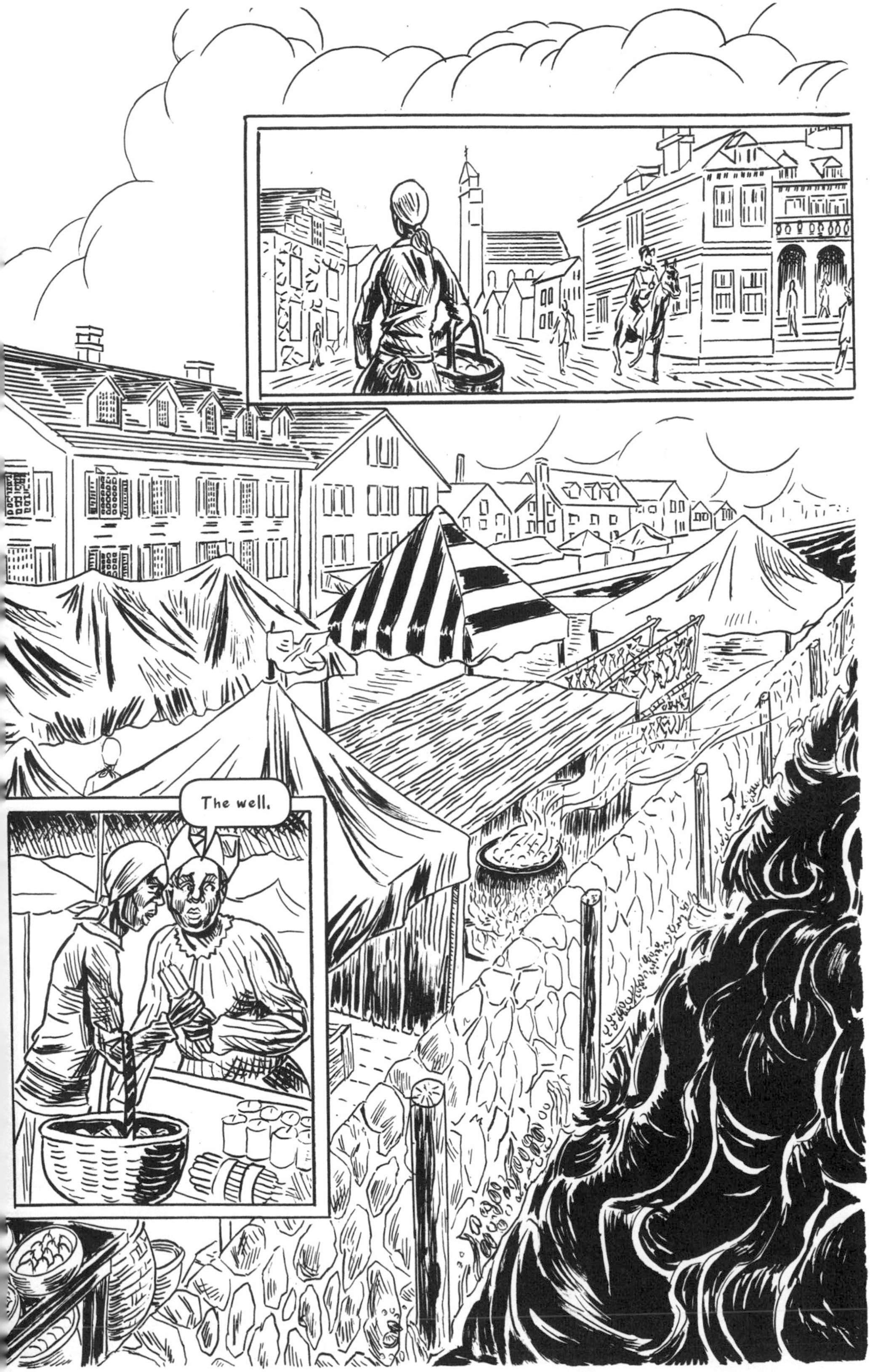
The well.

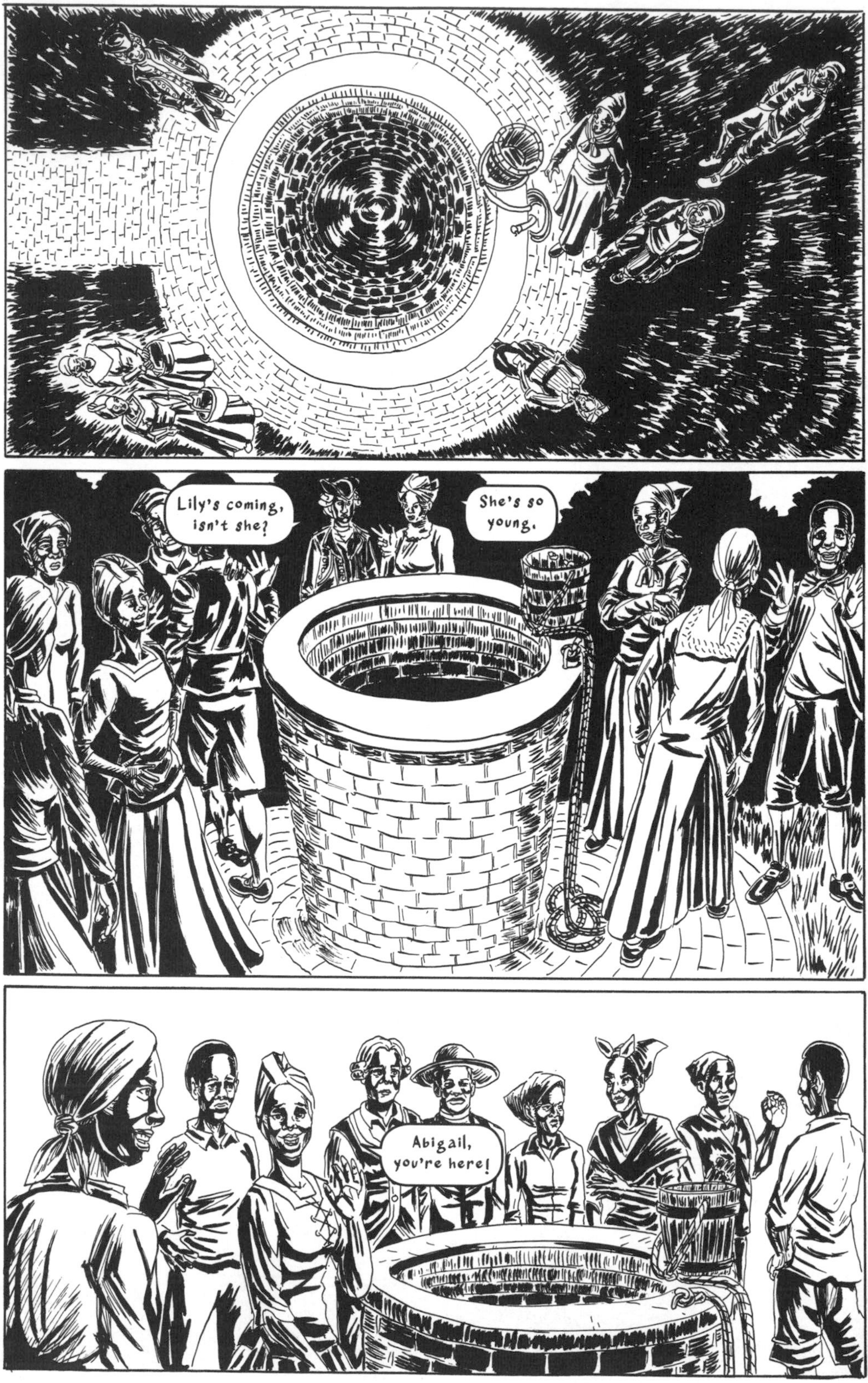

Lily's coming, isn't she?
She's so young.
Abigail, you're here!

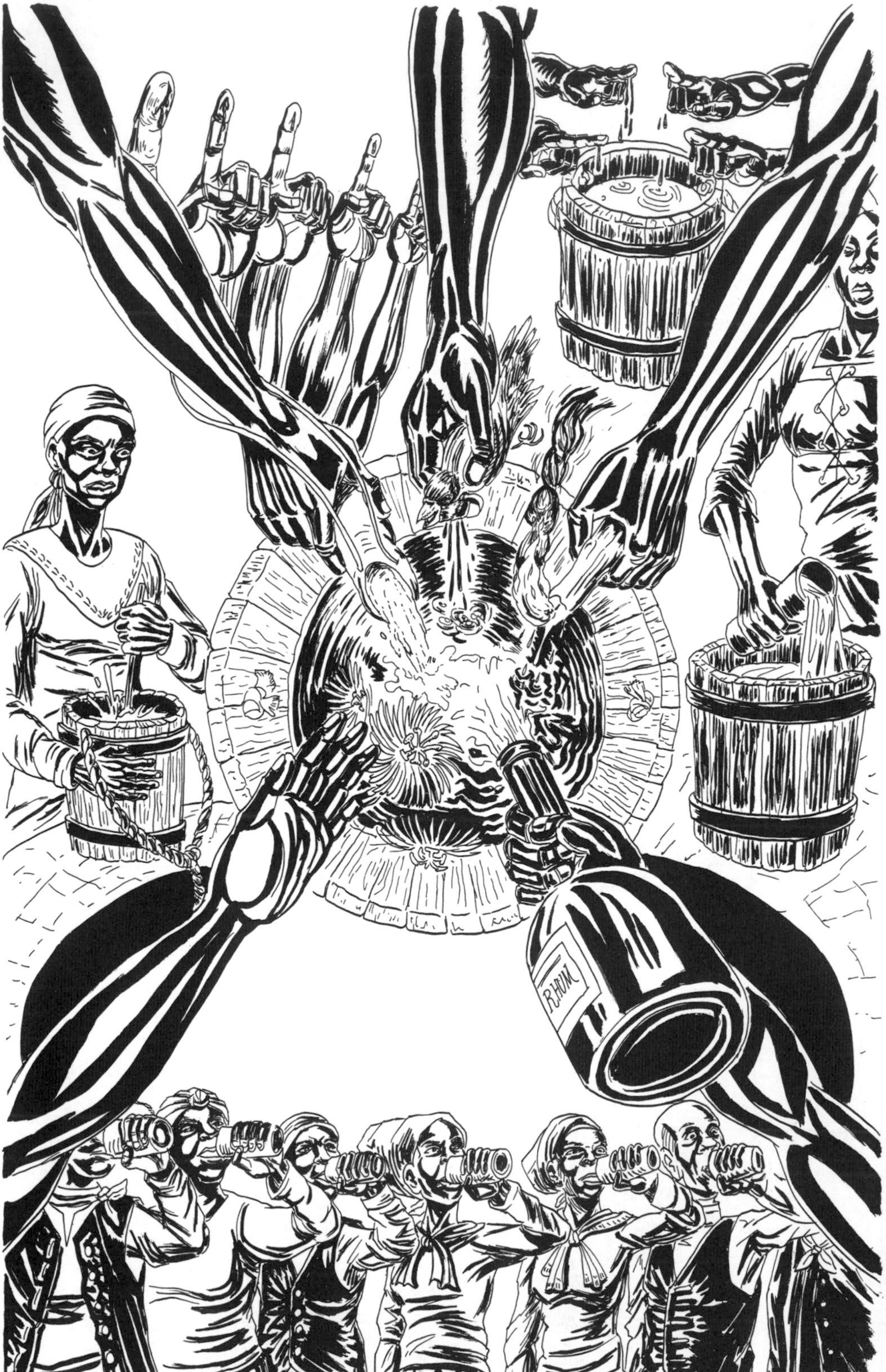
RHUM

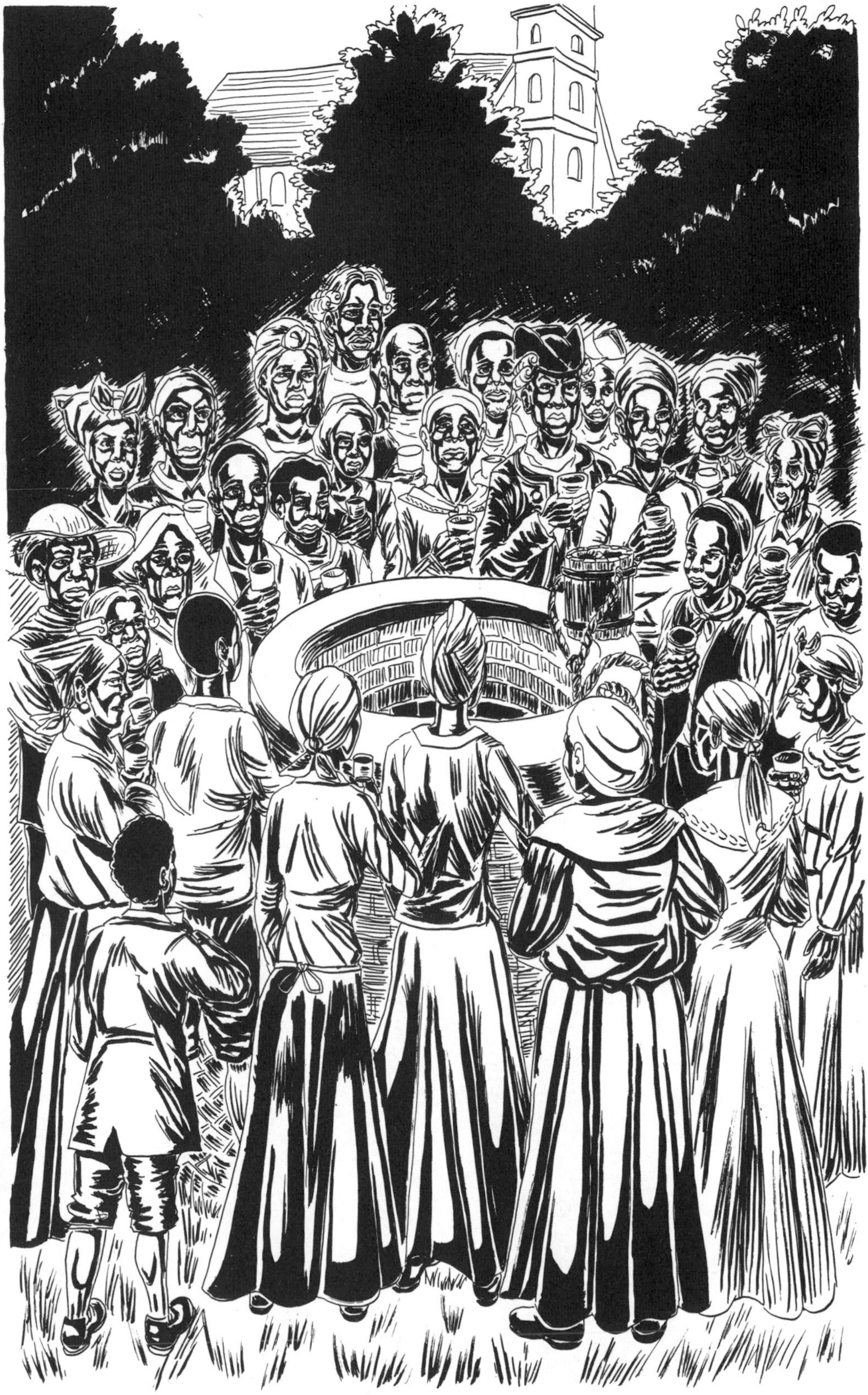

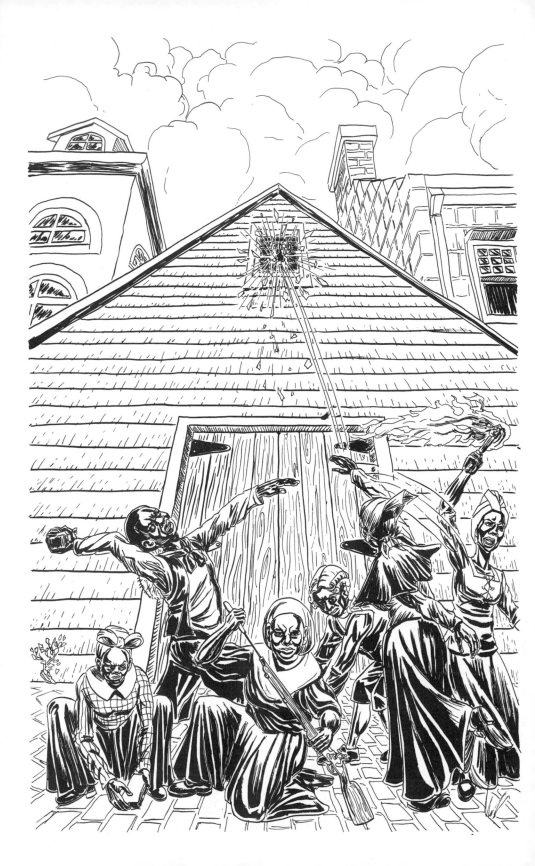

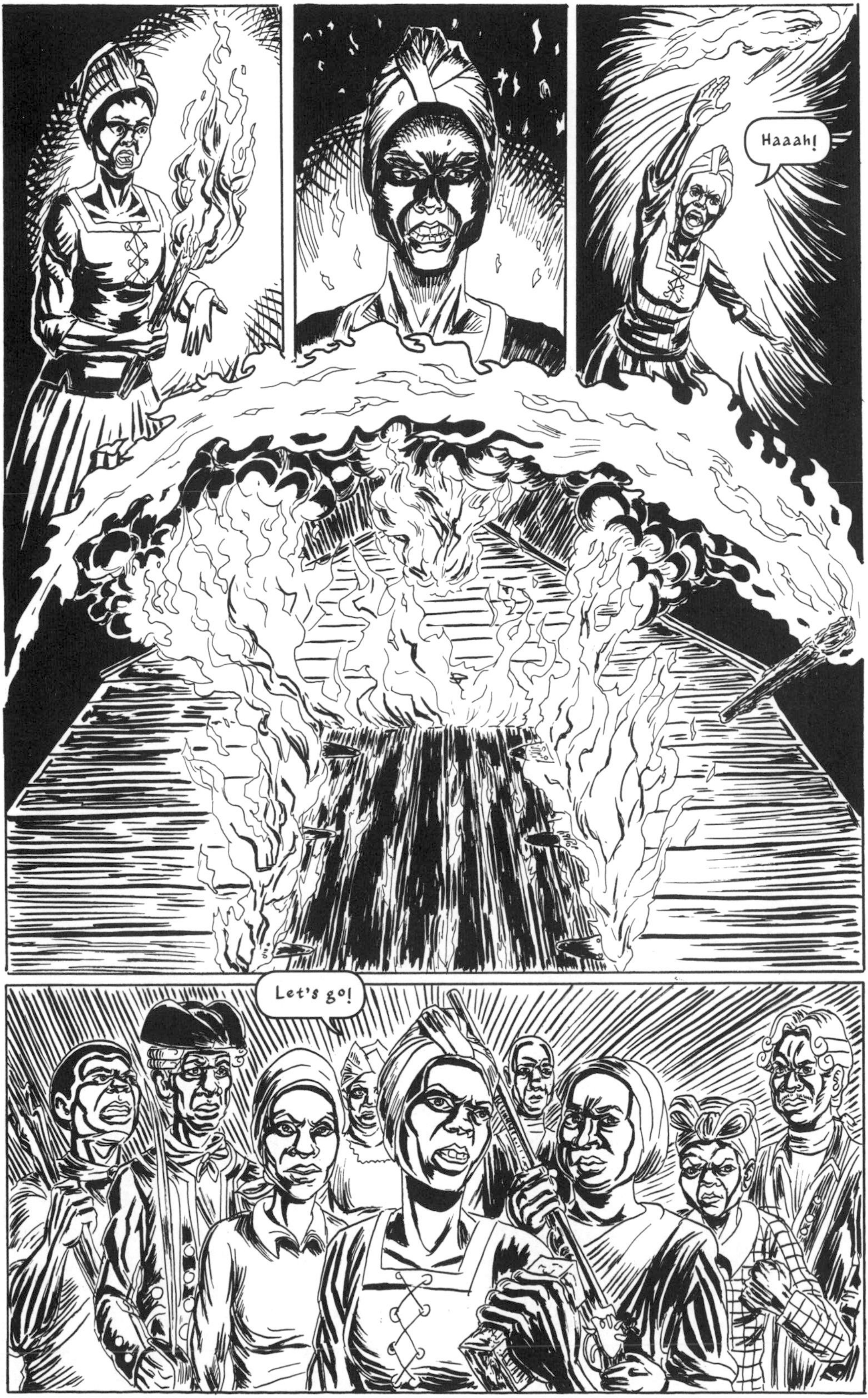
Haaah!
Let's go!

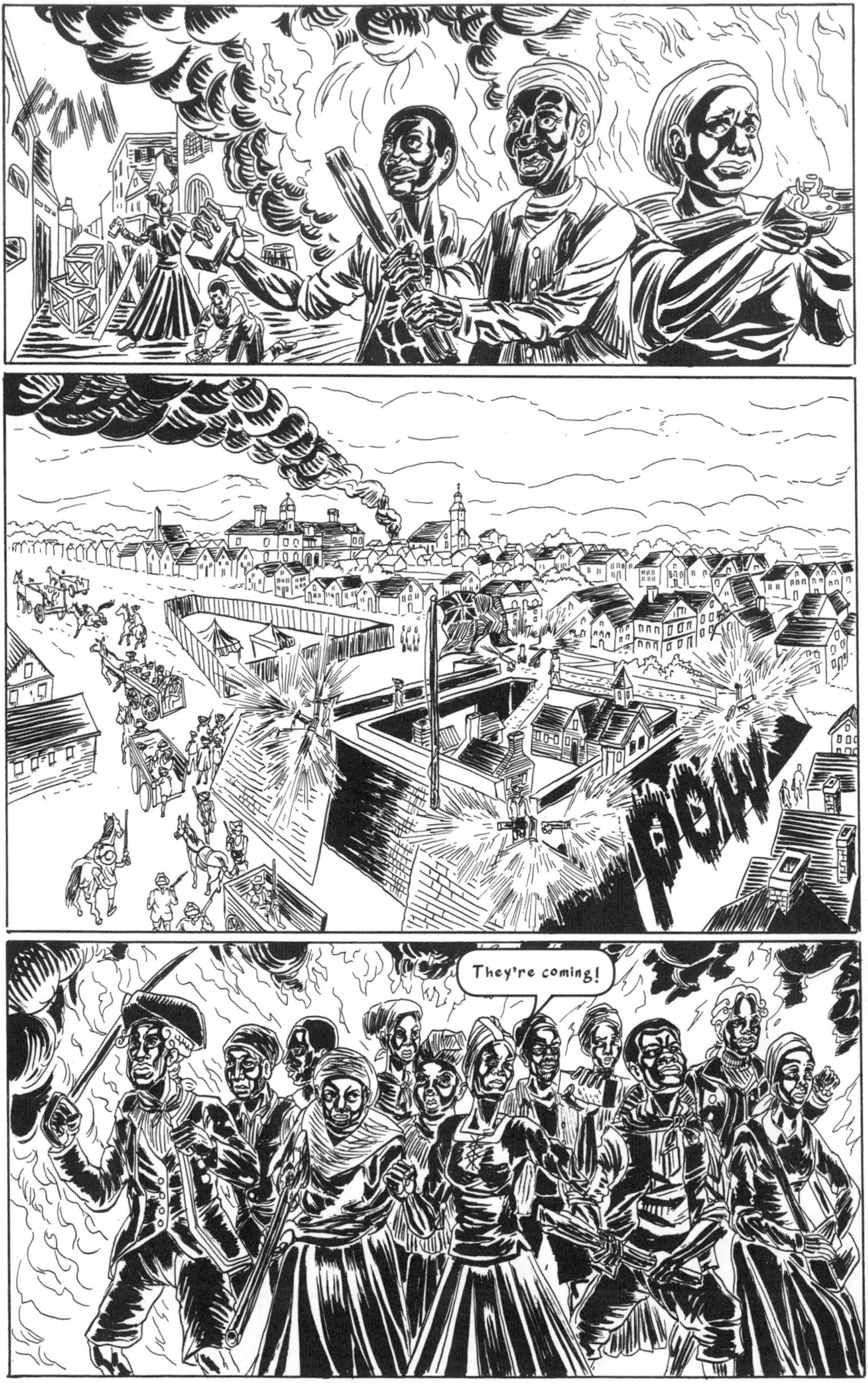
POW
POW
They're coming!

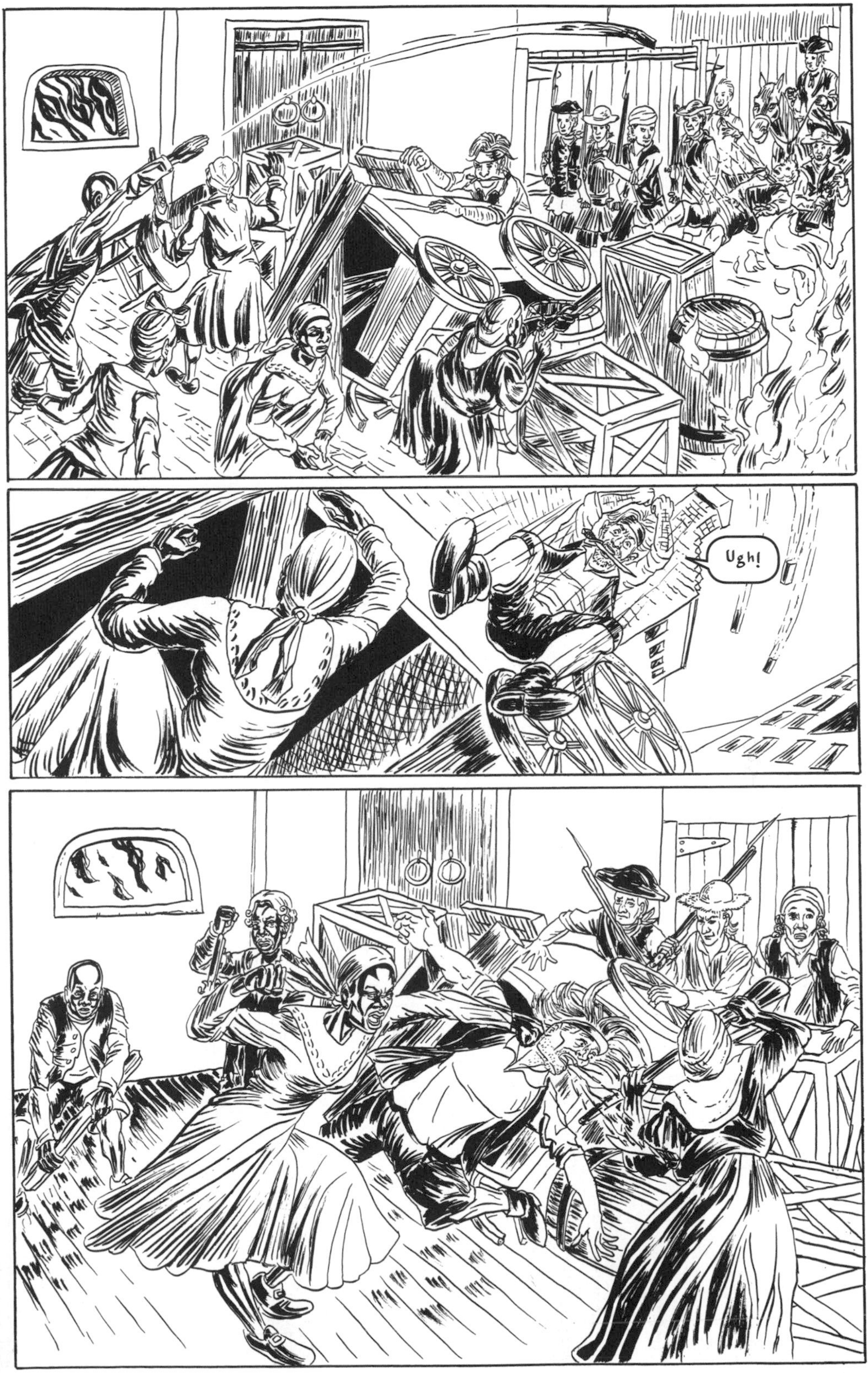
Ugh!

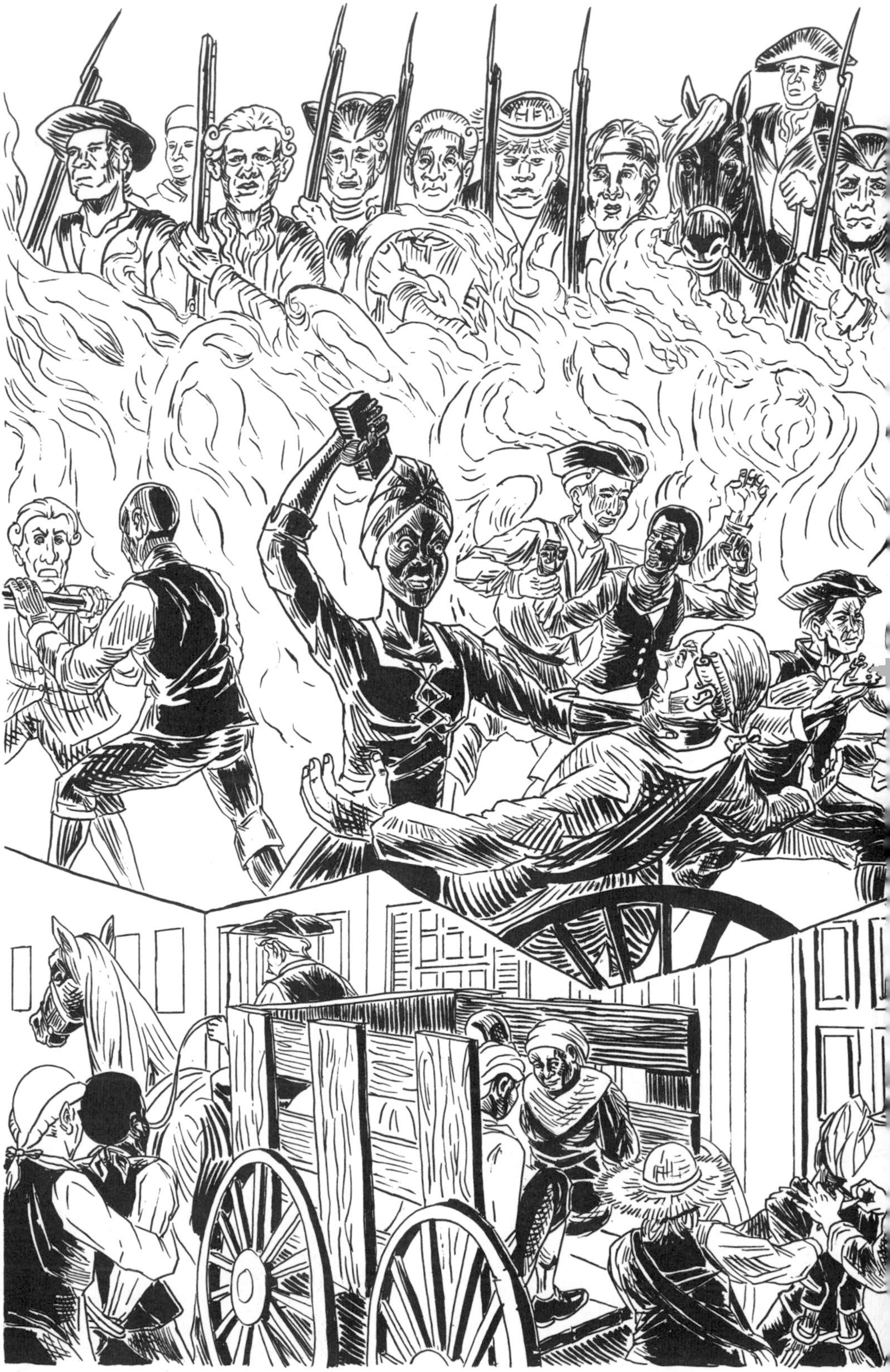

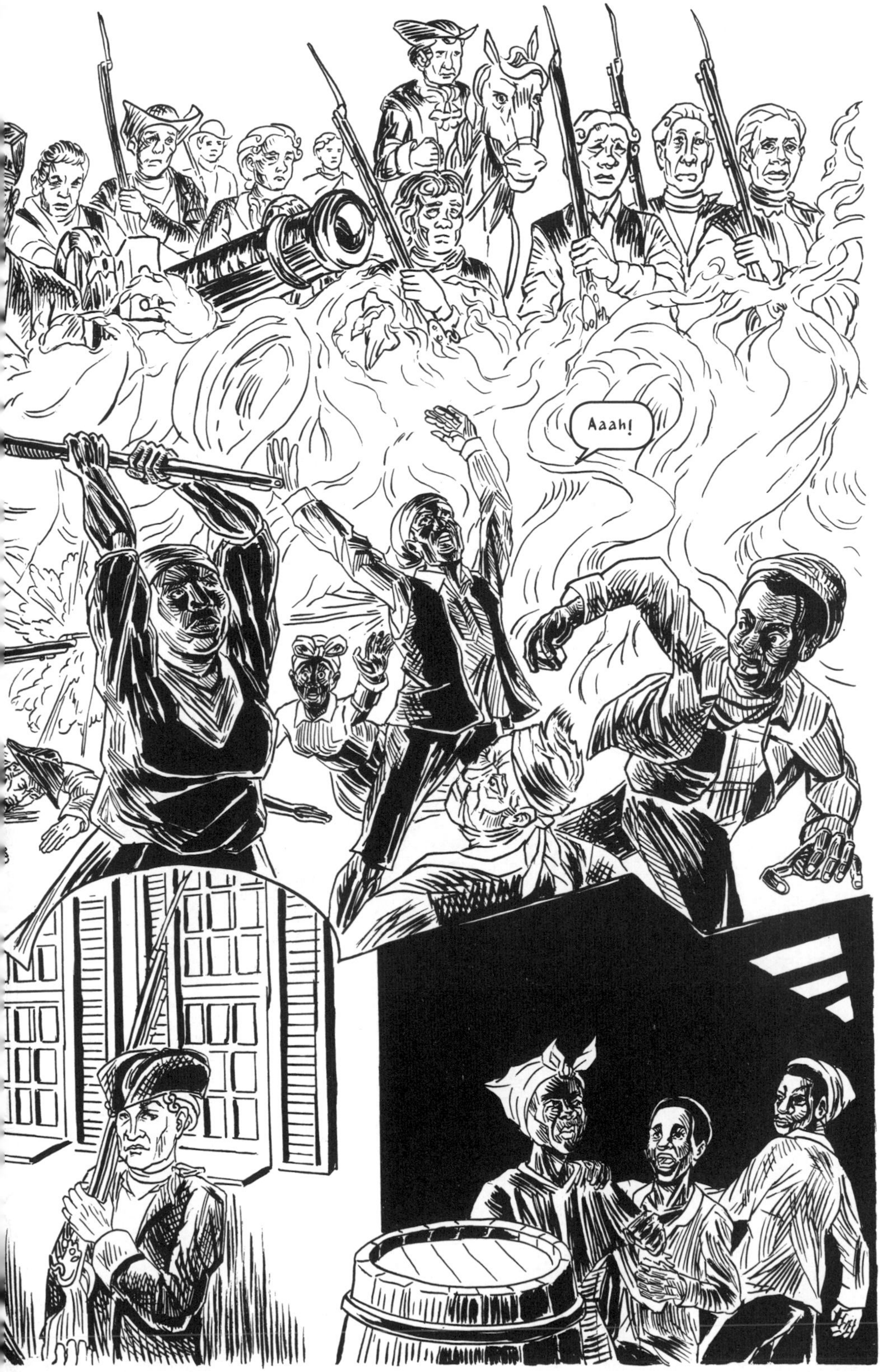
Aaah!

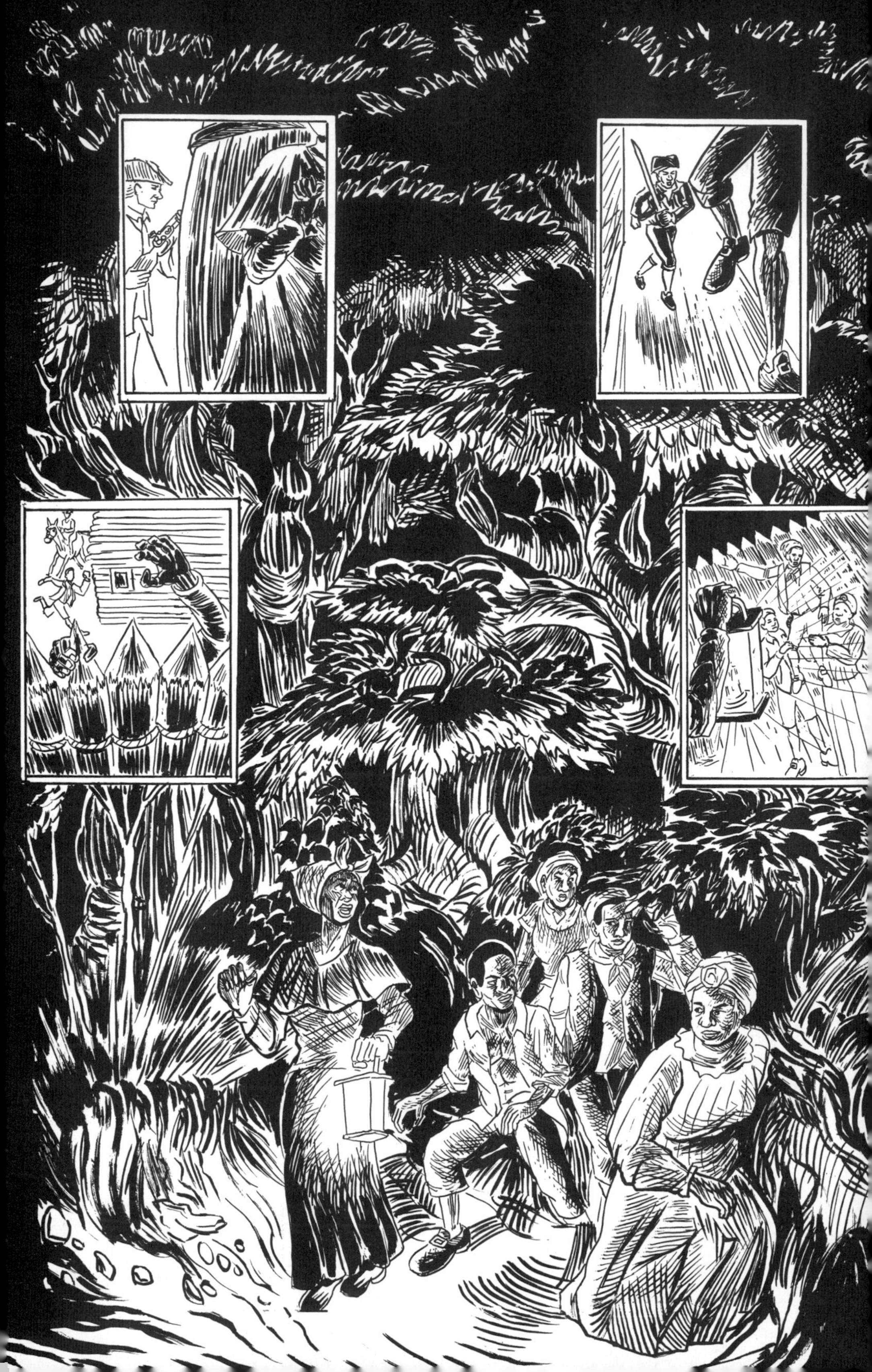

New York governor's letter to Dom Regina

June 23, 1712

We found all that put the design into execution, six of these
having first laid violent hands upon themselves, the rest
forthwith brought to trial before ye Justices of this place . . .

Twenty-seven condemned, whereof twenty-one
were executed, one being a woman with child,
her execution by that means suspended . . .

Some were burnt others hanged, one broke on the wheele,
and one hung a live in chains in the town, so that
there has been the most exemplary punishment inflicted
that can possibly be thought of . . .

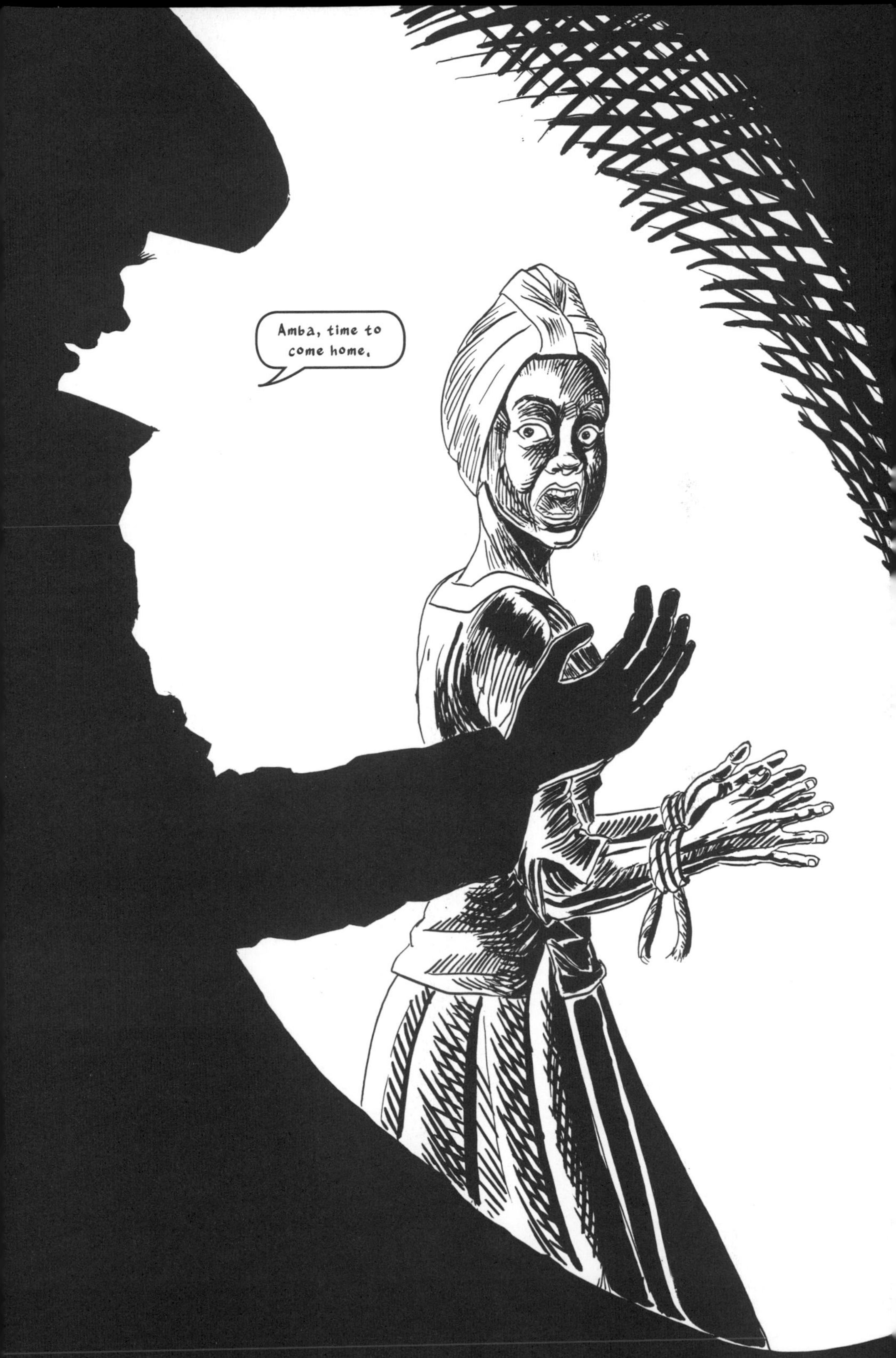
Amba, time to come home.

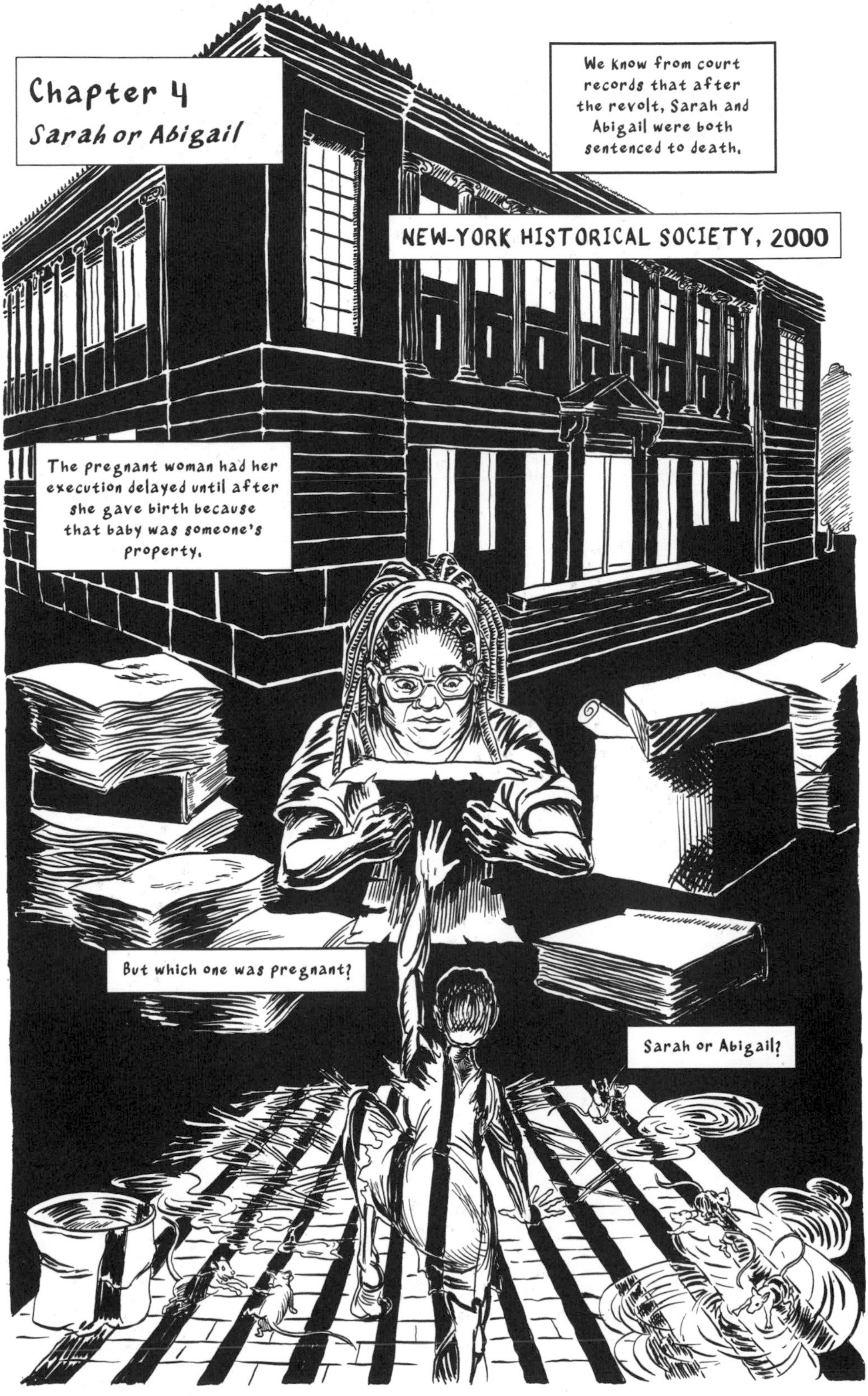
Chapter 4
Sarah or Abigail
We know from court records that after the revolt, Sarah and Abigail were both sentenced to death.
NEW-YORK HISTORICAL SOCIETY, 2000
The pregnant woman had her execution delayed until after she gave birth because that baby was someone's property.
But which one was pregnant?
Sarah or Abigail?

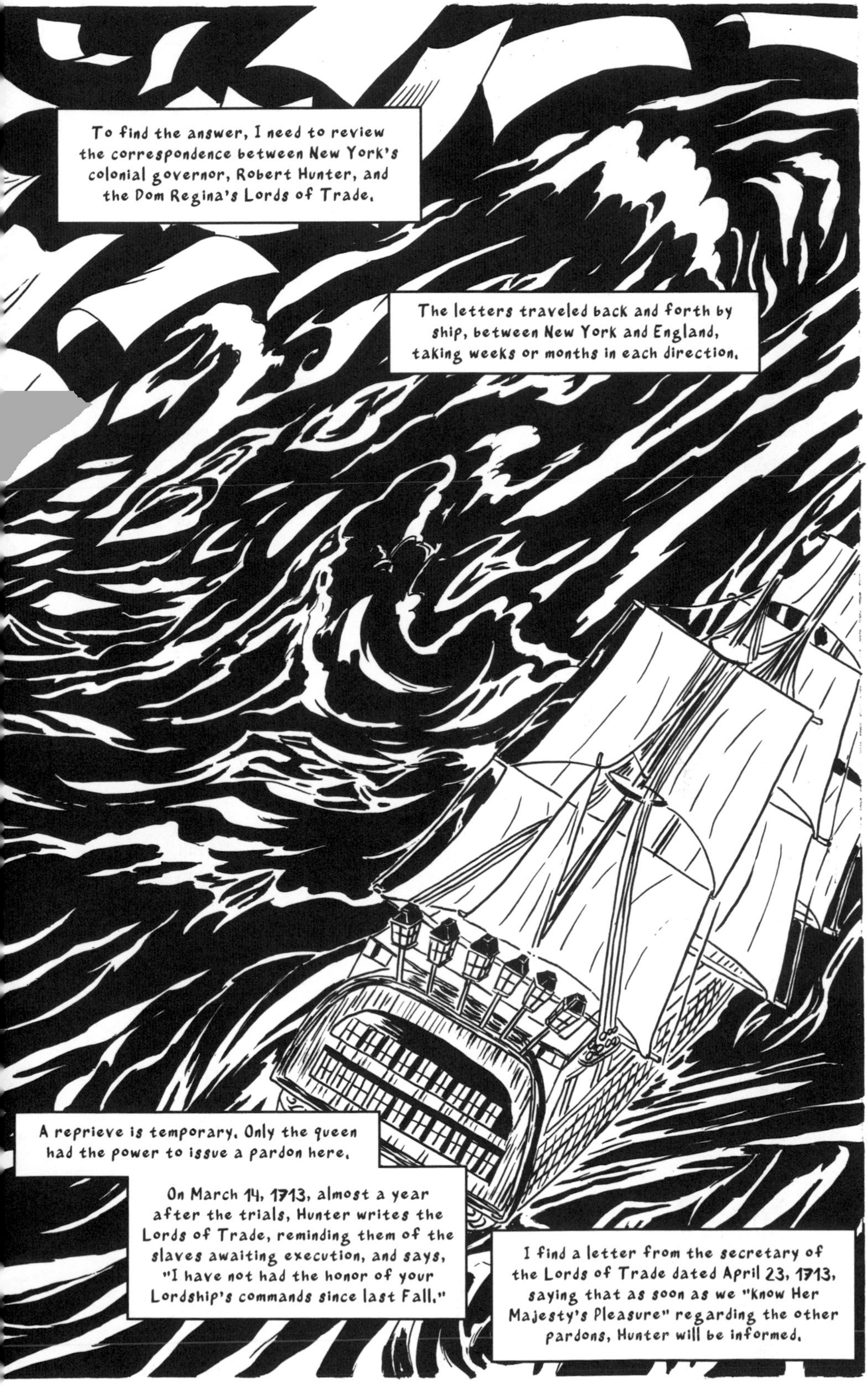
To find the answer, I need to review the correspondence between New York's colonial governor, Robert Hunter, and the Dom Regina's Lords of Trade.
The letters traveled back and forth by ship, between New York and England, taking weeks or months in each direction.
A reprieve is temporary. Only the queen had the power to issue a pardon here.
On March 14, 1713, almost a year after the trials, Hunter writes the Lords of Trade, reminding them of the slaves awaiting execution, and says, "I have not had the honor of your Lordship's commands since last Fall."
I find a letter from the secretary of the Lords of Trade dated April 23, 1713, saying that as soon as we "Know Her Majesty's Pleasure" regarding the other pardons, Hunter will be informed.

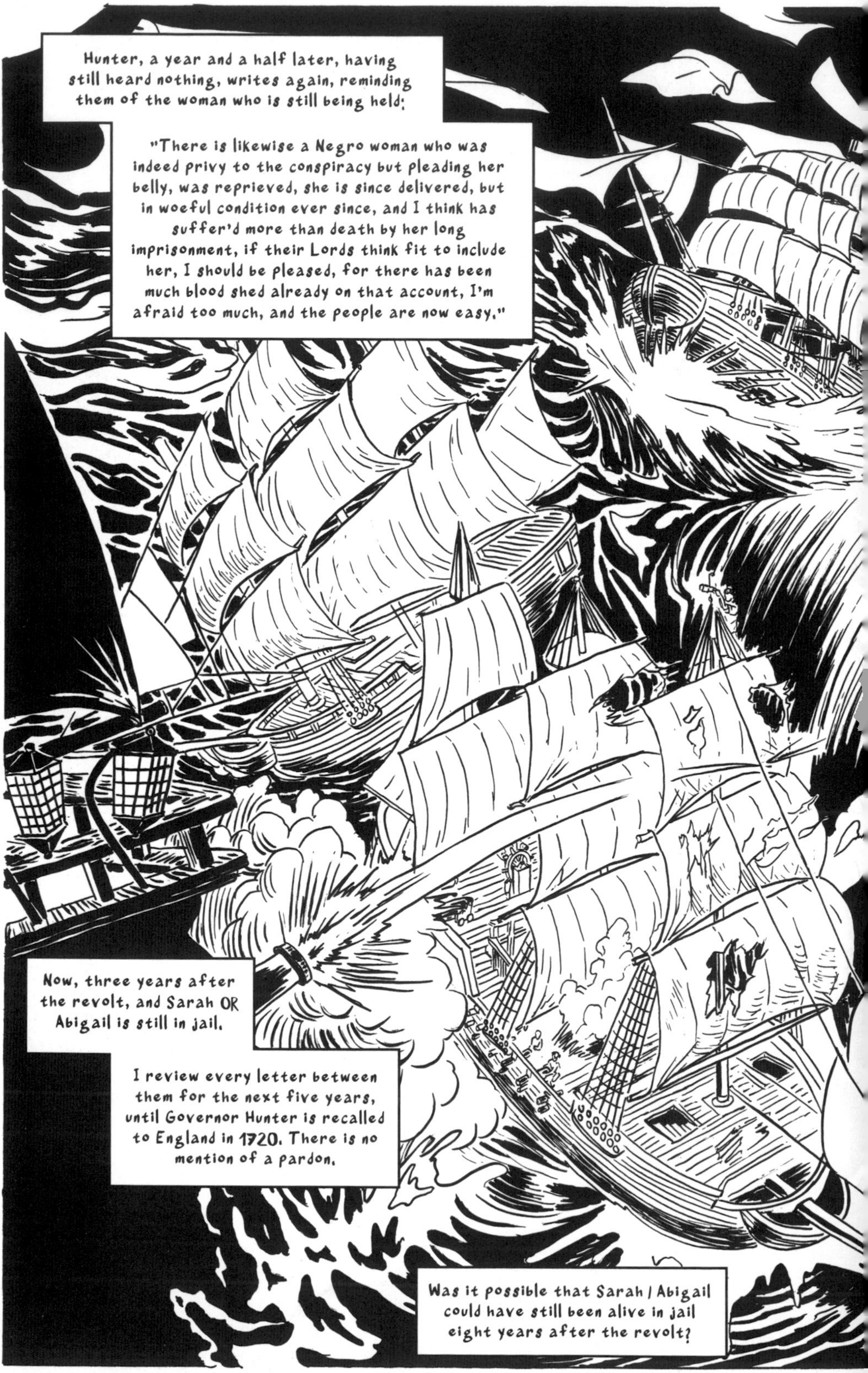
Hunter, a year and a half later, having still heard nothing, writes again, reminding them of the woman who is still being held:
"There is likewise a Negro woman who was indeed privy to the conspiracy but pleading her belly, was reprieved, she is since delivered, but in woeful condition ever since, and I think has suffer'd more than death by her long imprisonment, if their Lords think fit to include her, I should be pleased, for there has been much blood shed already on that account, I'm afraid too much, and the people are now easy."
Now, three years after the revolt, and Sarah OR Abigail is still in jail.
I review every letter between them for the next five years, until Governor Hunter is recalled to England in 1720. There is no mention of a pardon.
Was it possible that Sarah / Abigail could have still been alive in jail eight years after the revolt?

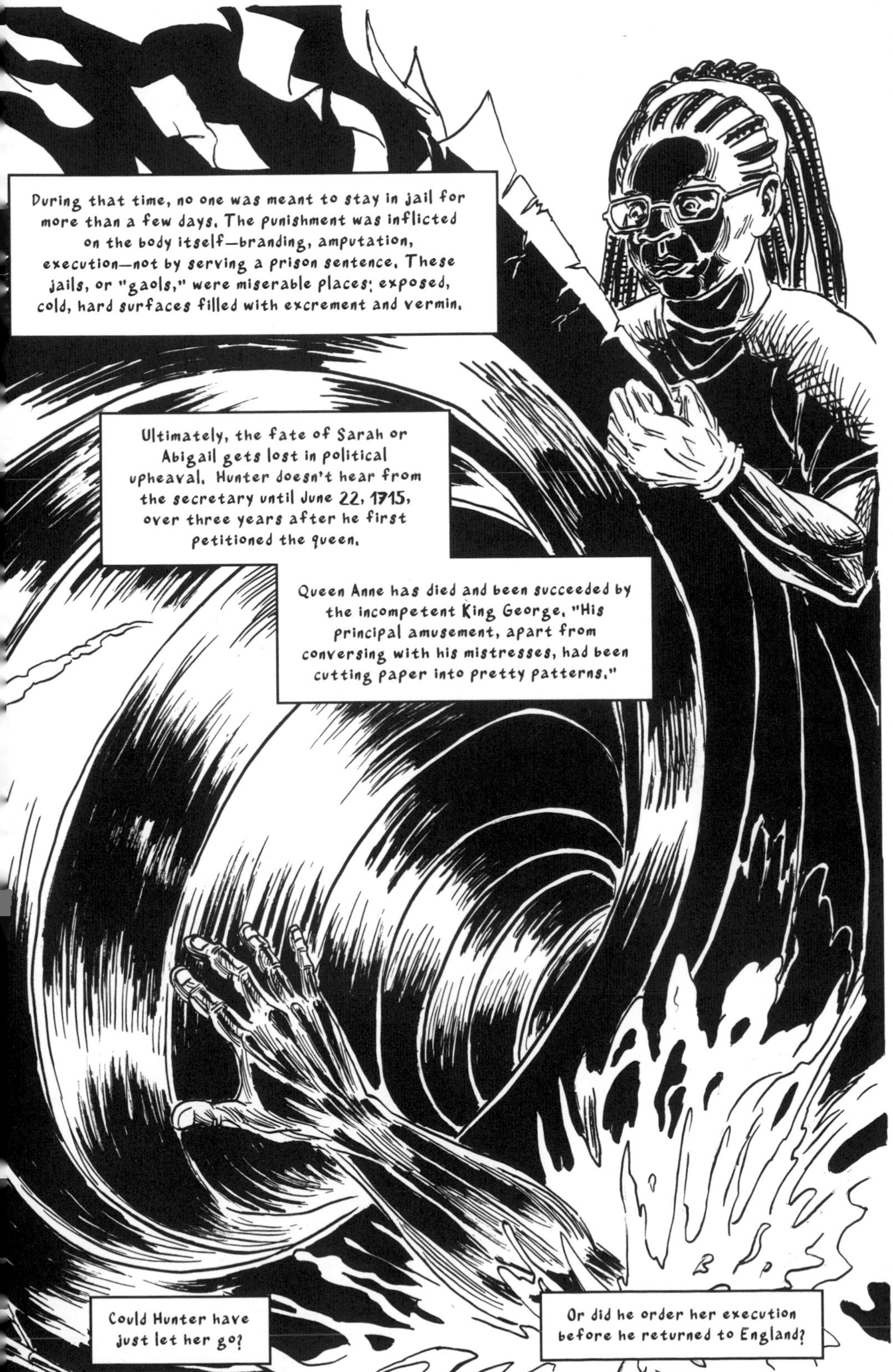
During that time, no one was meant to stay in jail for more than a few days. The punishment was inflicted on the body itself—branding, amputation, execution—not by serving a prison sentence. These jails, or "gaols," were miserable places: exposed, cold, hard surfaces filled with excrement and vermin.
Ultimately, the fate of Sarah or Abigail gets lost in political upheaval. Hunter doesn't hear from the secretary until June 22, 1715, over three years after he first petitioned the queen.
Queen Anne has died and been succeeded by the incompetent King George. "His principal amusement, apart from conversing with his mistresses, had been cutting paper into pretty patterns."
Could Hunter have just let her go?
Or did he order her execution before he returned to England?

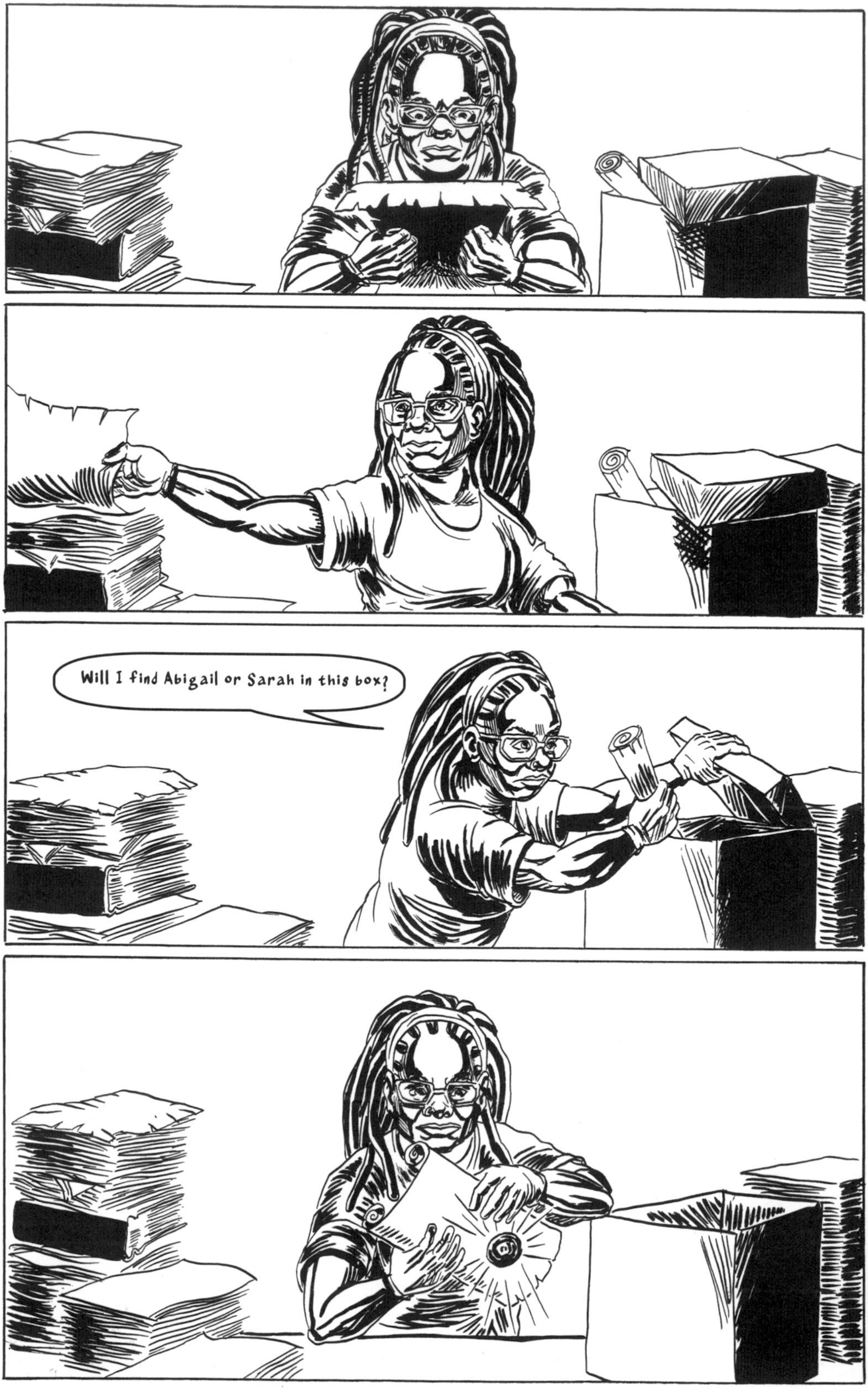
Will I find Abigail or Sarah in this box?

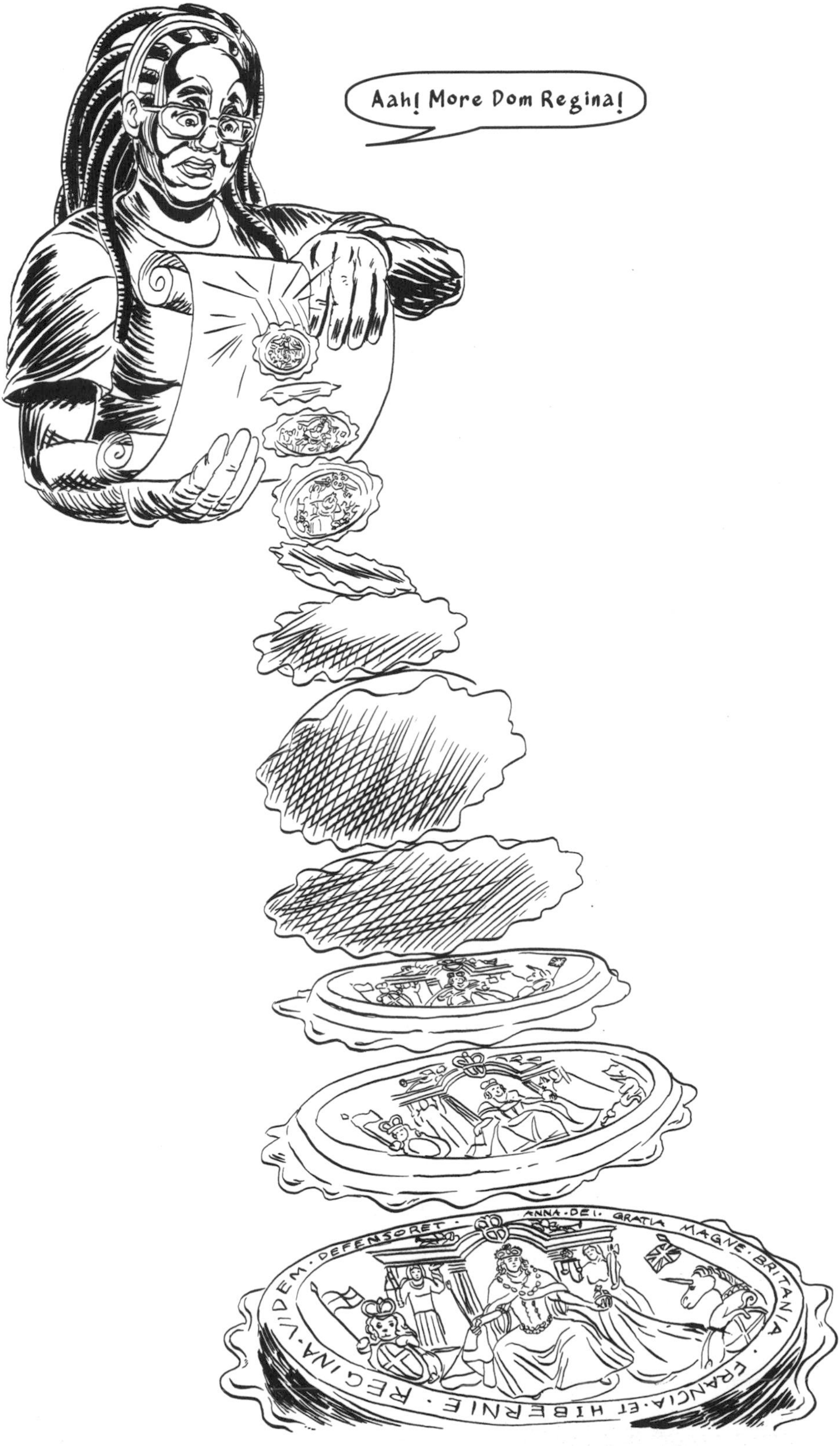
Aah! More Dom Regina!
ANNA·DEI· GRATIA MAGNE·BRITANIA· FRANCIA·ET HIBERNIE· REGINA·VIDEM·DEFENSORET·

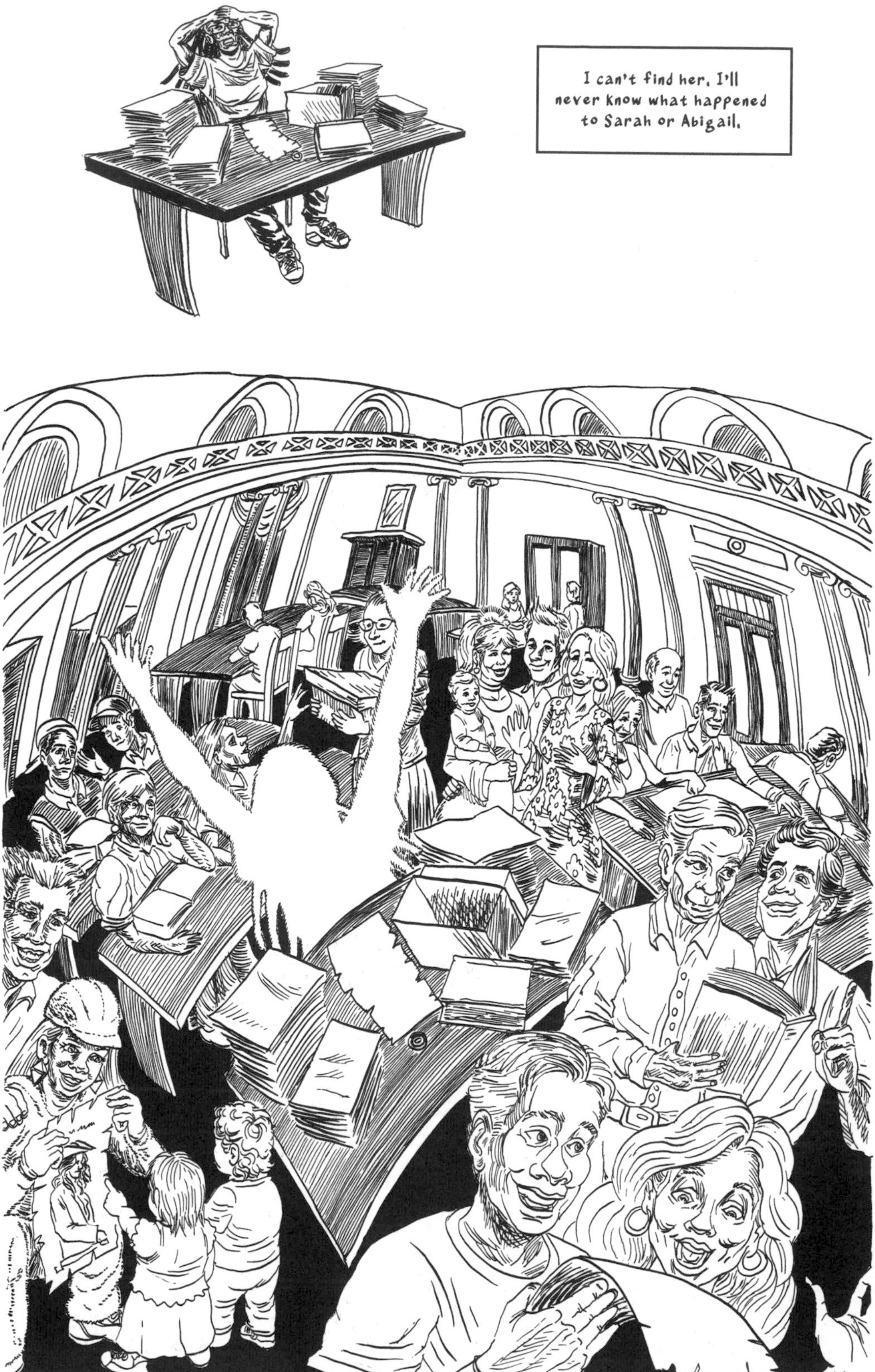
I can't find her. I'll never know what happened to Sarah or Abigail.

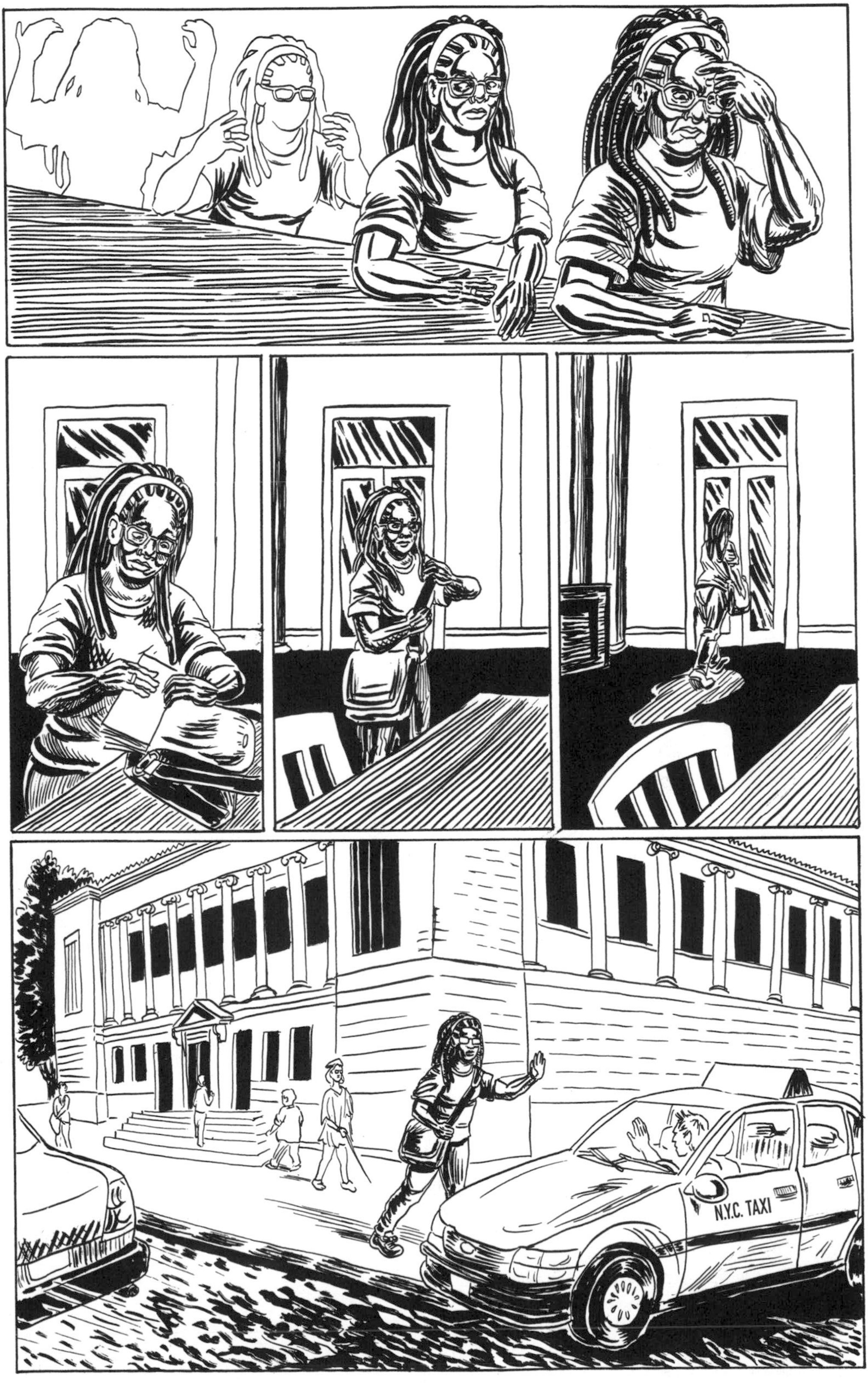
N.Y.C. TAXI

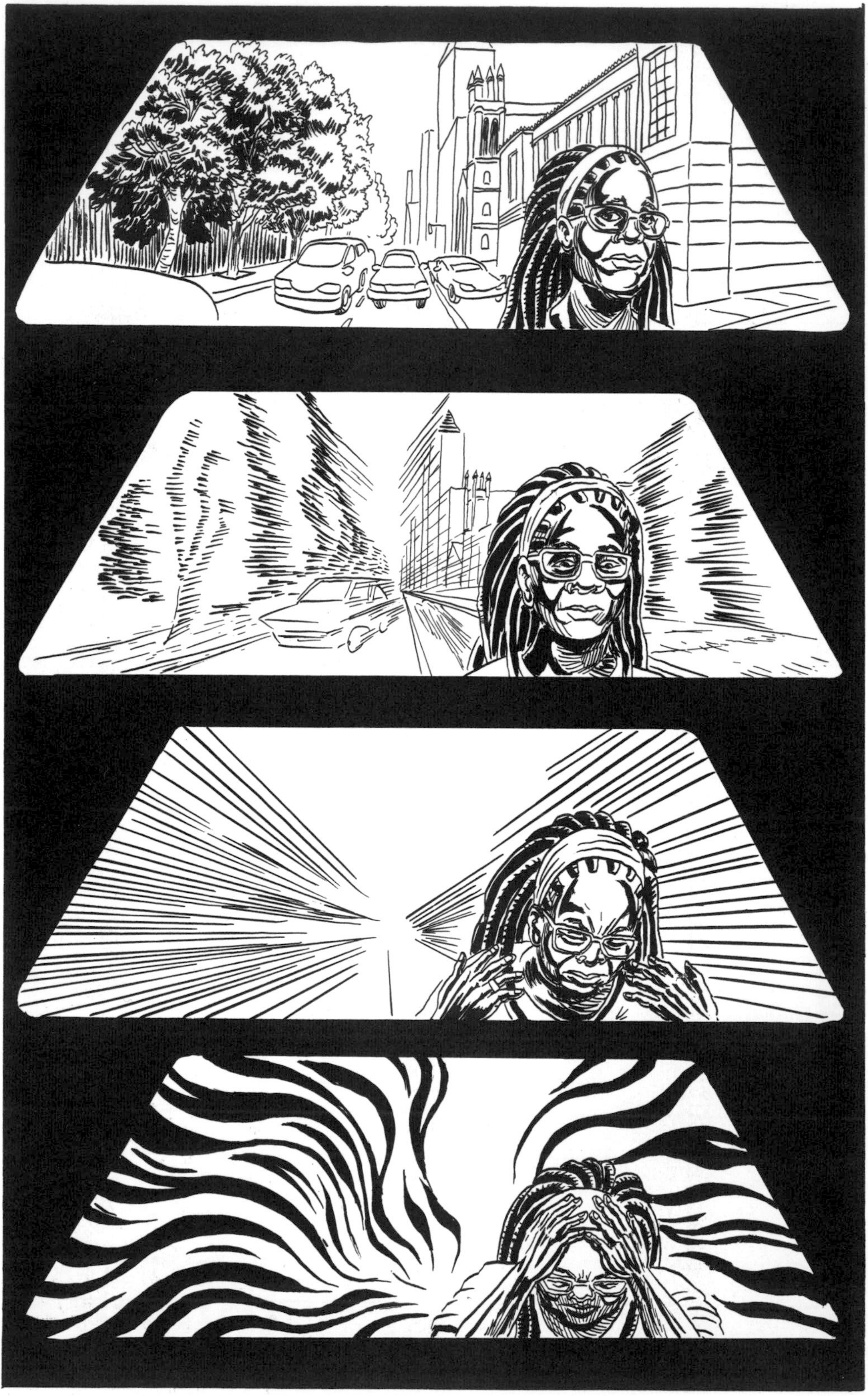

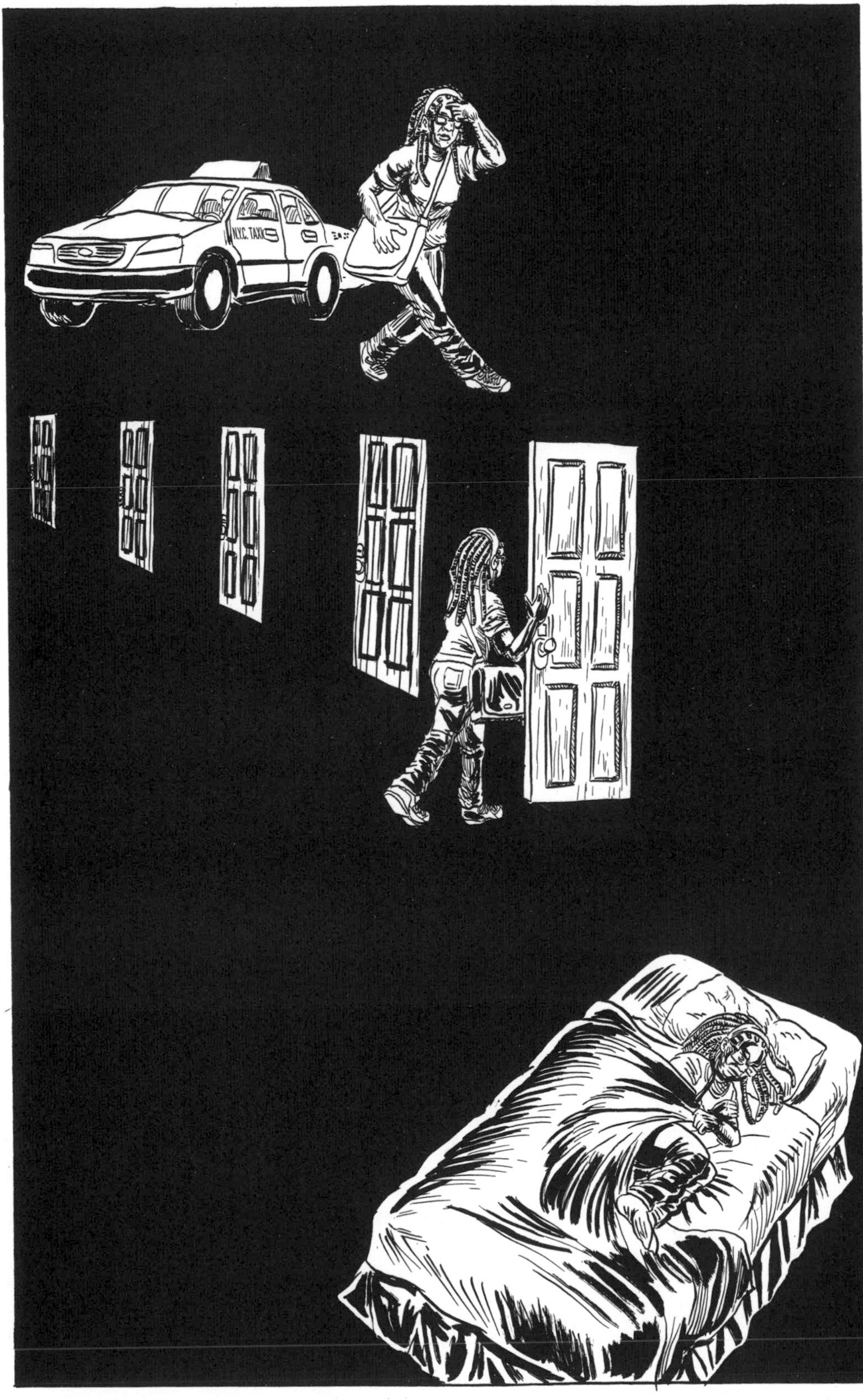
N.Y.C. TAXI

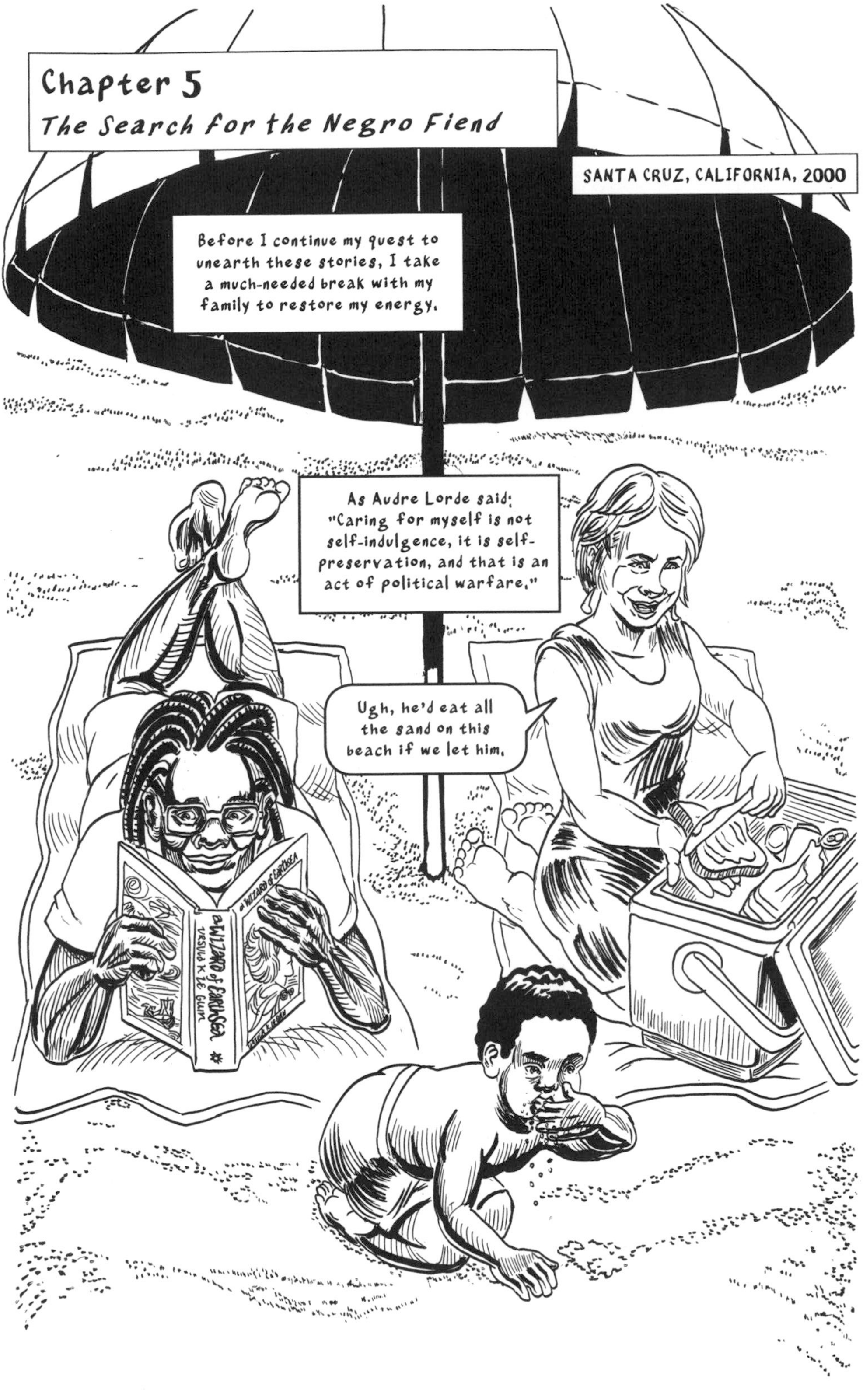
Chapter 5
The Search for the Negro Fiend
SANTA CRUZ, CALIFORNIA, 2000
Before I continue my quest to unearth these stories, I take a much-needed break with my family to restore my energy.
As Audre Lorde said: "Caring for myself is not self-indulgence, it is self-preservation, and that is an act of political warfare."
Ugh, he'd eat all the sand on this beach if we let him.

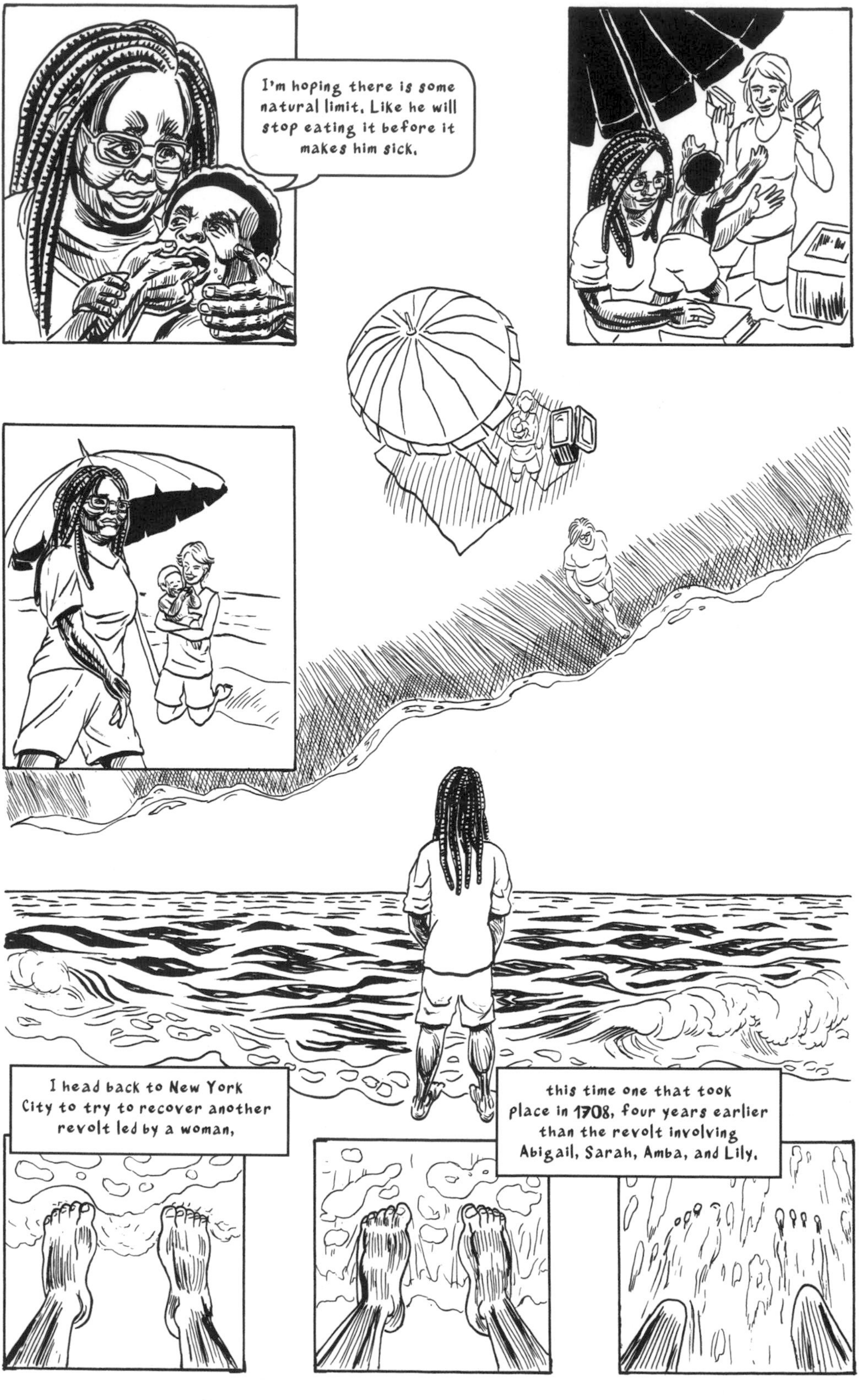
I'm hoping there is some natural limit. Like he will stop eating it before it makes him sick.
I head back to New York City to try to recover another revolt led by a woman,
this time one that took place in 1708, four years earlier than the revolt involving Abigail, Sarah, Amba, and Lily.

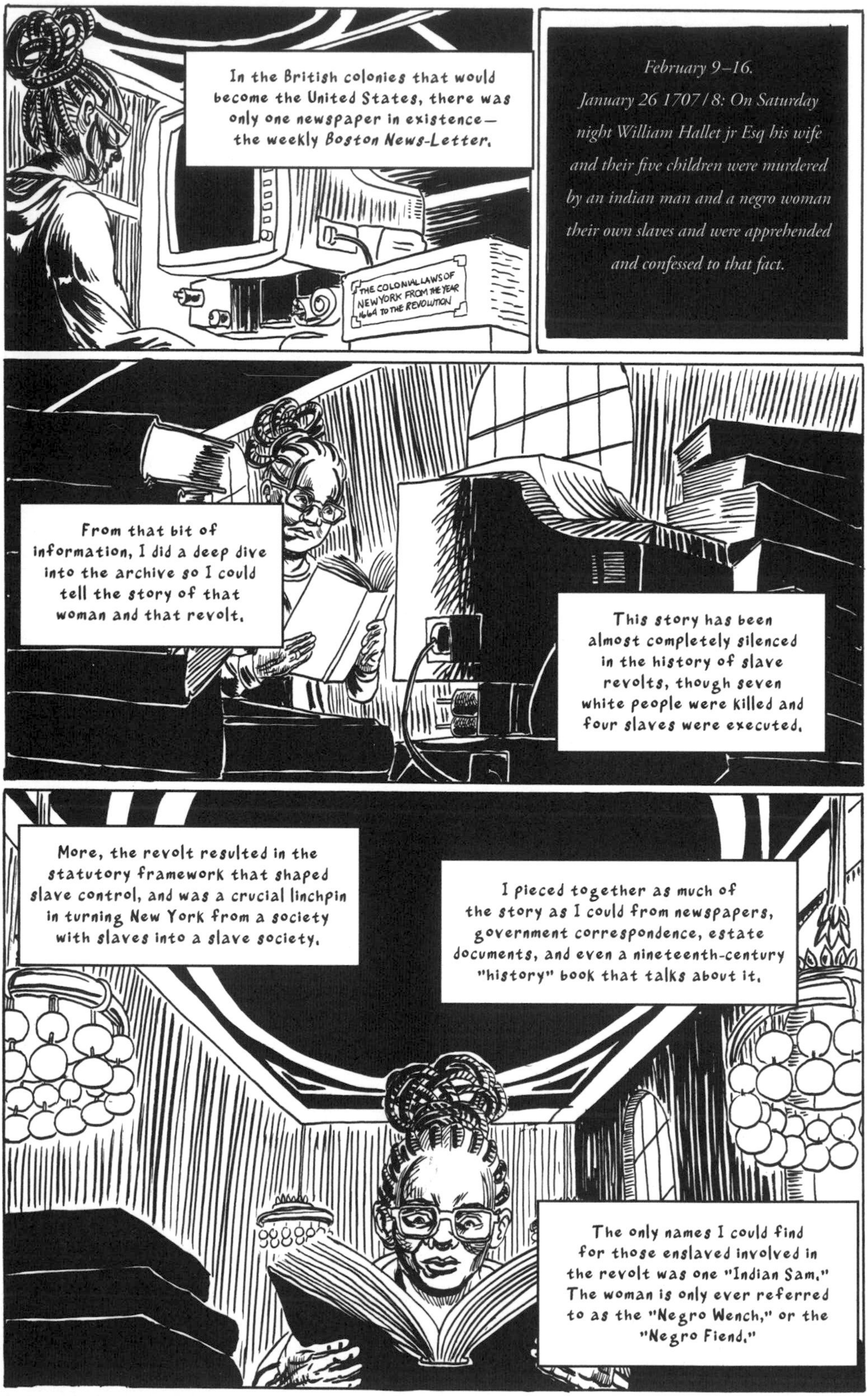
In the British colonies that would become the United States, there was only one newspaper in existence—the weekly *Boston News-Letter*.
THE COLONIAL LAWS OF NEW YORK FROM THE YEAR 1664 TO THE REVOLUTION
February 9–16. January 26 1707/8: On Saturday night William Hallet jr Esq his wife and their five children were murdered by an indian man and a negro woman their own slaves and were apprehended and confessed to that fact.
From that bit of information, I did a deep dive into the archive so I could tell the story of that woman and that revolt.
This story has been almost completely silenced in the history of slave revolts, though seven white people were killed and four slaves were executed.
More, the revolt resulted in the statutory framework that shaped slave control, and was a crucial linchpin in turning New York from a society with slaves into a slave society.
I pieced together as much of the story as I could from newspapers, government correspondence, estate documents, and even a nineteenth-century "history" book that talks about it.
The only names I could find for those enslaved involved in the revolt was one "Indian Sam." The woman is only ever referred to as the "Negro Wench," or the "Negro Fiend."

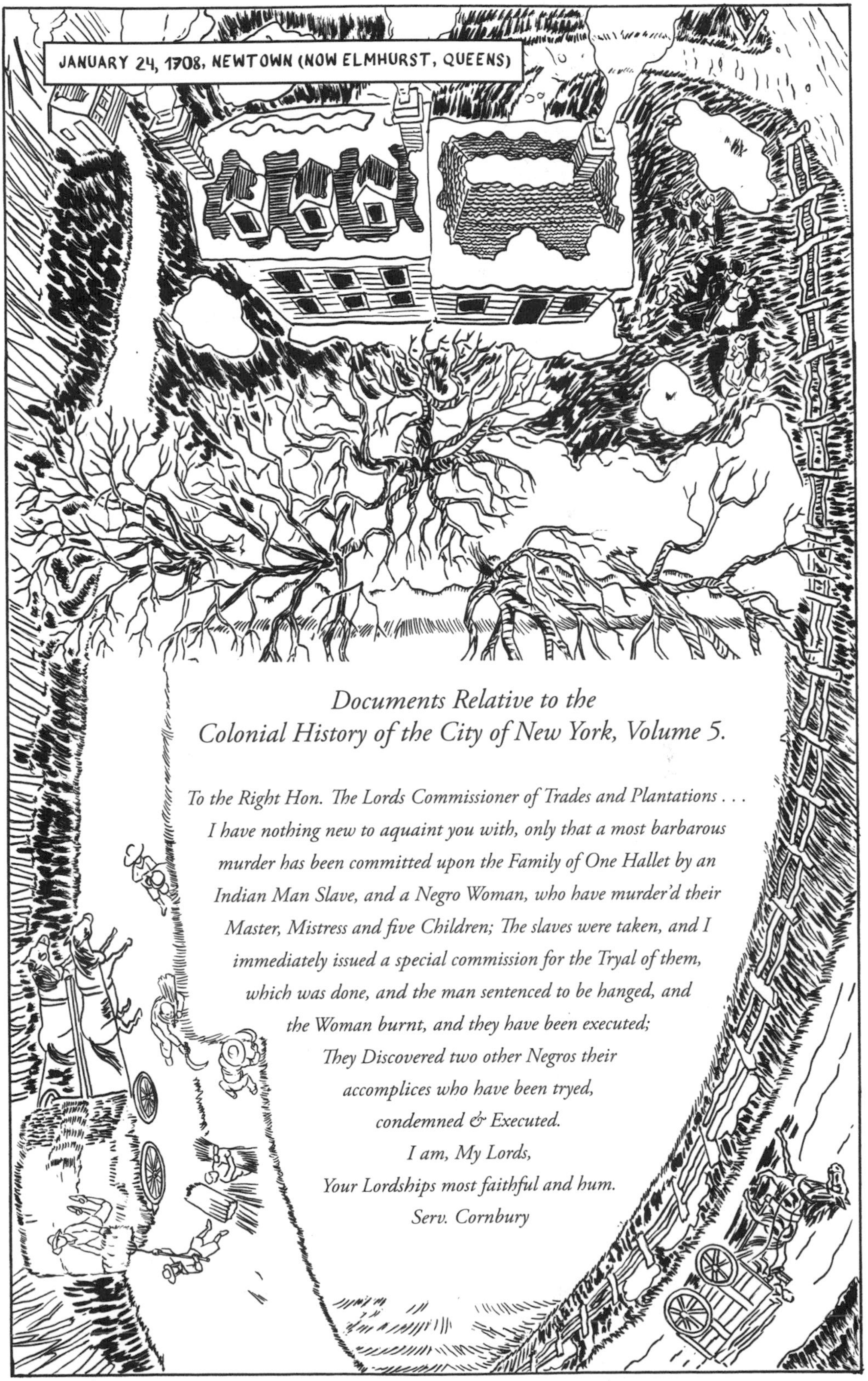
JANUARY 24, 1708, NEWTOWN (NOW ELMHURST, QUEENS)
Documents Relative to the Colonial History of the City of New York, Volume 5.
To the Right Hon. The Lords Commissioner of Trades and Plantations . . . I have nothing new to aquaint you with, only that a most barbarous murder has been committed upon the Family of One Hallet by an Indian Man Slave, and a Negro Woman, who have murder'd their Master, Mistress and five Children; The slaves were taken, and I immediately issued a special commission for the Tryal of them, which was done, and the man sentenced to be hanged, and the Woman burnt, and they have been executed; They Discovered two other Negros their accomplices who have been tryed, condemned & Executed.
I am, My Lords,
Your Lordships most faithful and hum.
Serv. Cornbury

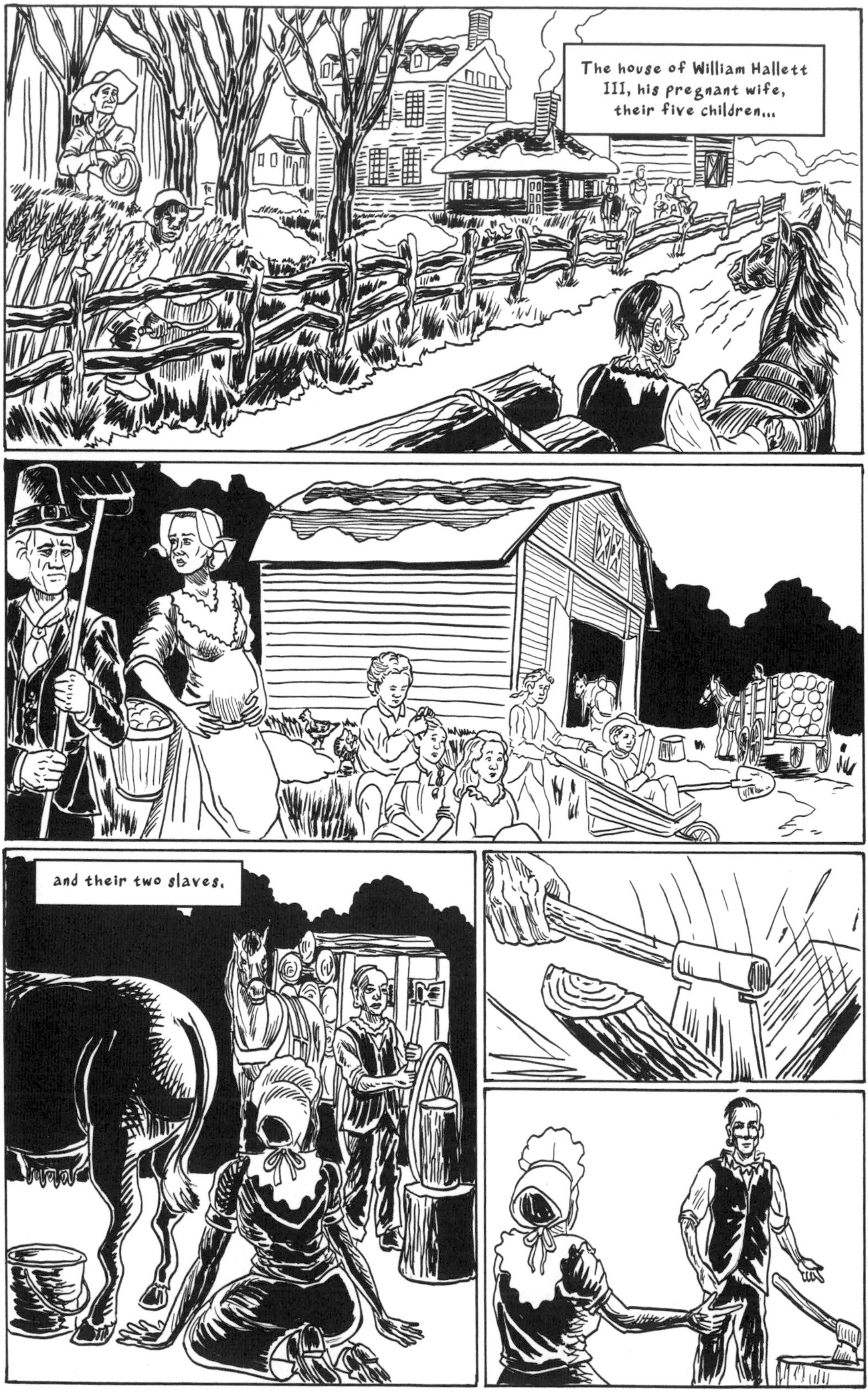
The house of William Hallett III, his pregnant wife, their five children...
and their two slaves.

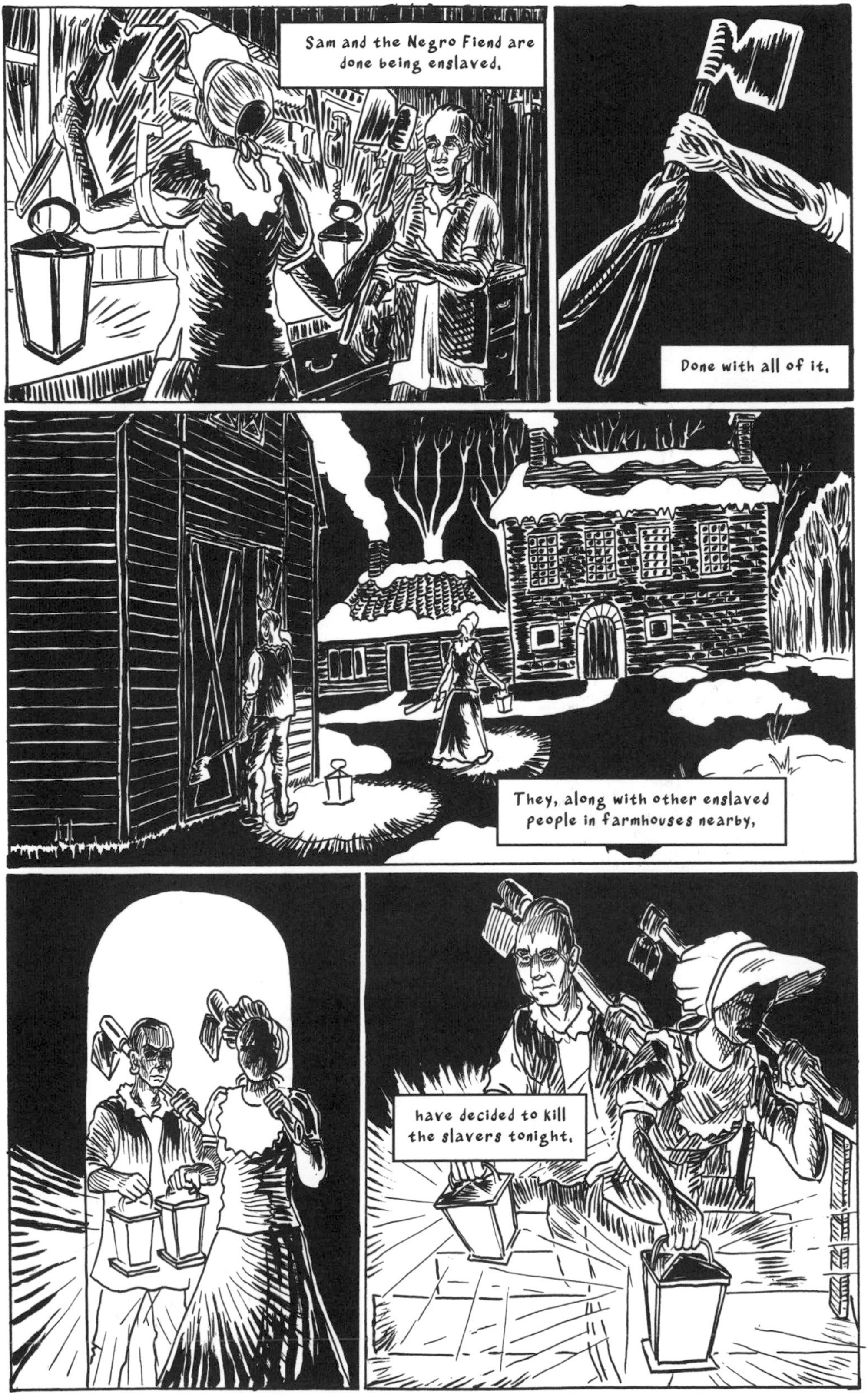
Sam and the Negro Fiend are done being enslaved.
Done with all of it.
They, along with other enslaved people in farmhouses nearby,
have decided to kill the slavers tonight.

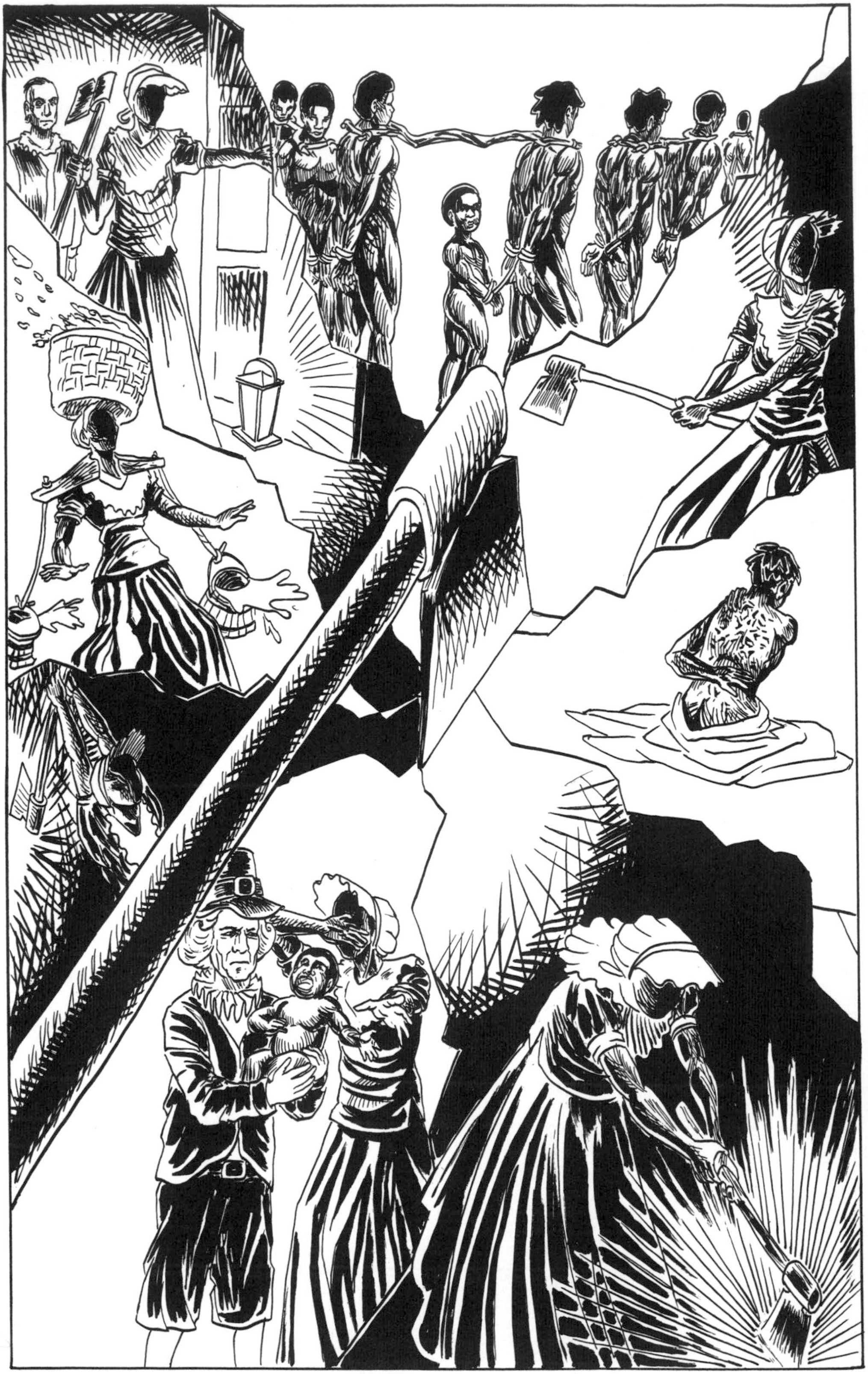

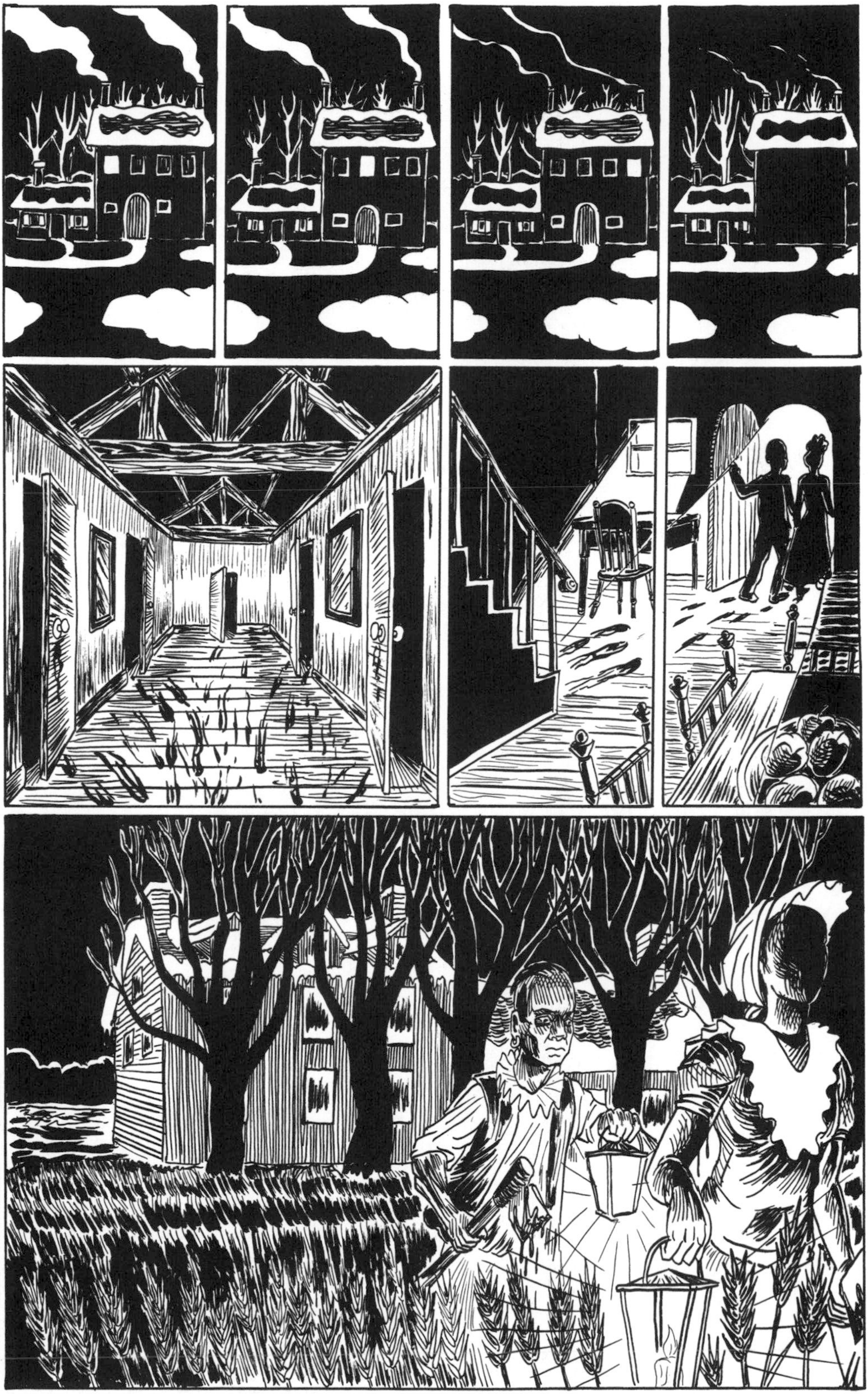

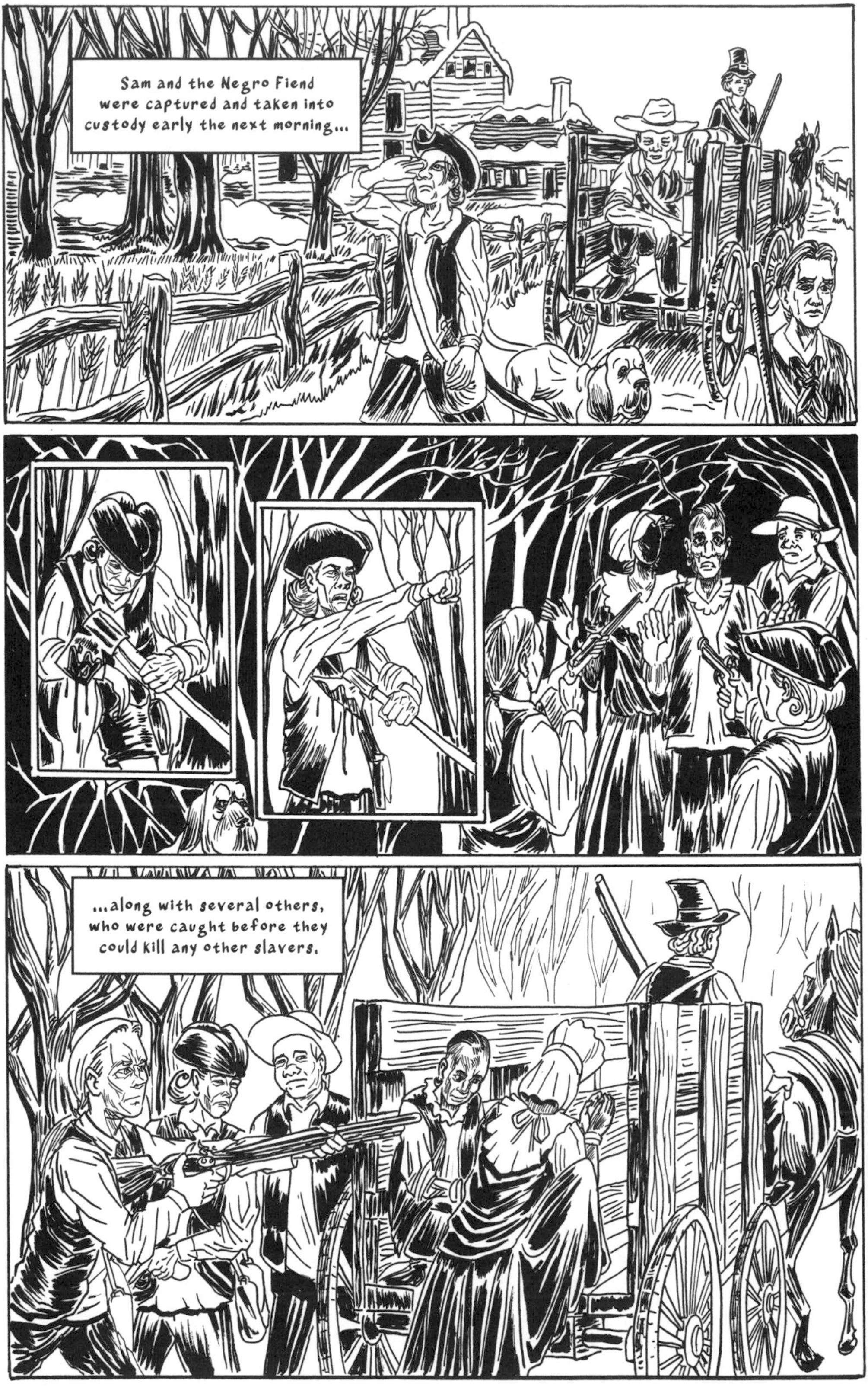
Sam and the Negro Fiend were captured and taken into custody early the next morning...
...along with several others, who were caught before they could kill any other slavers.

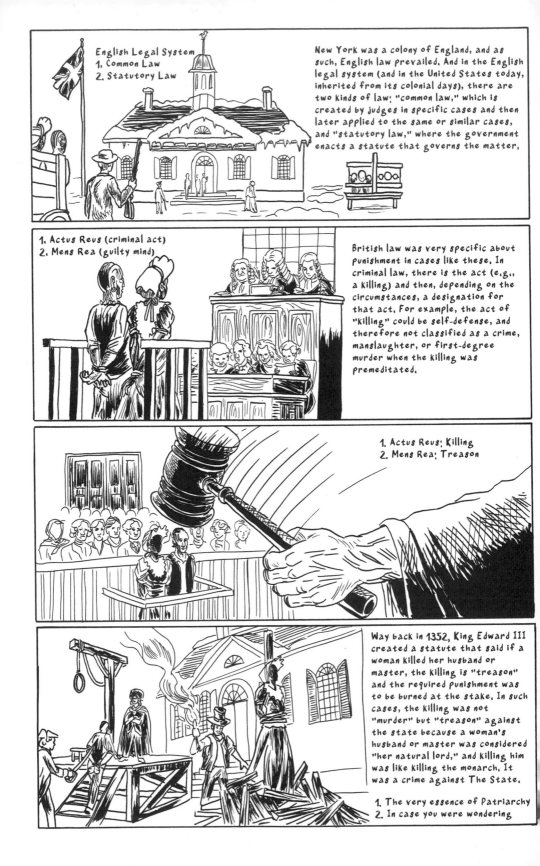

English Legal System
1. Common Law
2. Statutory Law

New York was a colony of England, and as such, English law prevailed. And in the English legal system (and in the United States today, inherited from its colonial days), there are two kinds of law: "common law," which is created by judges in specific cases and then later applied to the same or similar cases, and "statutory law," where the government enacts a statute that governs the matter.

1. Actus Reus (criminal act)
2. Mens Rea (guilty mind)

British law was very specific about punishment in cases like these. In criminal law, there is the act (e.g., a killing) and then, depending on the circumstances, a designation for that act. For example, the act of "killing" could be self-defense, and therefore not classified as a crime, manslaughter, or first-degree murder when the killing was premeditated.

1. Actus Reus: Killing
2. Mens Rea: Treason

Way back in 1352, King Edward III created a statute that said if a woman killed her husband or master, the killing is "treason" and the required punishment was to be burned at the stake. In such cases, the killing was not "murder" but "treason" against the state because a woman's husband or master was considered "her natural lord," and killing him was like killing the monarch. It was a crime against The State.

1. The very essence of Patriarchy
2. In case you were wondering

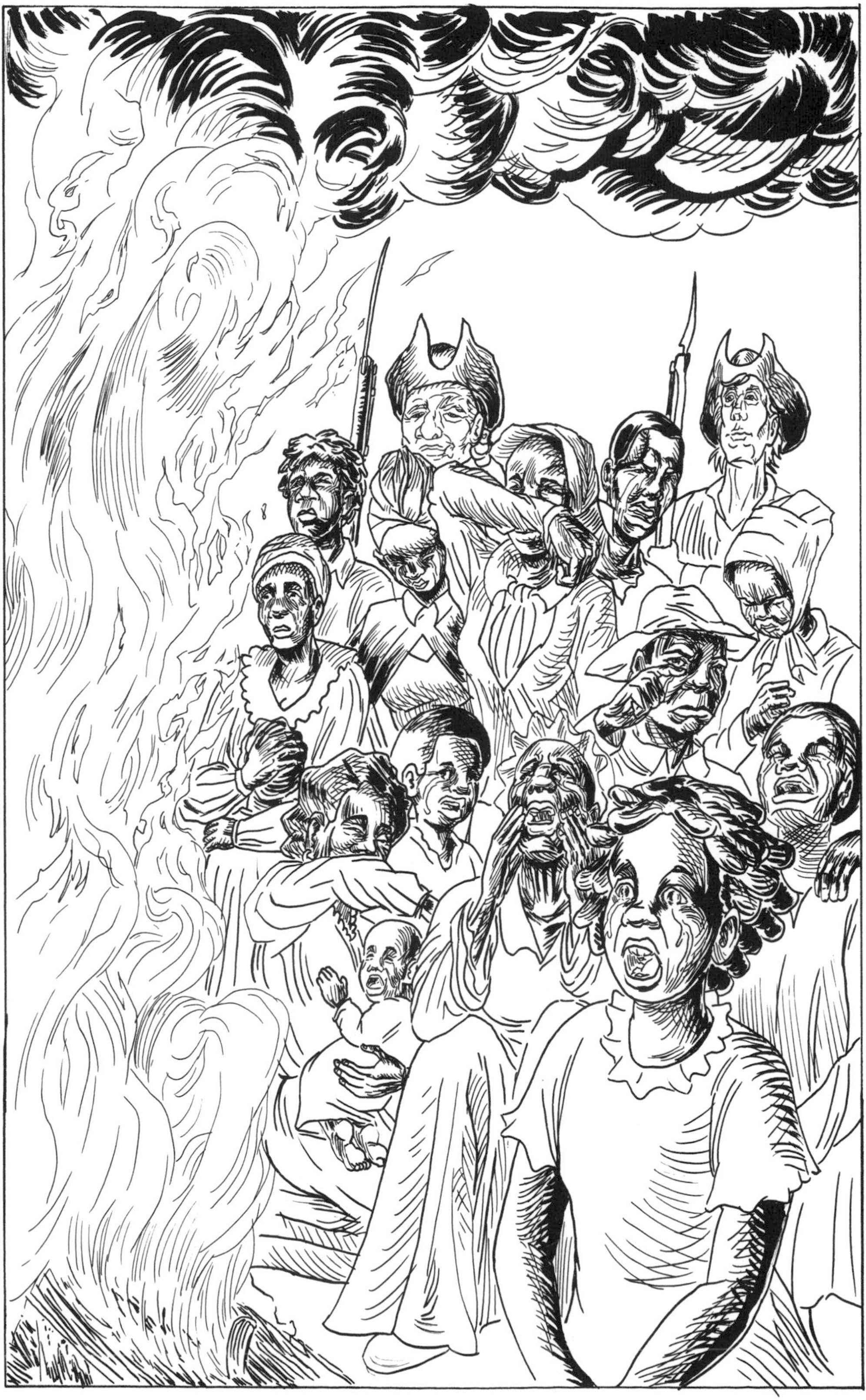

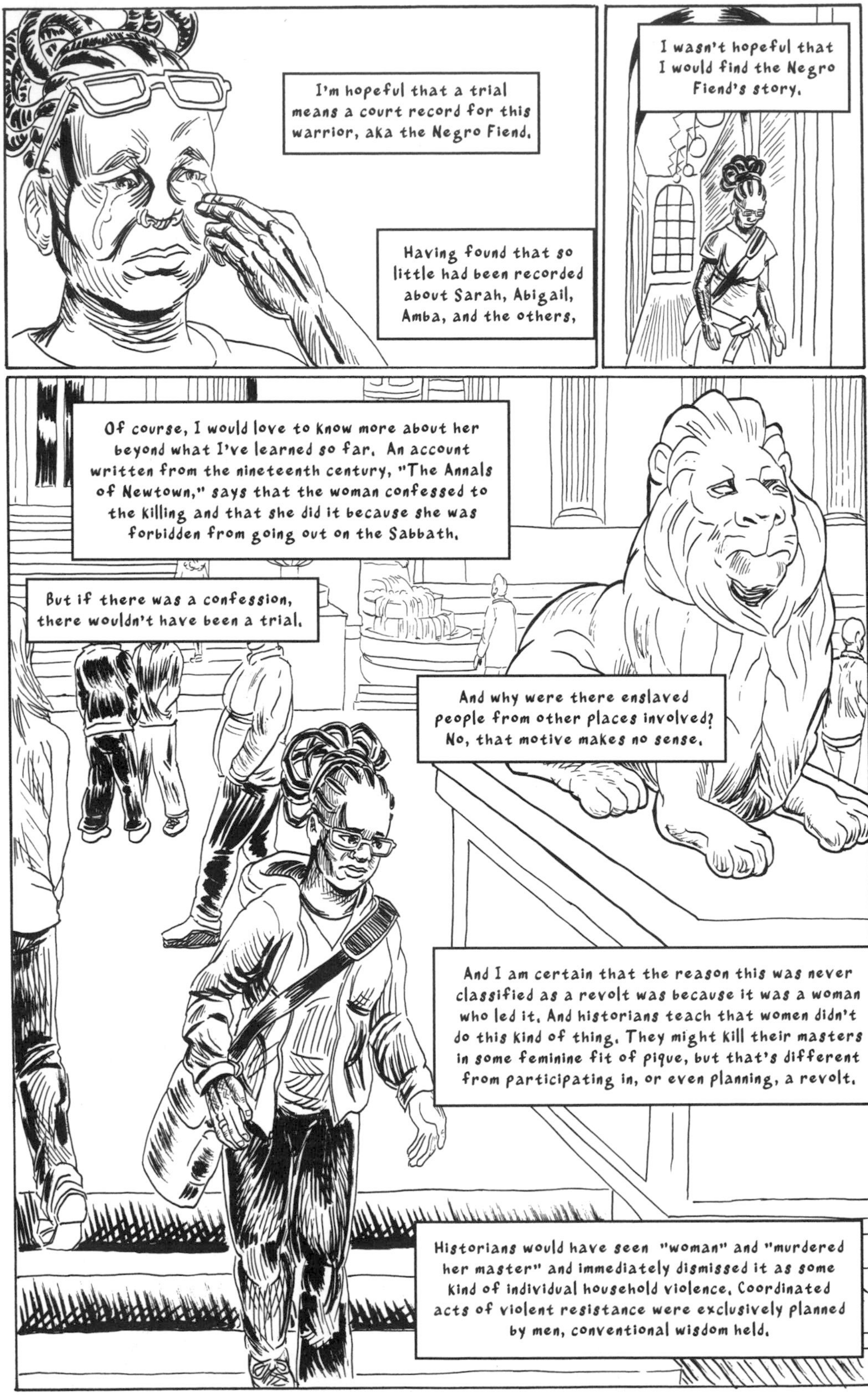
I'm hopeful that a trial means a court record for this warrior, aka the Negro Fiend.
Having found that so little had been recorded about Sarah, Abigail, Amba, and the others,
I wasn't hopeful that I would find the Negro Fiend's story.
Of course, I would love to know more about her beyond what I've learned so far. An account written from the nineteenth century, "The Annals of Newtown," says that the woman confessed to the killing and that she did it because she was forbidden from going out on the Sabbath.
But if there was a confession, there wouldn't have been a trial.
And why were there enslaved people from other places involved? No, that motive makes no sense.
And I am certain that the reason this was never classified as a revolt was because it was a woman who led it. And historians teach that women didn't do this kind of thing. They might kill their masters in some feminine fit of pique, but that's different from participating in, or even planning, a revolt.
Historians would have seen "woman" and "murdered her master" and immediately dismissed it as some kind of individual household violence. Coordinated acts of violent resistance were exclusively planned by men, conventional wisdom held.

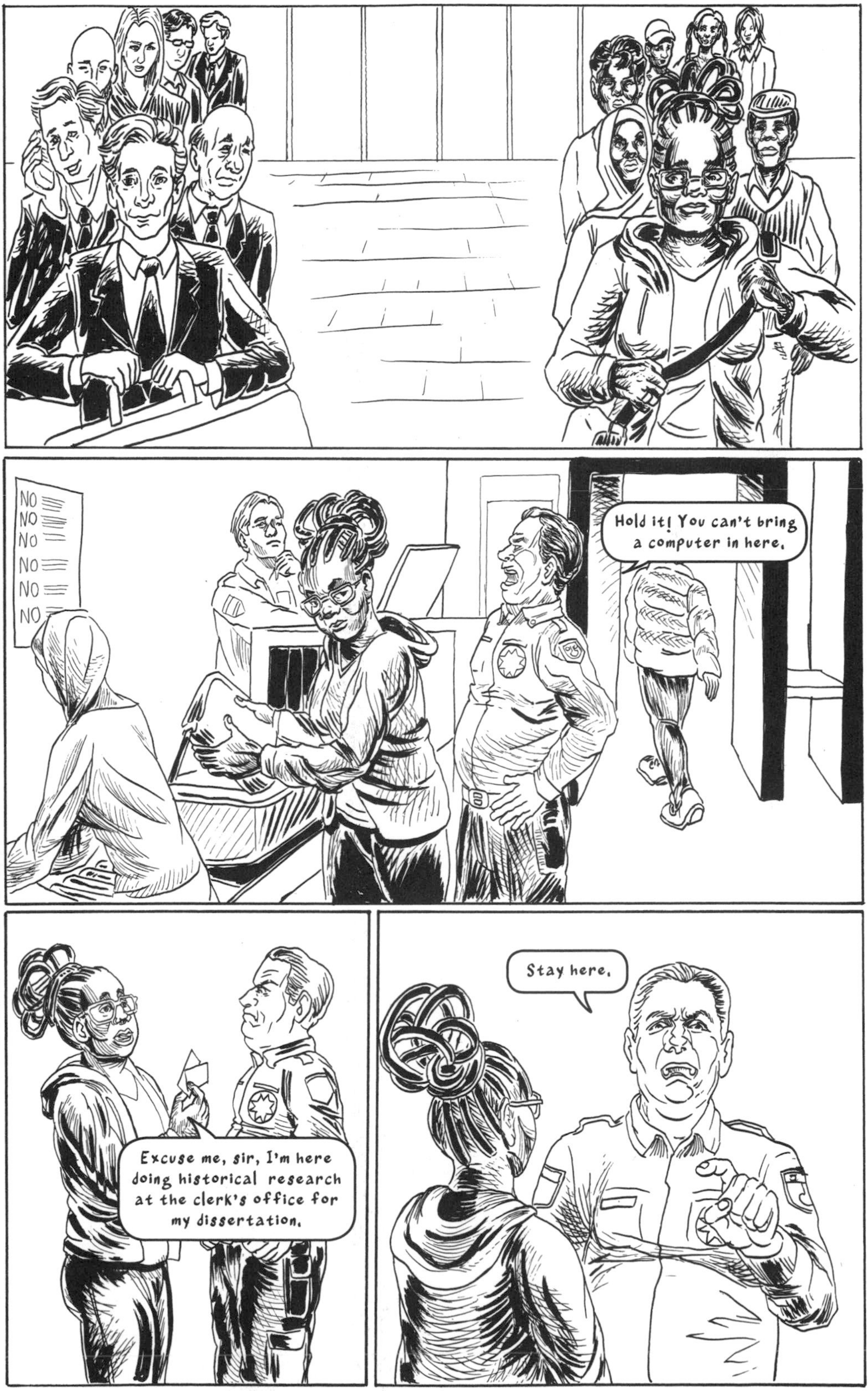
NO
NO
NO
NO
NO
NO
Hold it! You can't bring a computer in here.
Excuse me, sir, I'm here doing historical research at the clerk's office for my dissertation.
Stay here.

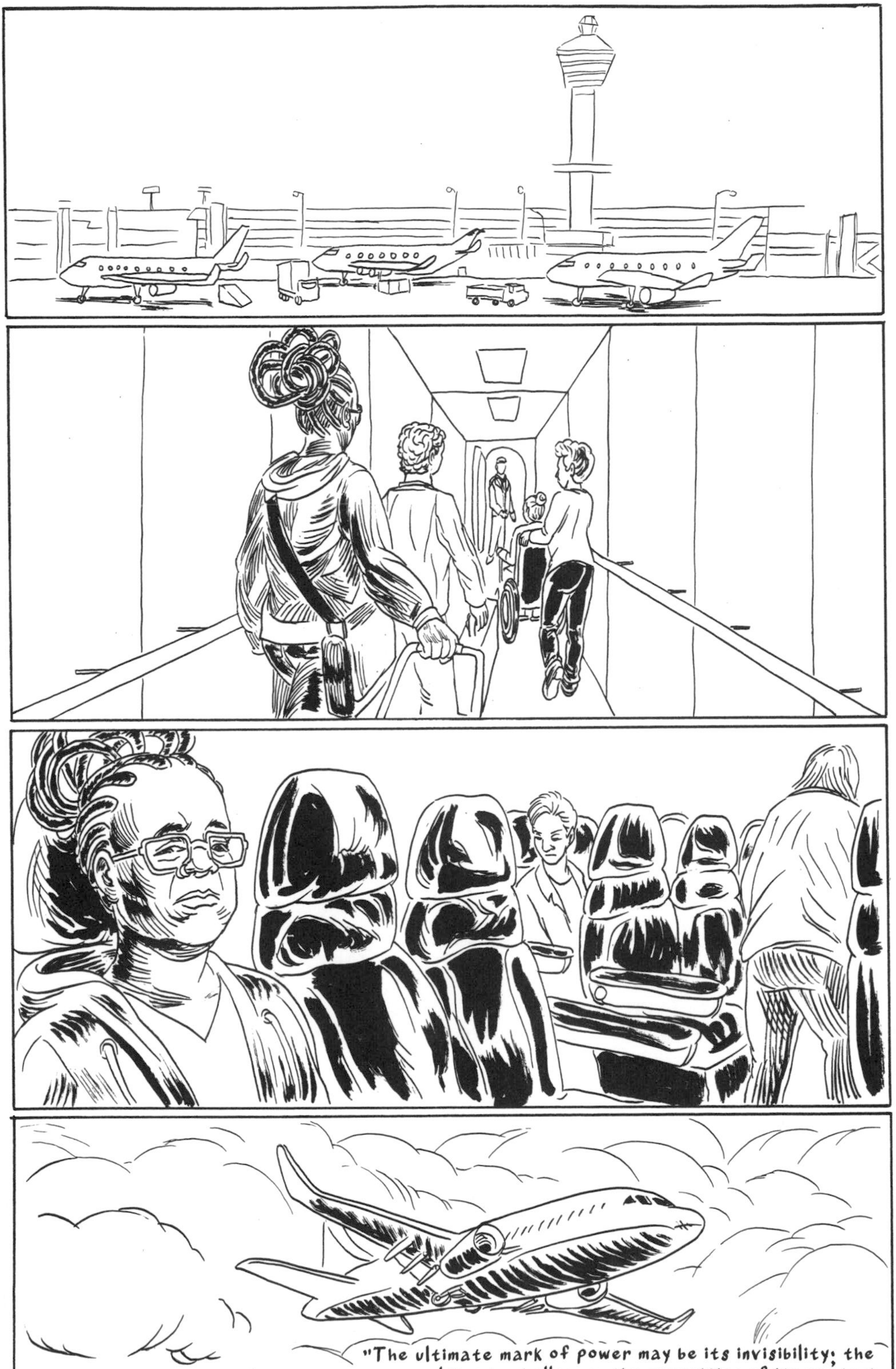
"The ultimate mark of power may be its invisibility; the ultimate challenge, the exposition of its roots."
—Michel-Rolph Trouillot

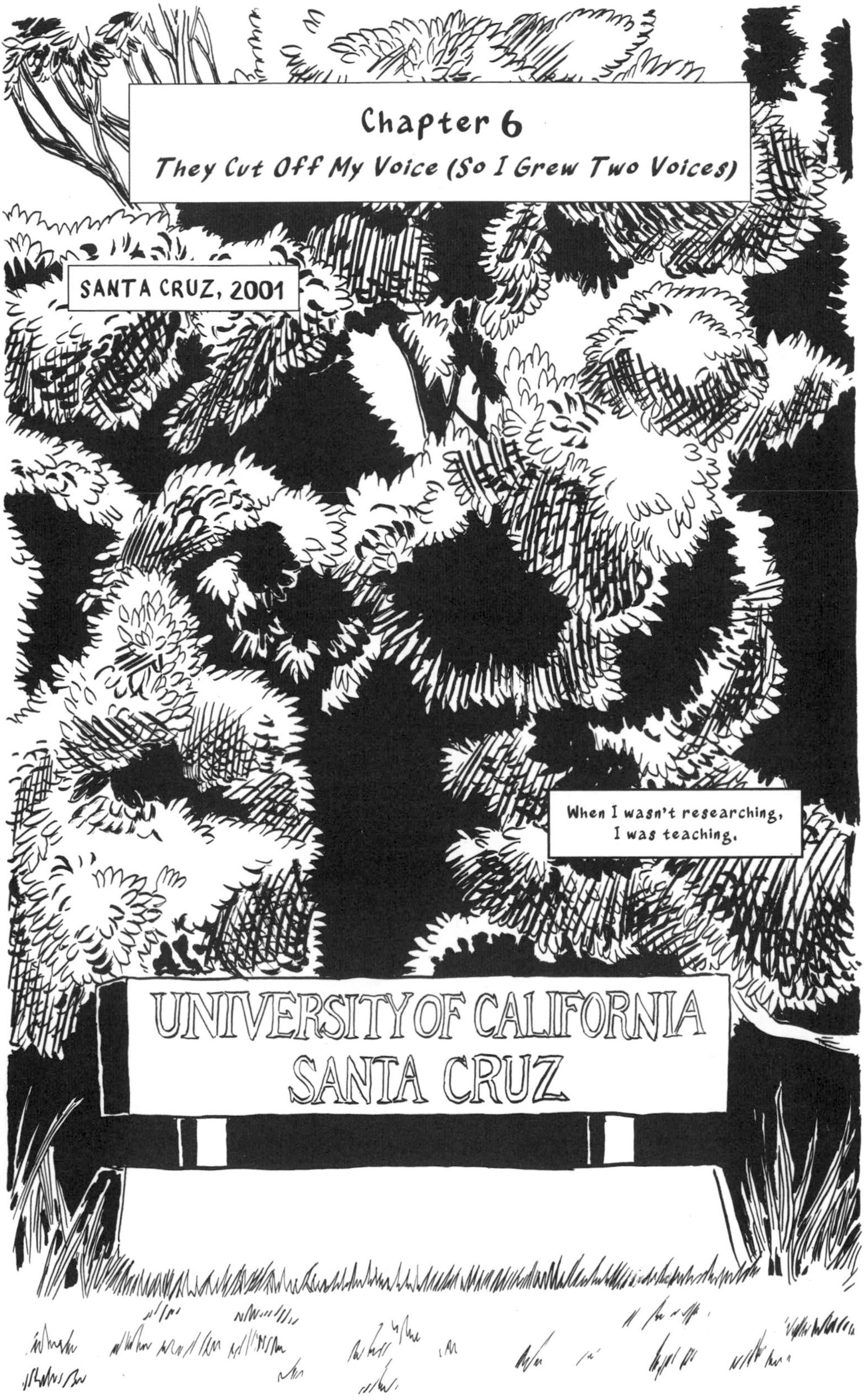
Chapter 6
They Cut Off My Voice (So I Grew Two Voices)
SANTA CRUZ, 2001
When I wasn't researching, I was teaching.
UNIVERSITY OF CALIFORNIA
SANTA CRUZ

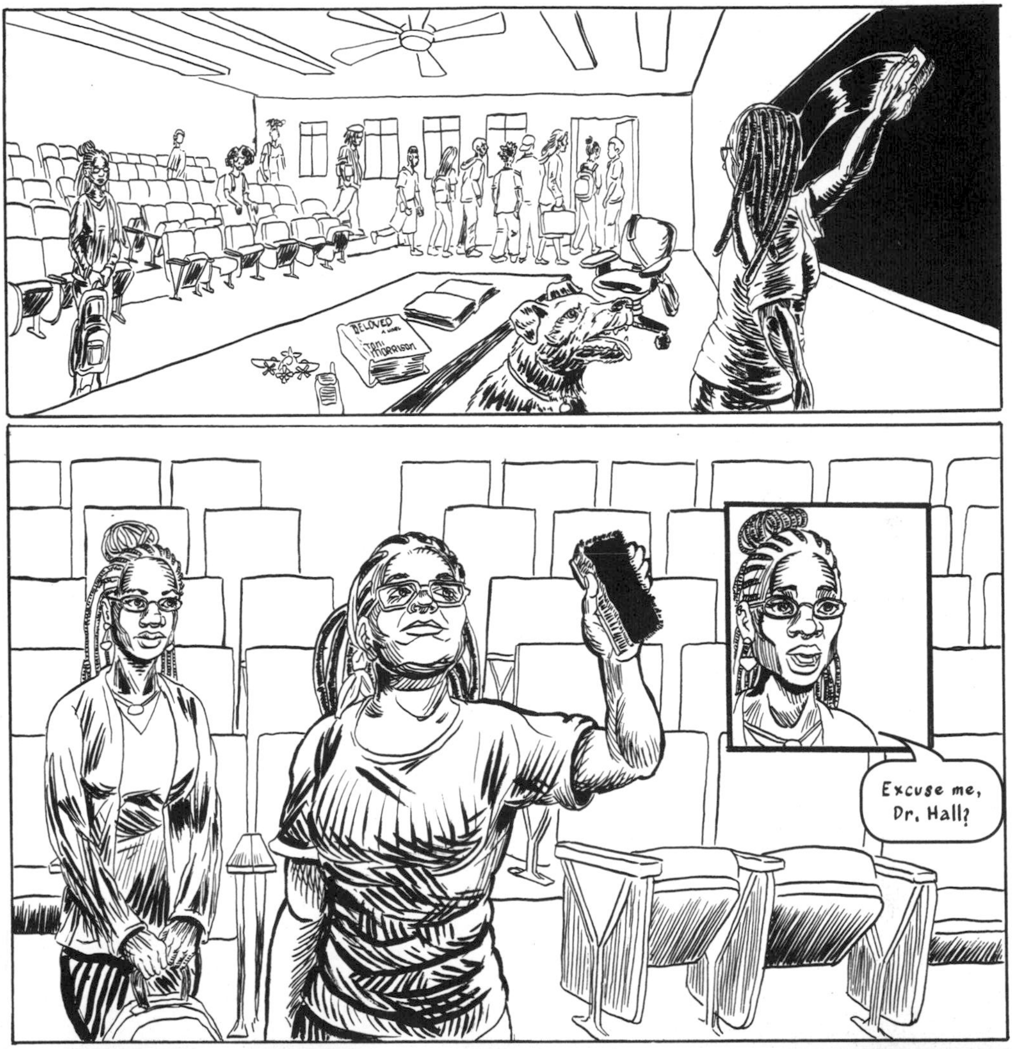
BELOVED
Toni Morrison
Excuse me, Dr. Hall?
Hey, Vicky, what's up?
Please just call me Rebecca.
Yes, Dr. Hall.

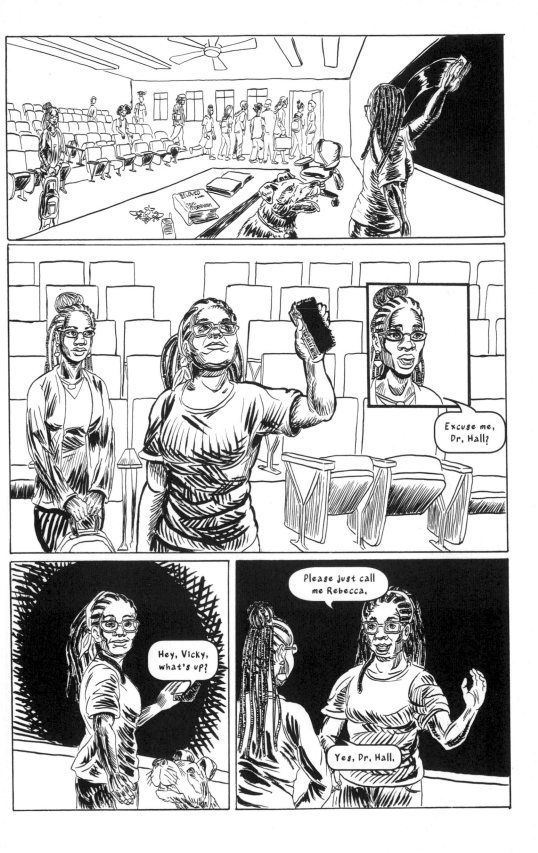

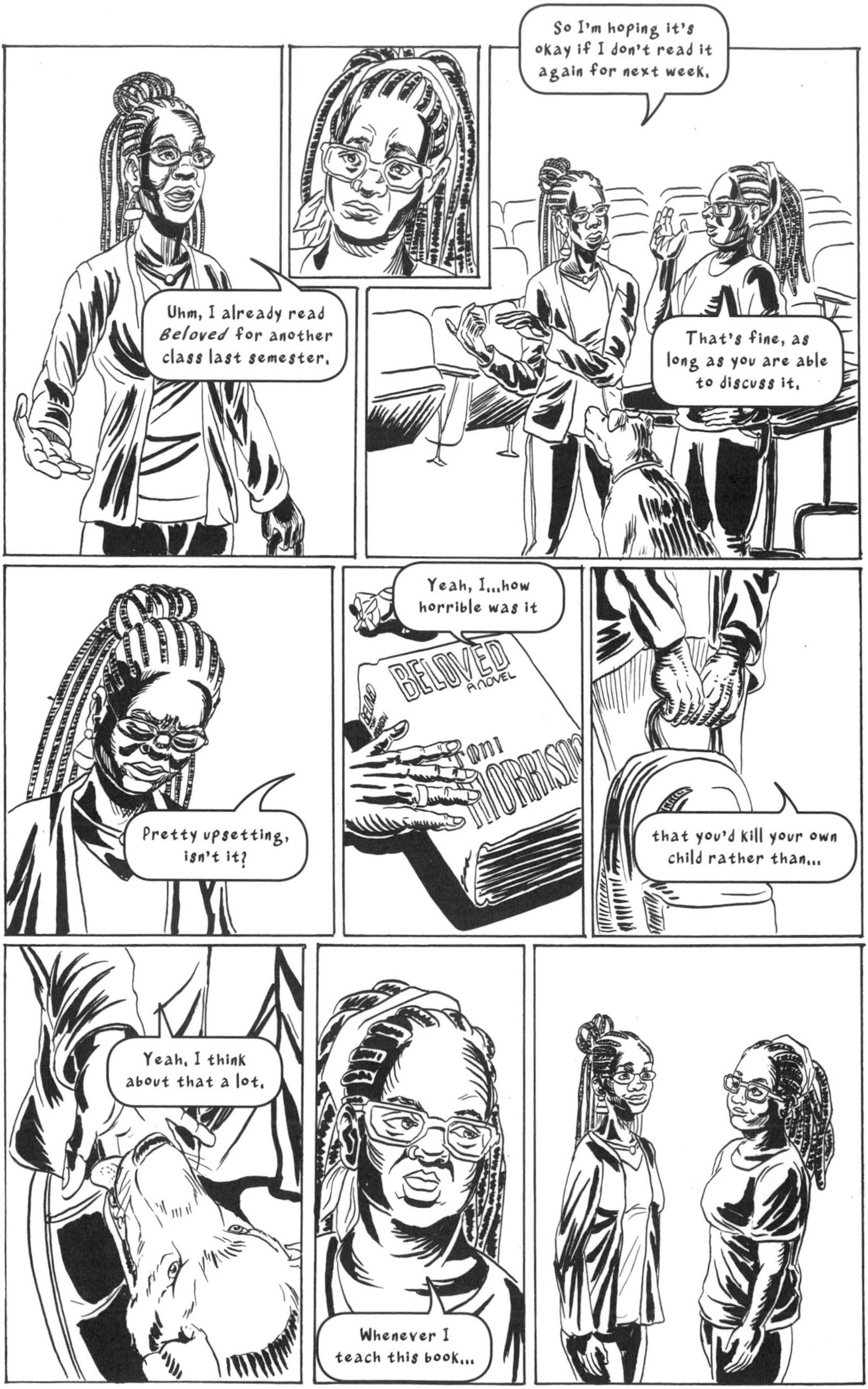
Uhm, I already read *Beloved* for another class last semester.
So I'm hoping it's okay if I don't read it again for next week.
That's fine, as long as you are able to discuss it.
Pretty upsetting, isn't it?
Yeah, I...how horrible was it
BELOVED
A NOVEL
TONI MORRISON
that you'd kill your own child rather than...
Yeah, I think about that a lot.
Whenever I teach this book...

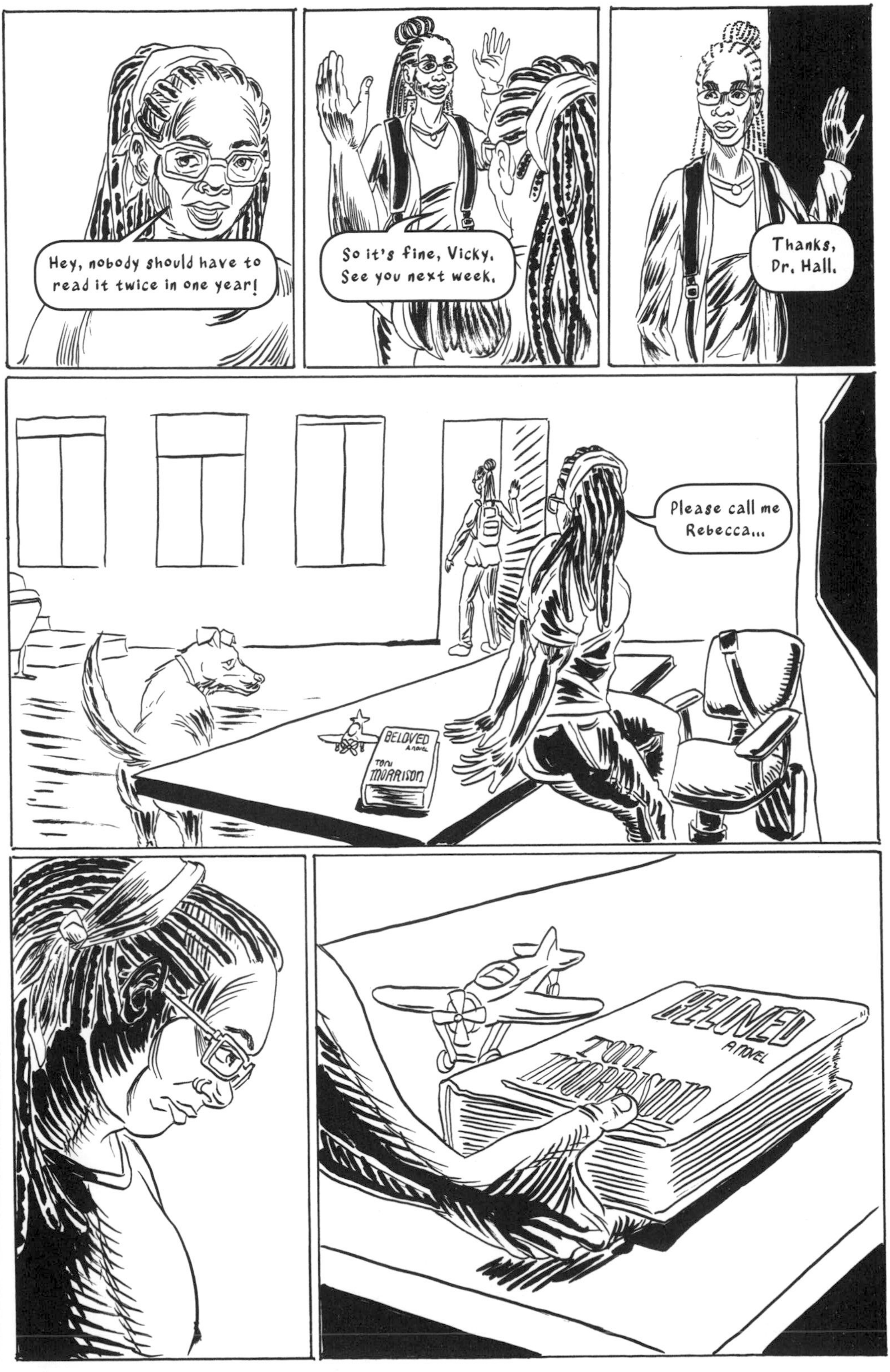
Hey, nobody should have to read it twice in one year!
So it's fine, Vicky. See you next week.
Thanks, Dr. Hall.
Please call me Rebecca...
BELOVED A NOVEL TONI MORRISON
BELOVED A NOVEL TONI MORRISON

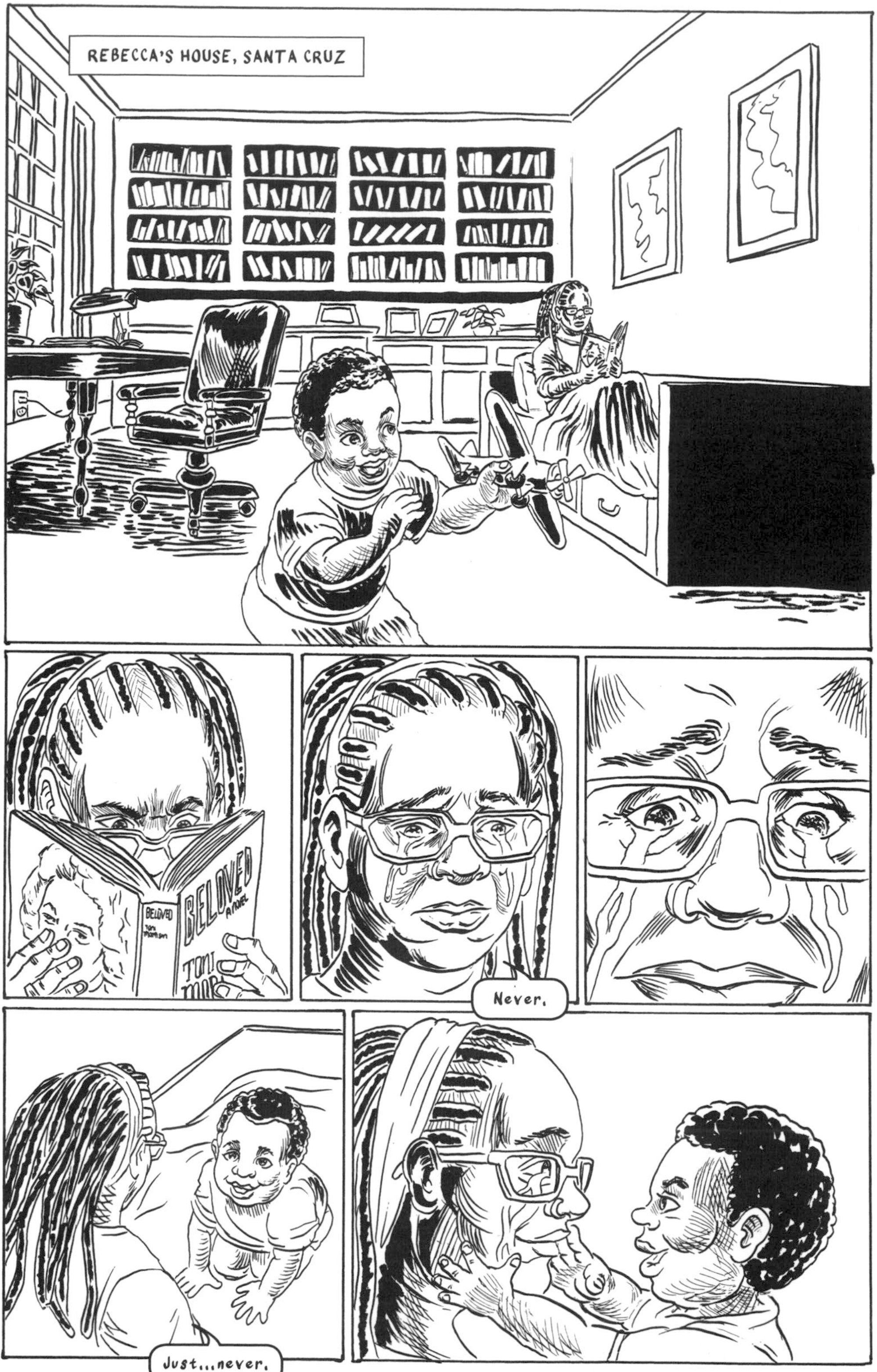
REBECCA'S HOUSE, SANTA CRUZ
BELOVED
Never.
Just...never.

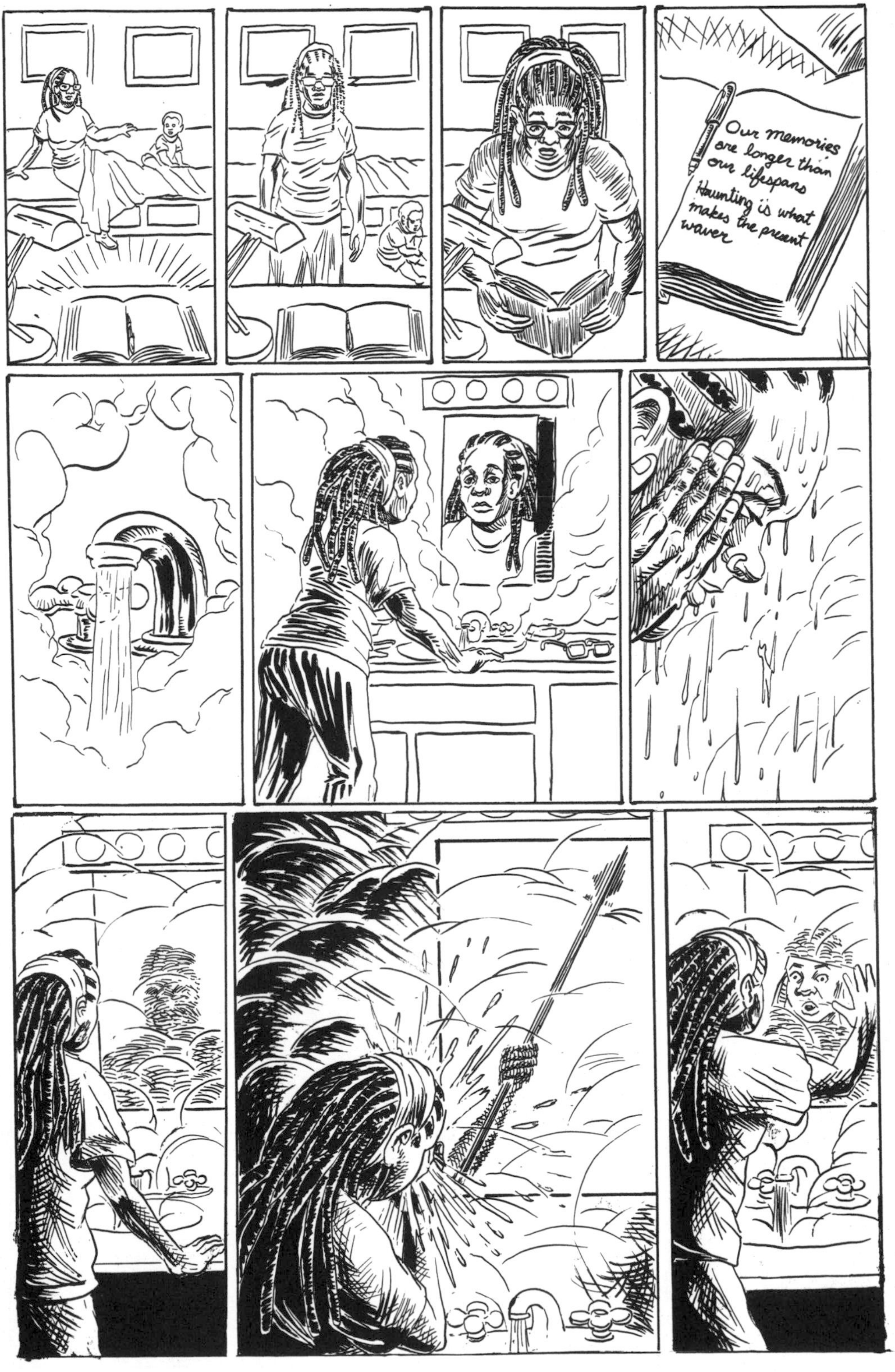
Our memories are longer than our lifespans
Haunting is what makes the present waver

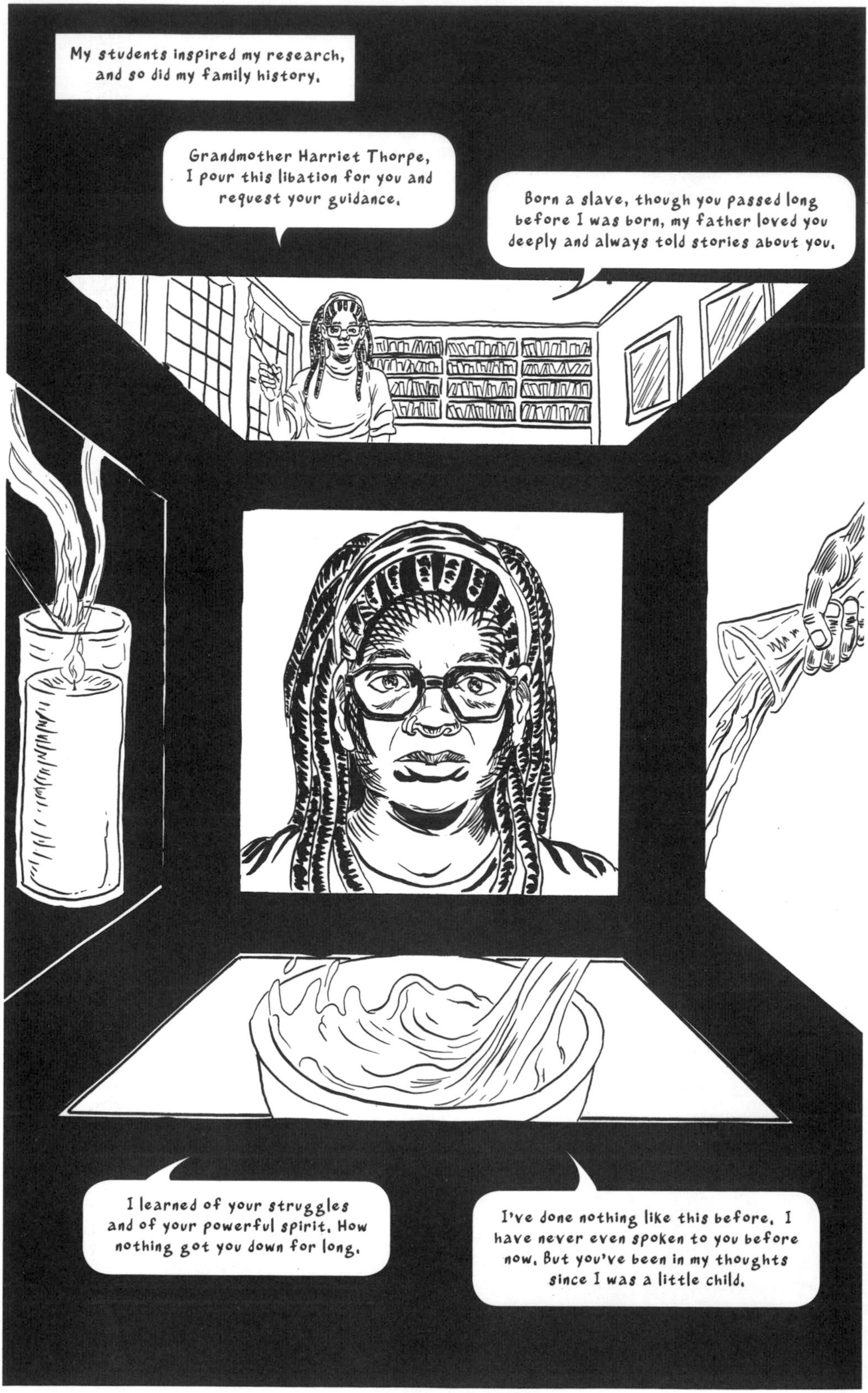

My students inspired my research, and so did my family history.
Grandmother Harriet Thorpe, I pour this libation for you and request your guidance.
Born a slave, though you passed long before I was born, my father loved you deeply and always told stories about you.
I learned of your struggles and of your powerful spirit. How nothing got you down for long.
I've done nothing like this before. I have never even spoken to you before now. But you've been in my thoughts since I was a little child.

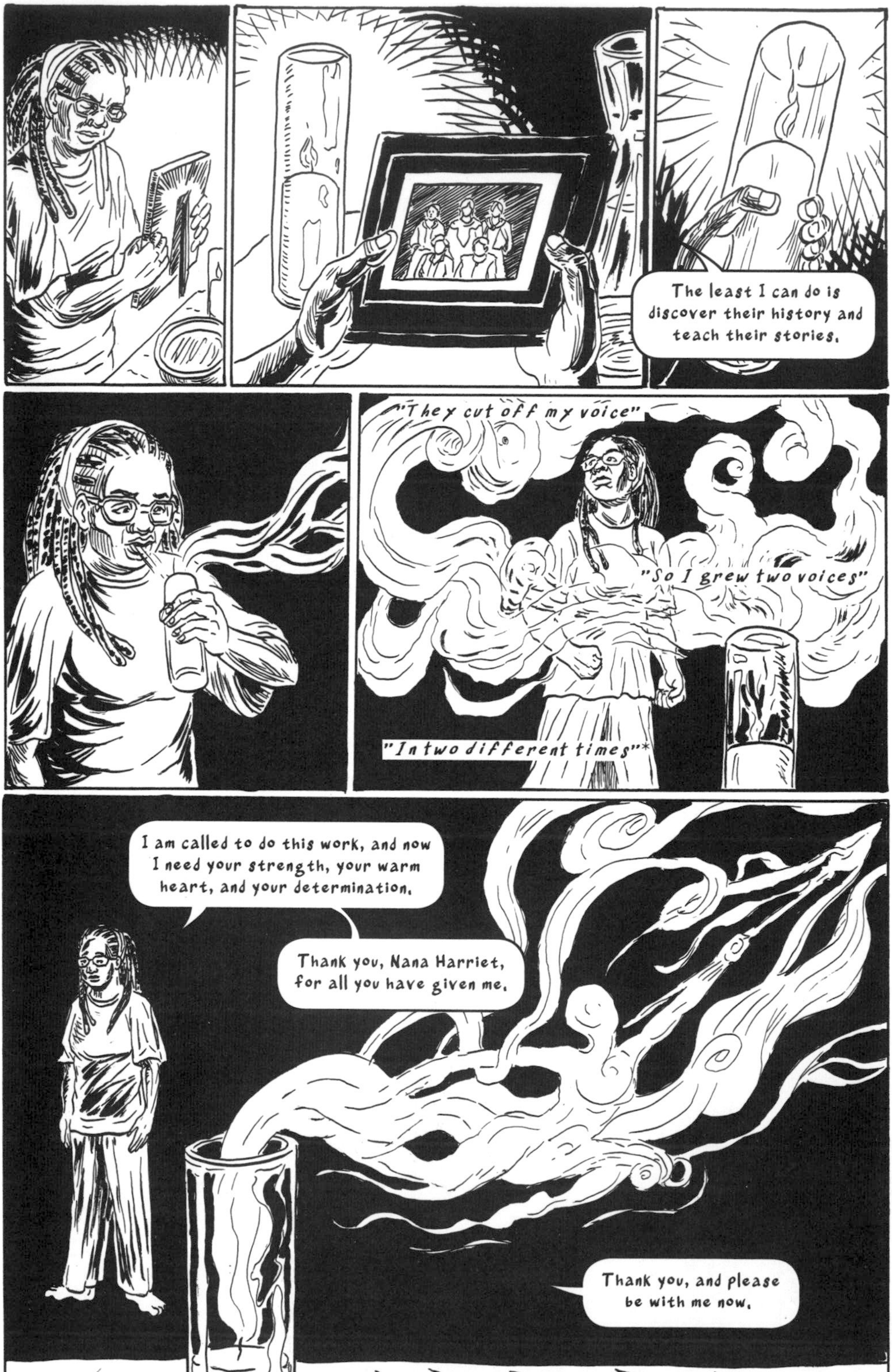
The least I can do is discover their history and teach their stories.
"They cut off my voice"
"So I grew two voices"
"In two different times"*
I am called to do this work, and now I need your strength, your warm heart, and your determination.
Thank you, Nana Harriet, for all you have given me.
Thank you, and please be with me now.

*Sweet Honey in the Rock, "Song of the Exiled," *Live at Carnegie Hall*, 1987.

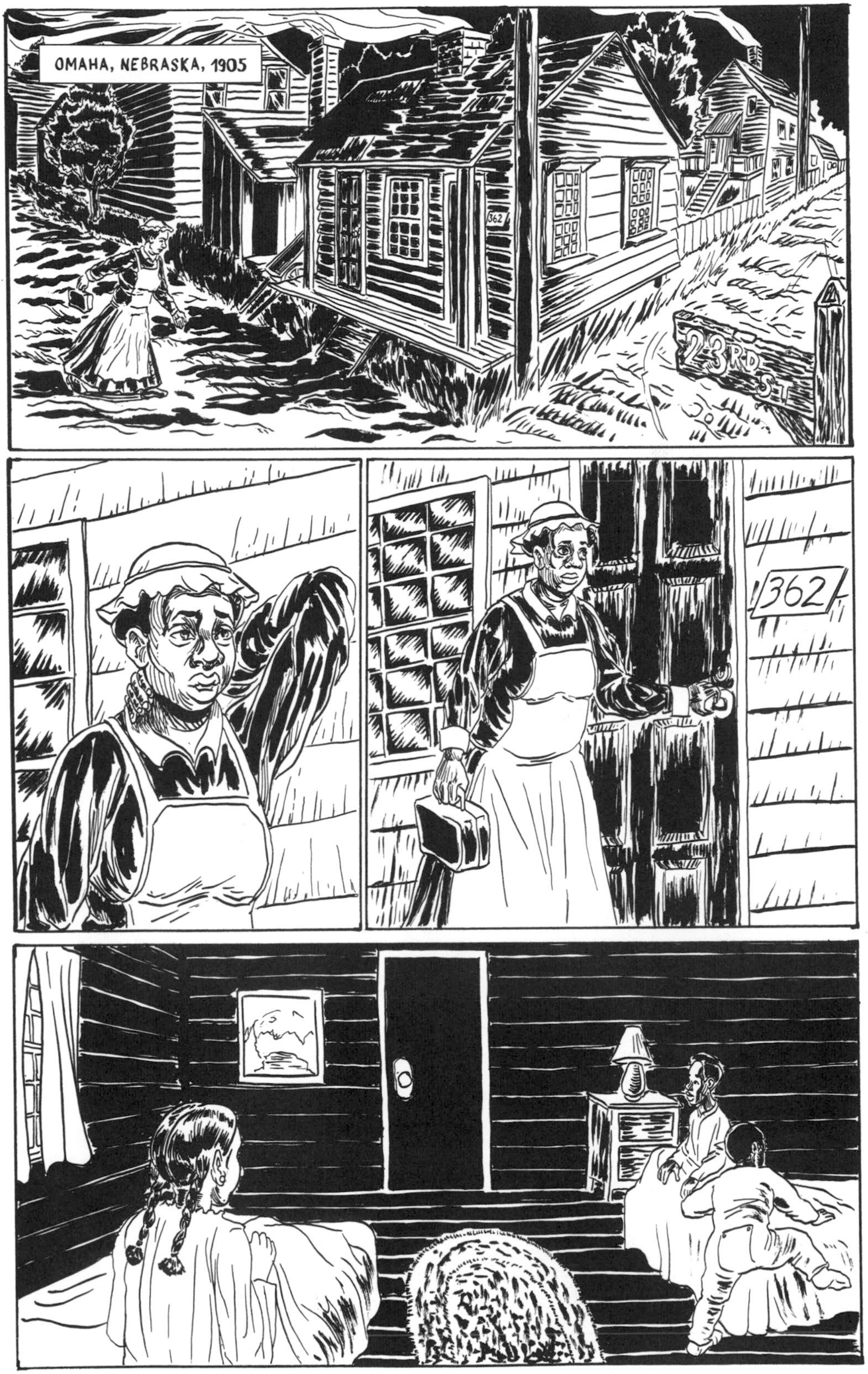
OMAHA, NEBRASKA, 1905
362
23RD ST
362

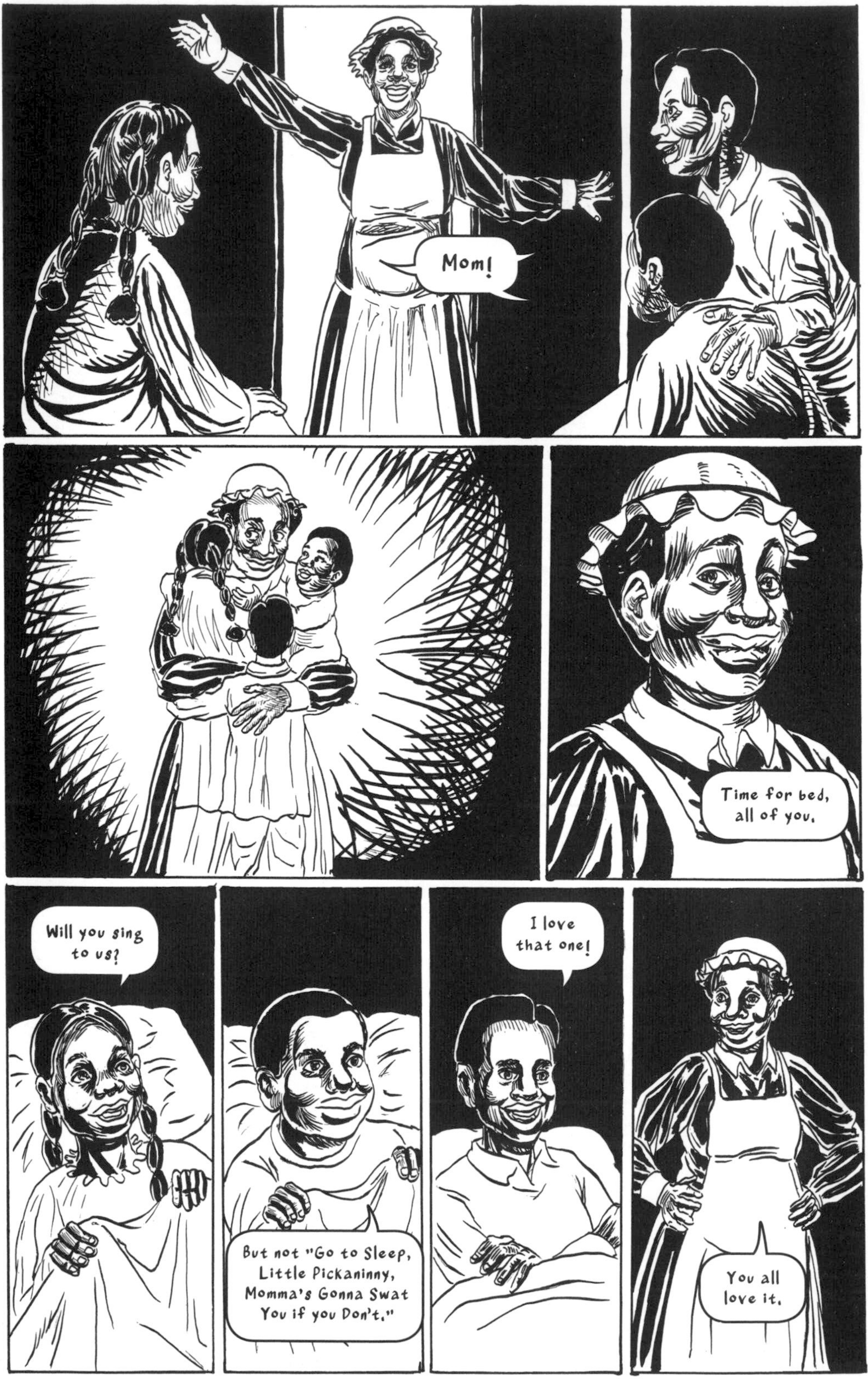
Mom!
Time for bed, all of you.
Will you sing to us?
But not "Go to Sleep, Little Pickaninny, Momma's Gonna Swat You if you Don't."
I love that one!
You all love it.

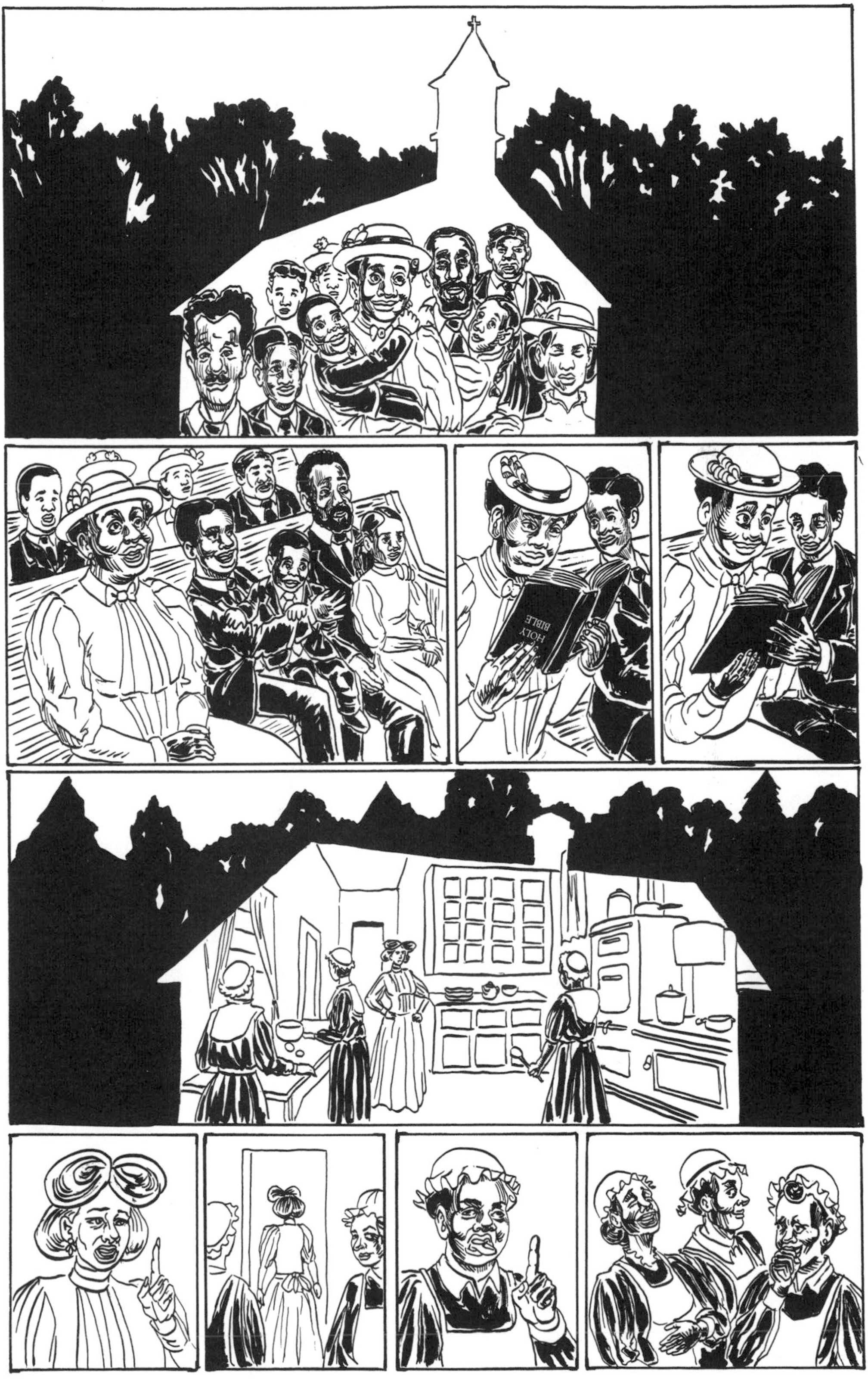
HOLY BIBLE

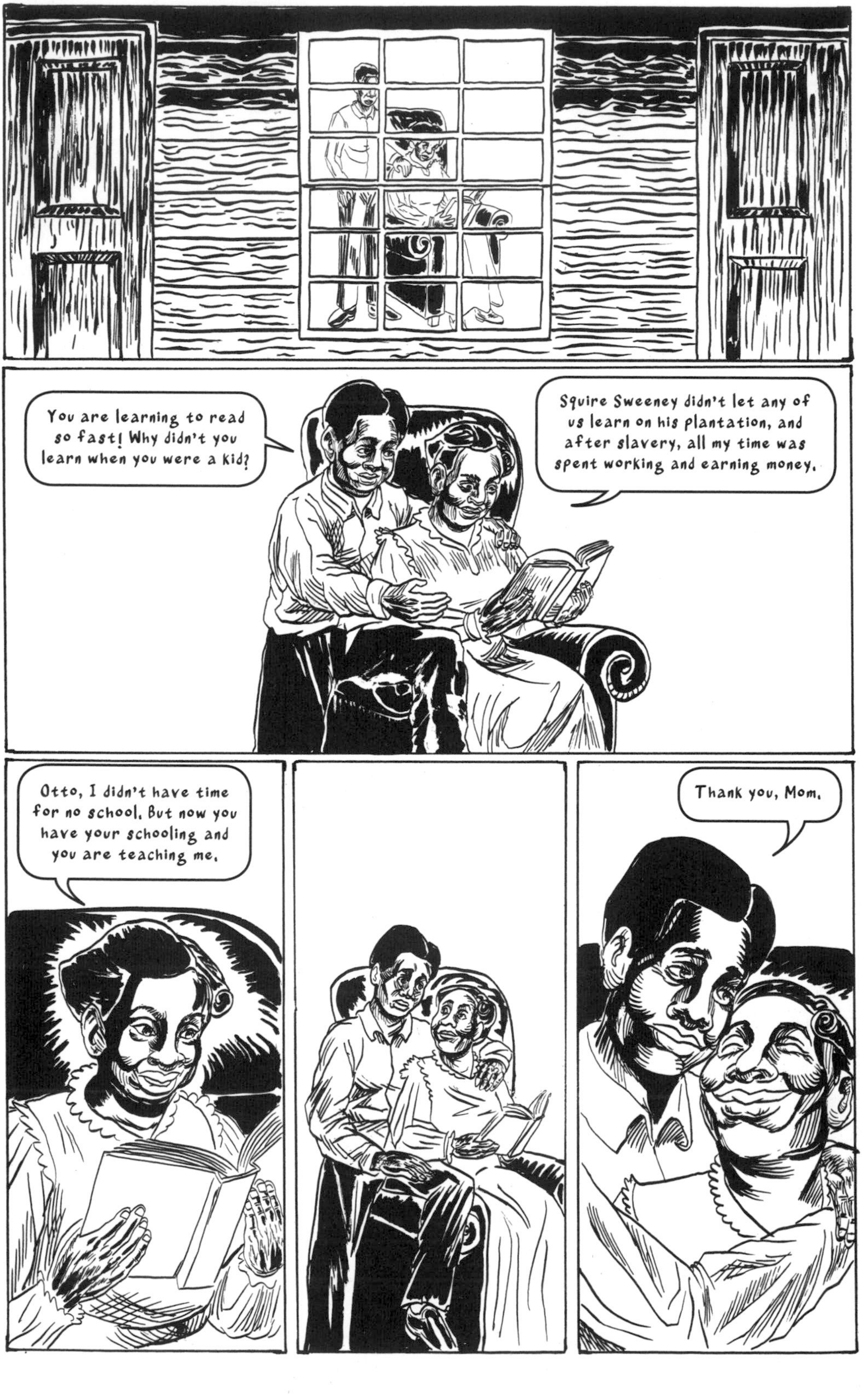
You are learning to read so fast! Why didn't you learn when you were a kid?
Squire Sweeney didn't let any of us learn on his plantation, and after slavery, all my time was spent working and earning money.
Otto, I didn't have time for no school. But now you have your schooling and you are teaching me.
Thank you, Mom.

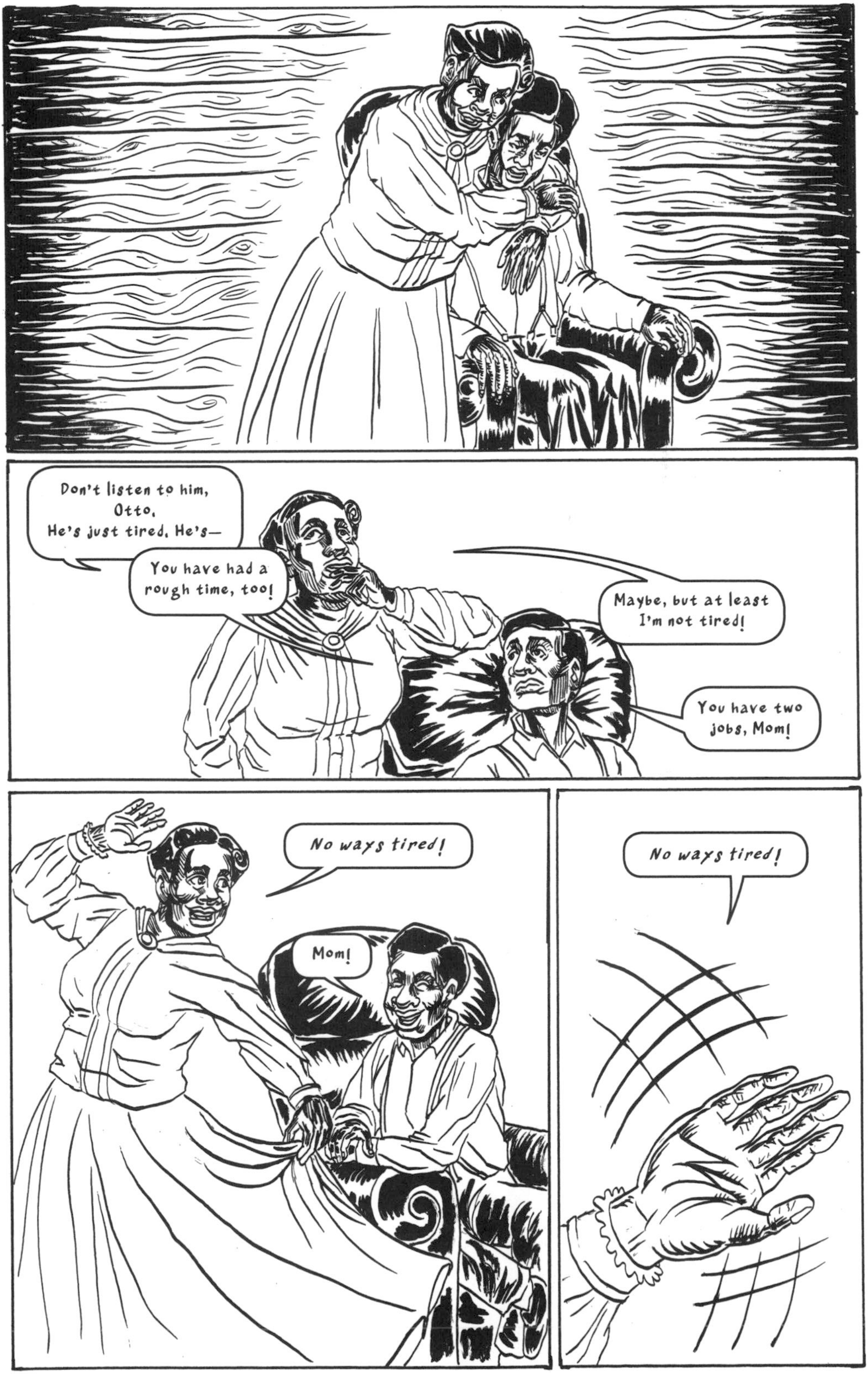
Don't listen to him, Otto. He's just tired. He's—
You have had a rough time, too!
Maybe, but at least I'm not tired!
You have two jobs, Mom!
No ways tired!
Mom!
No ways tired!

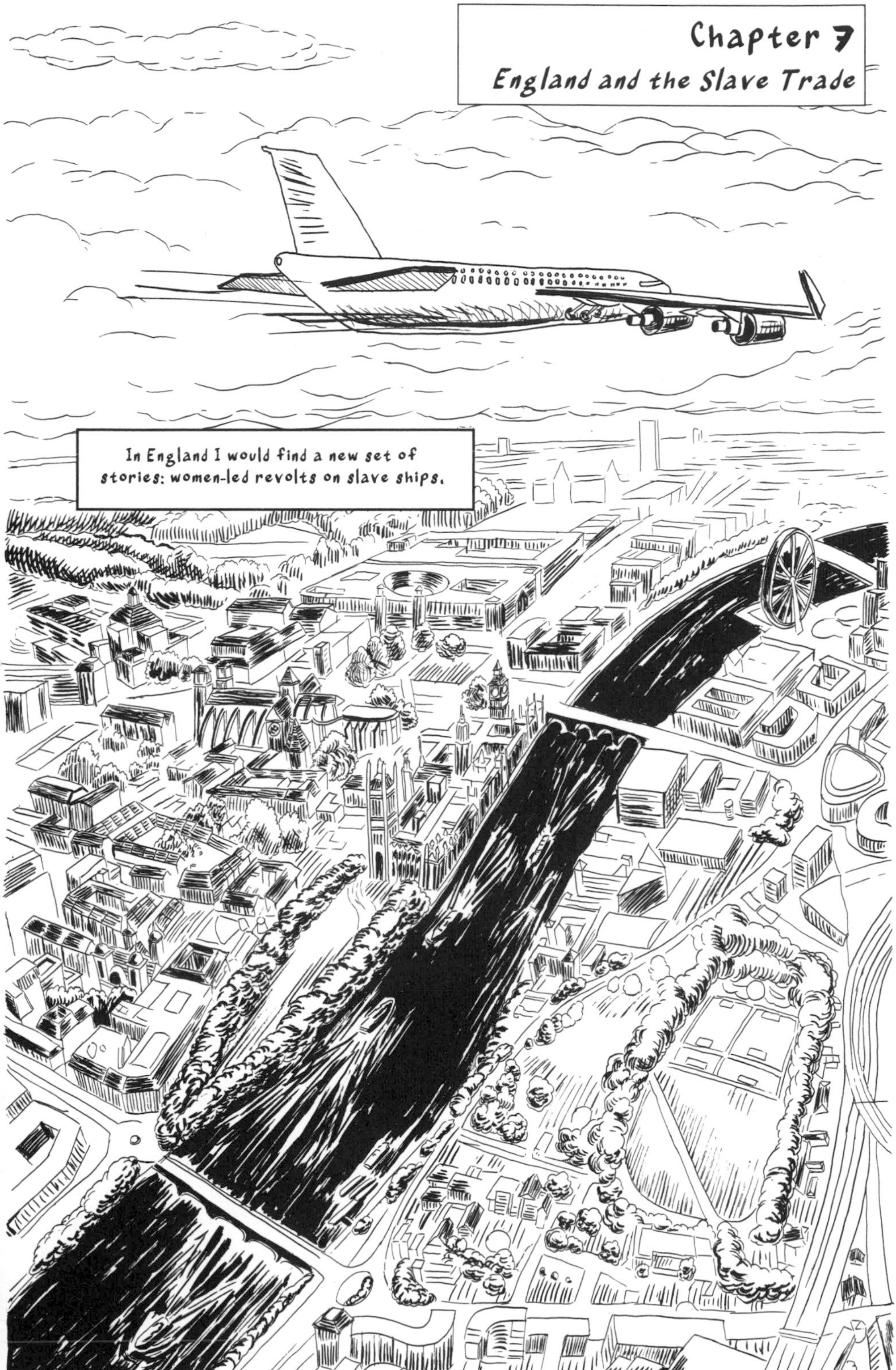
Chapter 7
England and the Slave Trade
In England I would find a new set of stories: women-led revolts on slave ships.

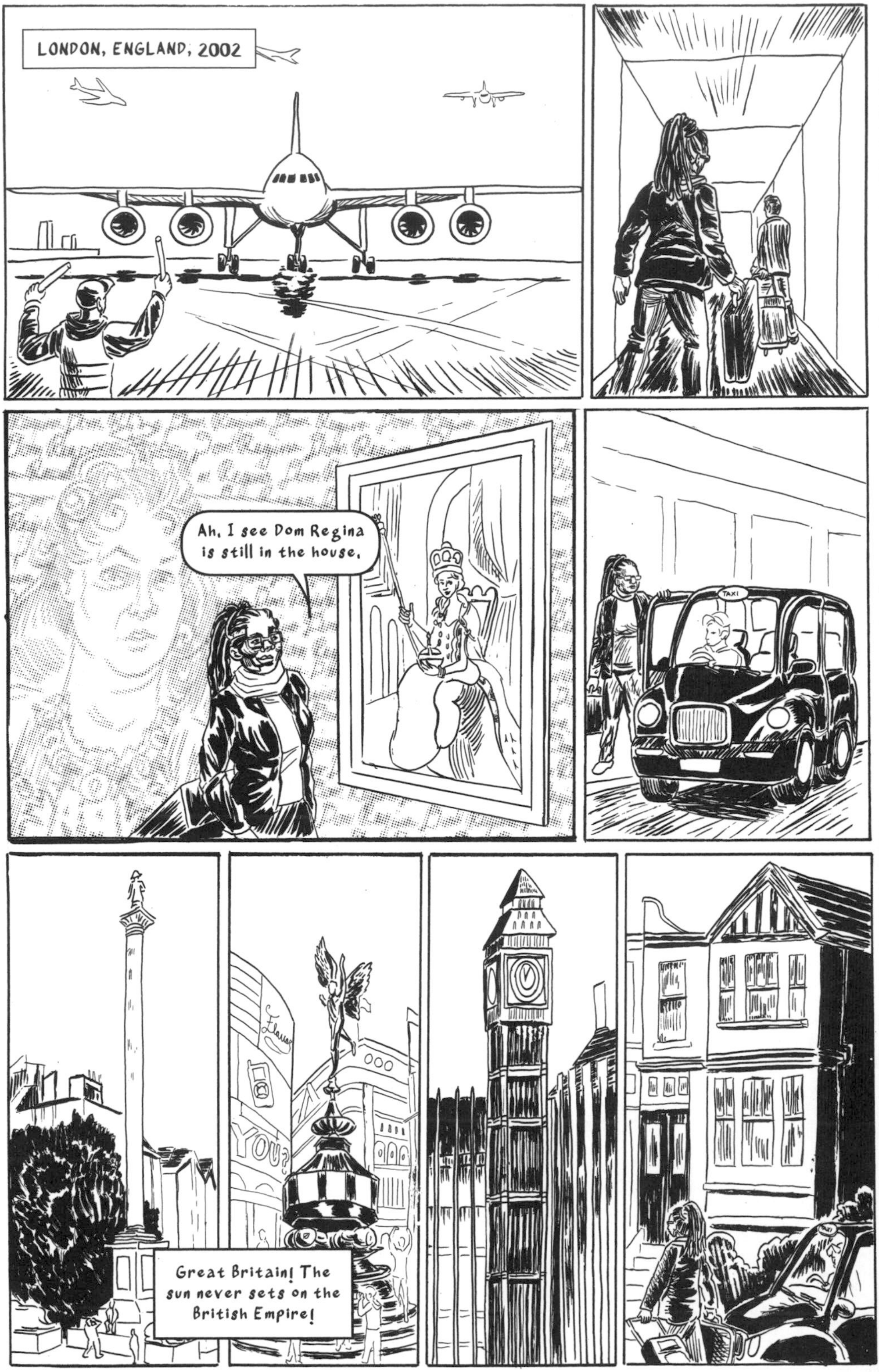
LONDON, ENGLAND, 2002
TAXI
Ah, I see Dom Regina is still in the house.
YOU?
Great Britain! The sun never sets on the British Empire!

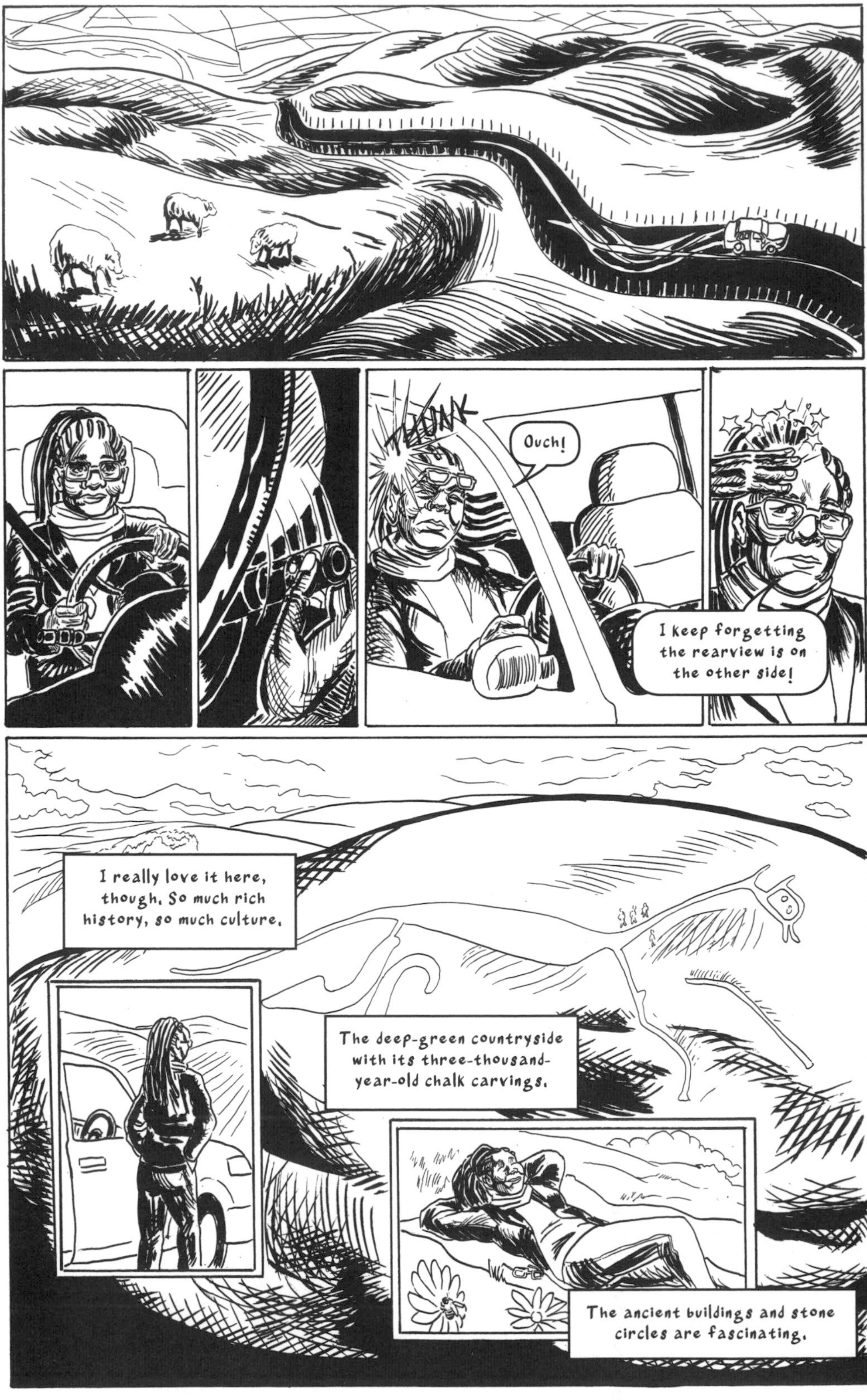
THUNK
Ouch!
I keep forgetting the rearview is on the other side!
I really love it here, though. So much rich history, so much culture.
The deep-green countryside with its three-thousand-year-old chalk carvings.
The ancient buildings and stone circles are fascinating.

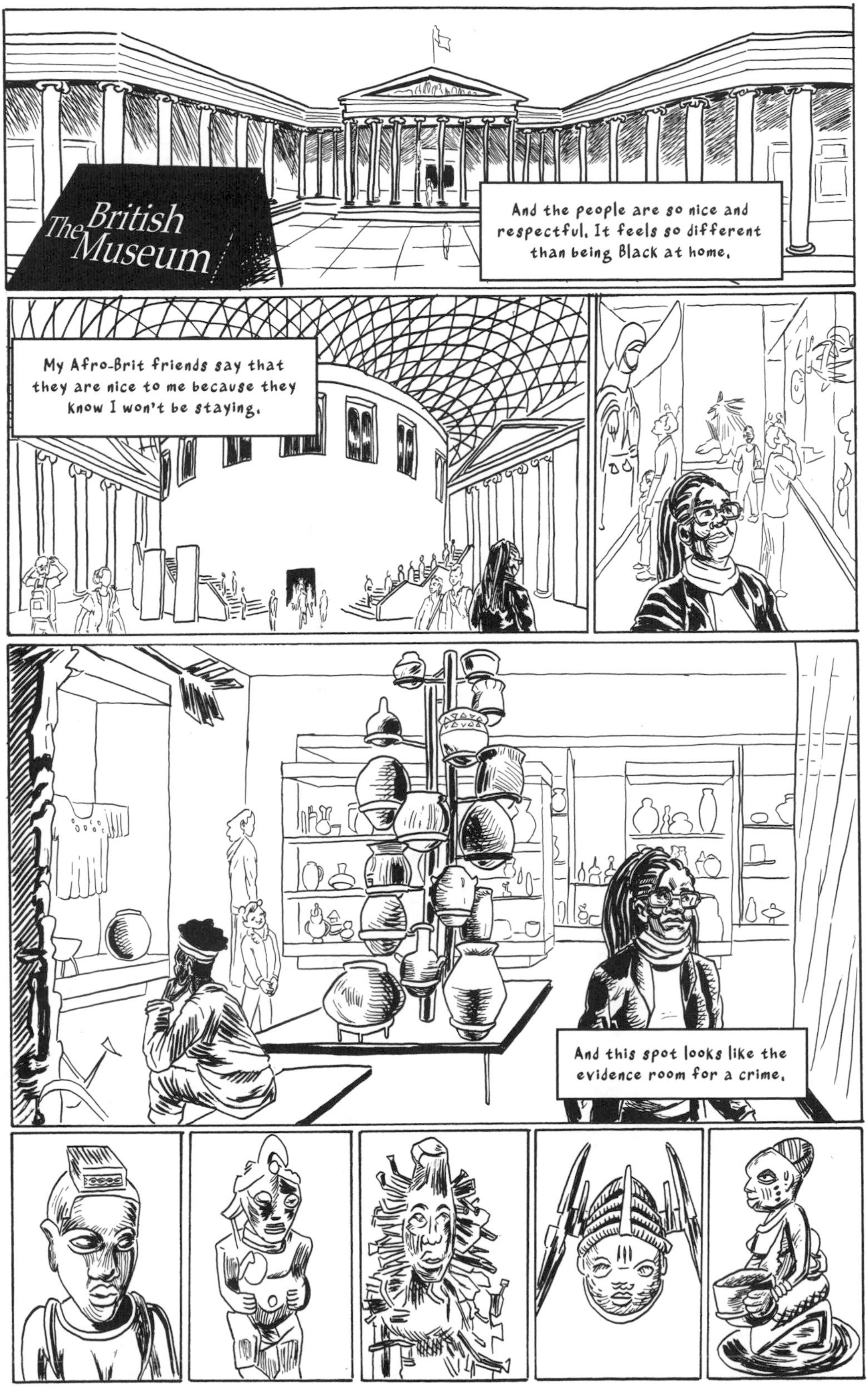
The British Museum
And the people are so nice and respectful. It feels so different than being Black at home.
My Afro-Brit friends say that they are nice to me because they know I won't be staying.
And this spot looks like the evidence room for a crime.

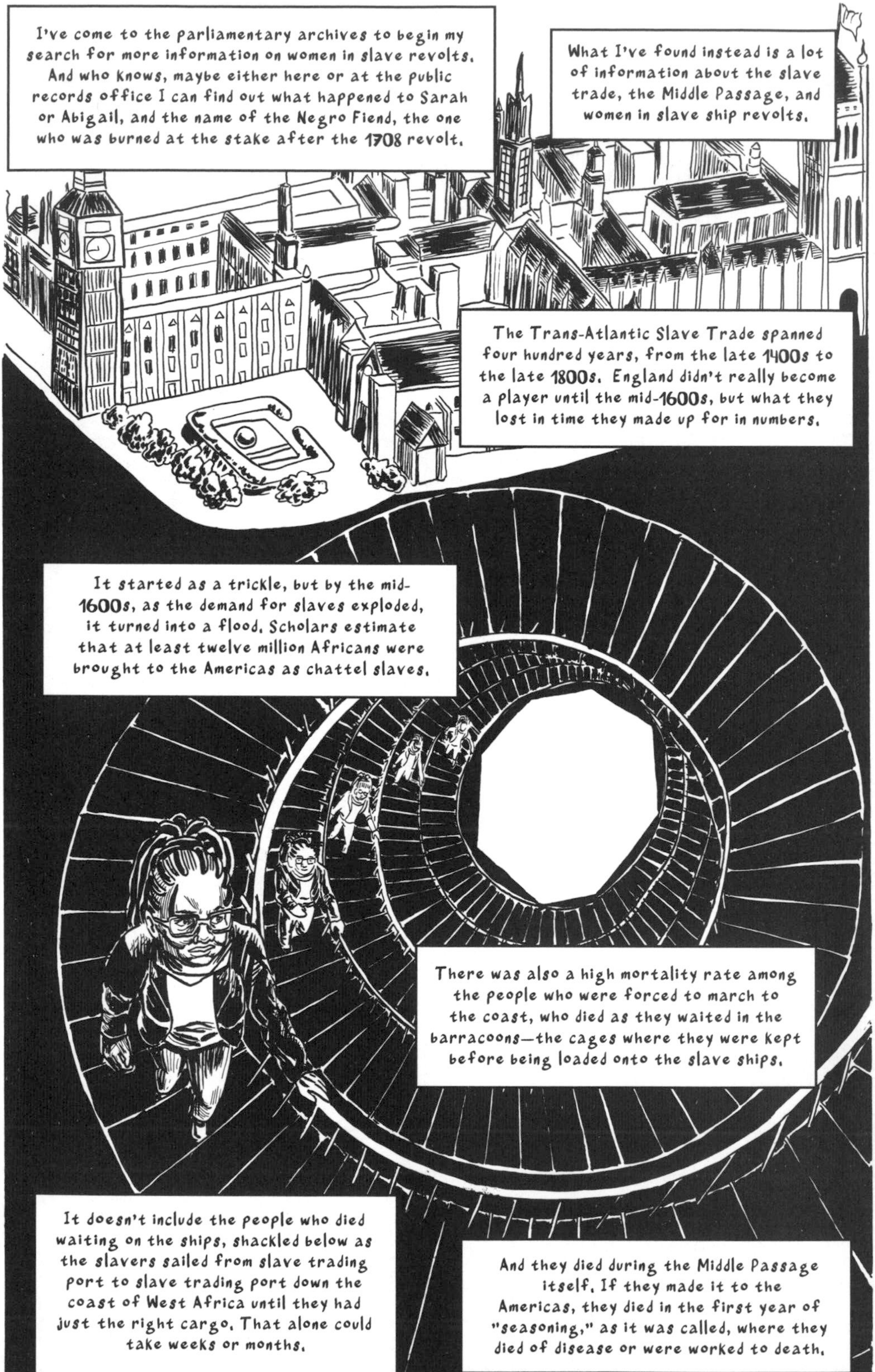
I've come to the parliamentary archives to begin my search for more information on women in slave revolts. And who knows, maybe either here or at the public records office I can find out what happened to Sarah or Abigail, and the name of the Negro Fiend, the one who was burned at the stake after the 1708 revolt.
What I've found instead is a lot of information about the slave trade, the Middle Passage, and women in slave ship revolts.
The Trans-Atlantic Slave Trade spanned four hundred years, from the late 1400s to the late 1800s. England didn't really become a player until the mid-1600s, but what they lost in time they made up for in numbers.
It started as a trickle, but by the mid-1600s, as the demand for slaves exploded, it turned into a flood. Scholars estimate that at least twelve million Africans were brought to the Americas as chattel slaves.
There was also a high mortality rate among the people who were forced to march to the coast, who died as they waited in the barracoons—the cages where they were kept before being loaded onto the slave ships.
It doesn't include the people who died waiting on the ships, shackled below as the slavers sailed from slave trading port to slave trading port down the coast of West Africa until they had just the right cargo. That alone could take weeks or months.
And they died during the Middle Passage itself. If they made it to the Americas, they died in the first year of "seasoning," as it was called, where they died of disease or were worked to death.

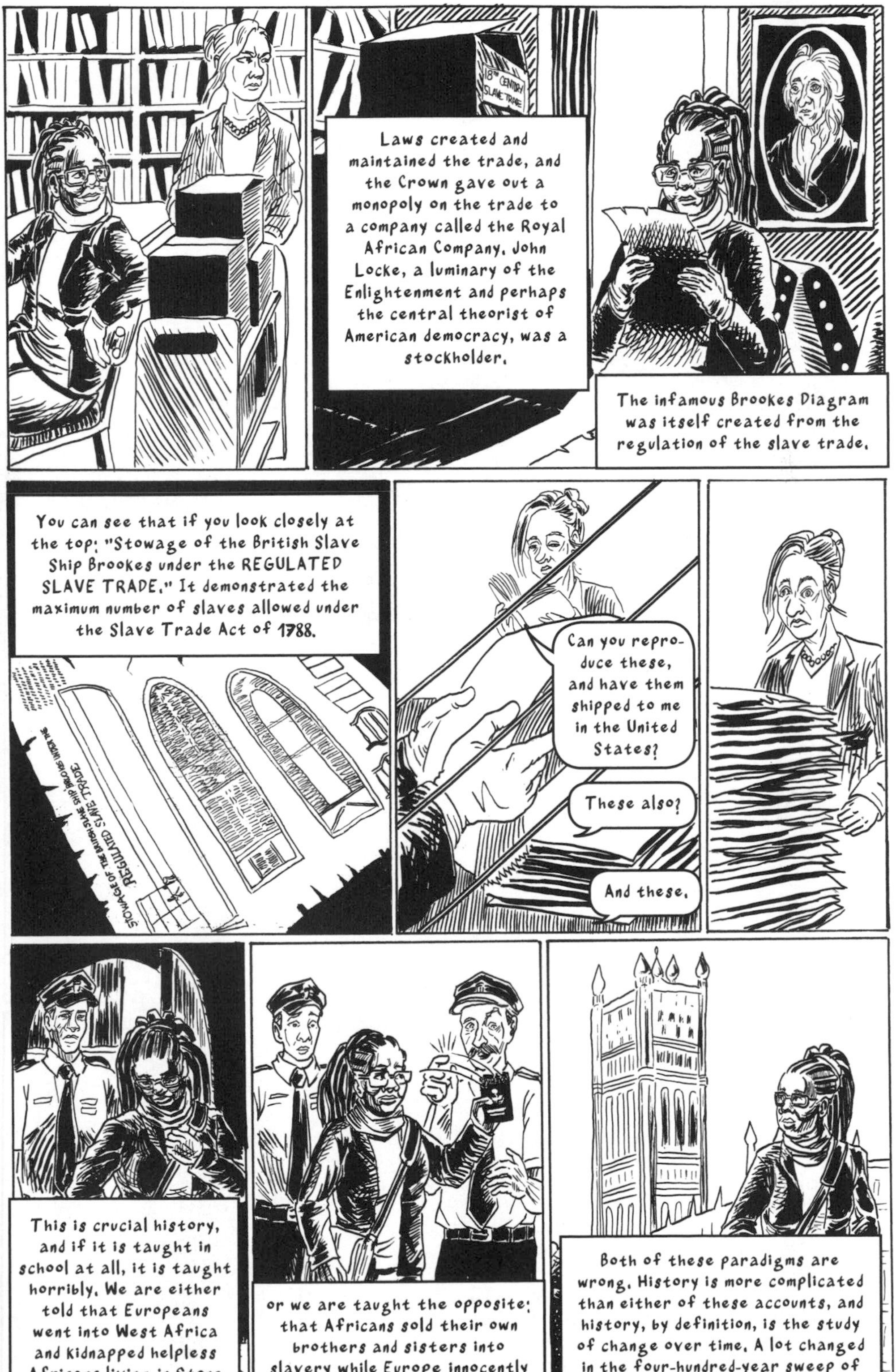
18TH CENTURY SLAVE TRADE
Laws created and maintained the trade, and the Crown gave out a monopoly on the trade to a company called the Royal African Company. John Locke, a luminary of the Enlightenment and perhaps the central theorist of American democracy, was a stockholder.
The infamous Brookes Diagram was itself created from the regulation of the slave trade.
You can see that if you look closely at the top: "Stowage of the British Slave Ship Brookes under the REGULATED SLAVE TRADE." It demonstrated the maximum number of slaves allowed under the Slave Trade Act of 1788.
STOWAGE OF THE BRITISH SLAVE SHIP BROOKES UNDER THE REGULATED SLAVE TRADE
Can you reproduce these, and have them shipped to me in the United States?
These also?
And these.
This is crucial history, and if it is taught in school at all, it is taught horribly. We are either told that Europeans went into West Africa and kidnapped helpless Africans living in Stone Age conditions,
or we are taught the opposite: that Africans sold their own brothers and sisters into slavery while Europe innocently tapped into an existing supply.
Both of these paradigms are wrong. History is more complicated than either of these accounts, and history, by definition, is the study of change over time. A lot changed in the four-hundred-year sweep of Atlantic slave trade history.

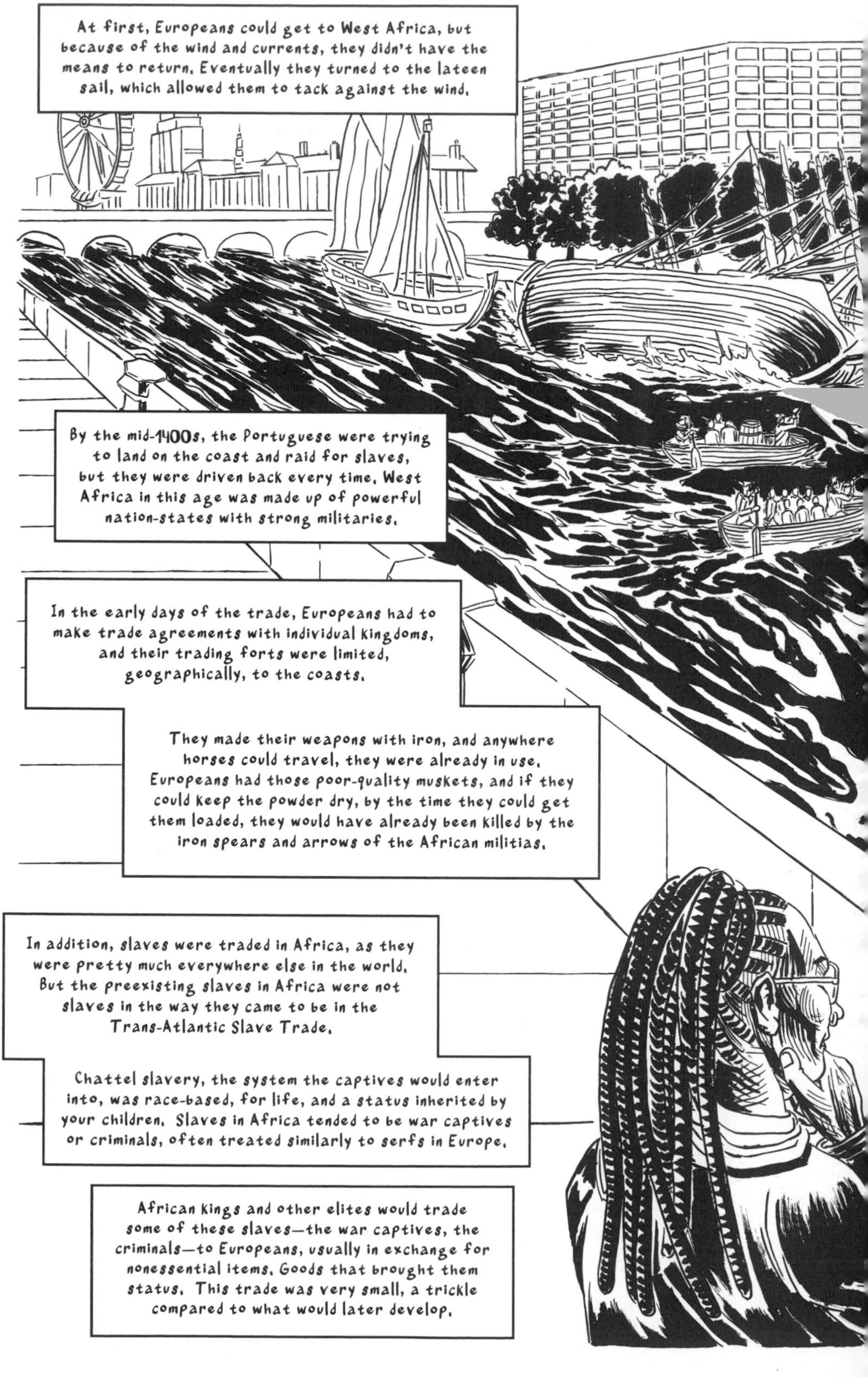
At first, Europeans could get to West Africa, but because of the wind and currents, they didn't have the means to return. Eventually they turned to the lateen sail, which allowed them to tack against the wind.
By the mid-1400s, the Portuguese were trying to land on the coast and raid for slaves, but they were driven back every time. West Africa in this age was made up of powerful nation-states with strong militaries.
In the early days of the trade, Europeans had to make trade agreements with individual kingdoms, and their trading forts were limited, geographically, to the coasts.
They made their weapons with iron, and anywhere horses could travel, they were already in use. Europeans had those poor-quality muskets, and if they could keep the powder dry, by the time they could get them loaded, they would have already been killed by the iron spears and arrows of the African militias.
In addition, slaves were traded in Africa, as they were pretty much everywhere else in the world. But the preexisting slaves in Africa were not slaves in the way they came to be in the Trans-Atlantic Slave Trade.
Chattel slavery, the system the captives would enter into, was race-based, for life, and a status inherited by your children. Slaves in Africa tended to be war captives or criminals, often treated similarly to serfs in Europe.
African kings and other elites would trade some of these slaves—the war captives, the criminals—to Europeans, usually in exchange for nonessential items. Goods that brought them status. This trade was very small, a trickle compared to what would later develop.

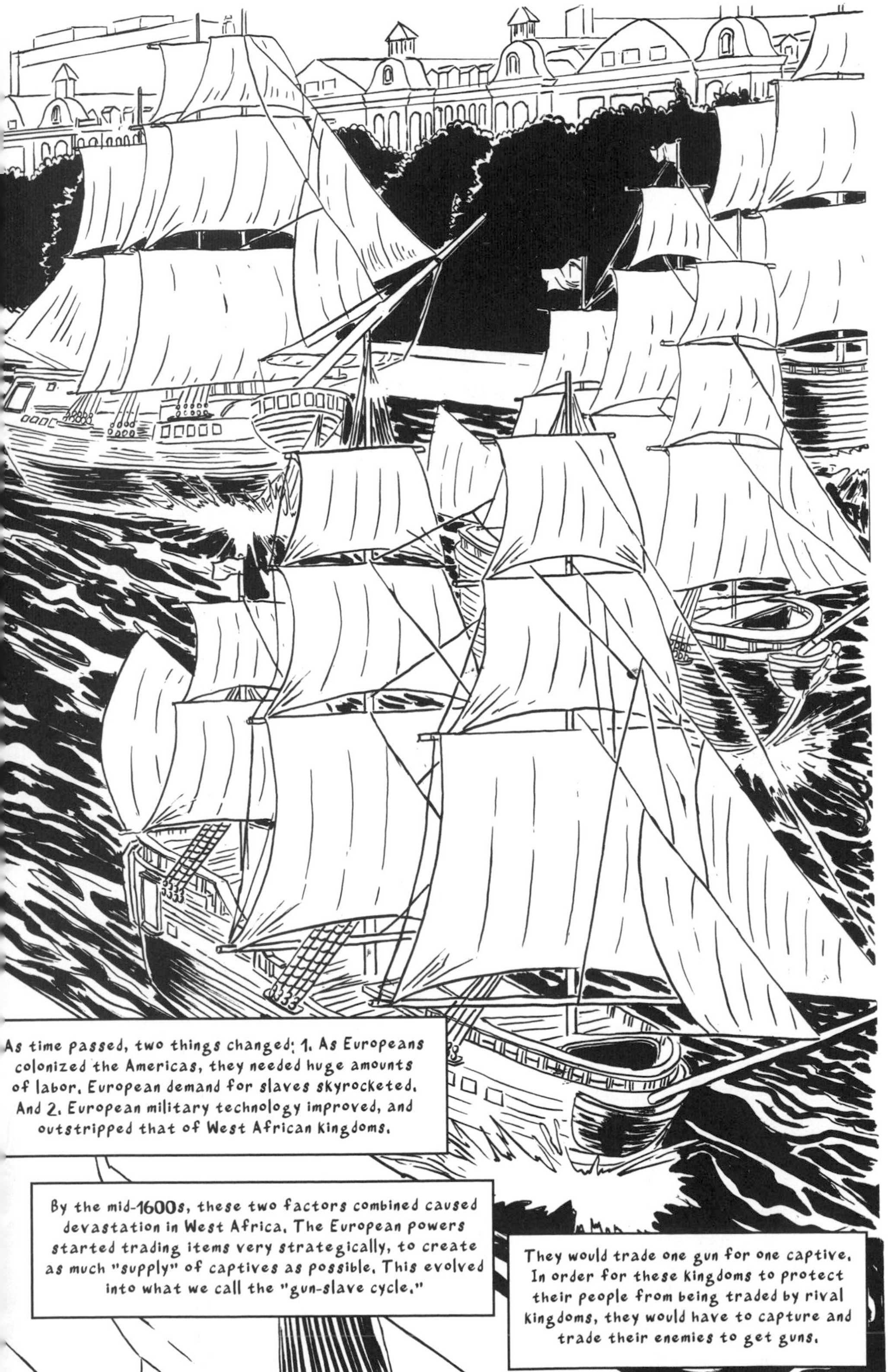
As time passed, two things changed: 1. As Europeans colonized the Americas, they needed huge amounts of labor. European demand for slaves skyrocketed. And 2. European military technology improved, and outstripped that of West African kingdoms.
By the mid-1600s, these two factors combined caused devastation in West Africa. The European powers started trading items very strategically, to create as much "supply" of captives as possible. This evolved into what we call the "gun-slave cycle."
They would trade one gun for one captive. In order for these kingdoms to protect their people from being traded by rival kingdoms, they would have to capture and trade their enemies to get guns.

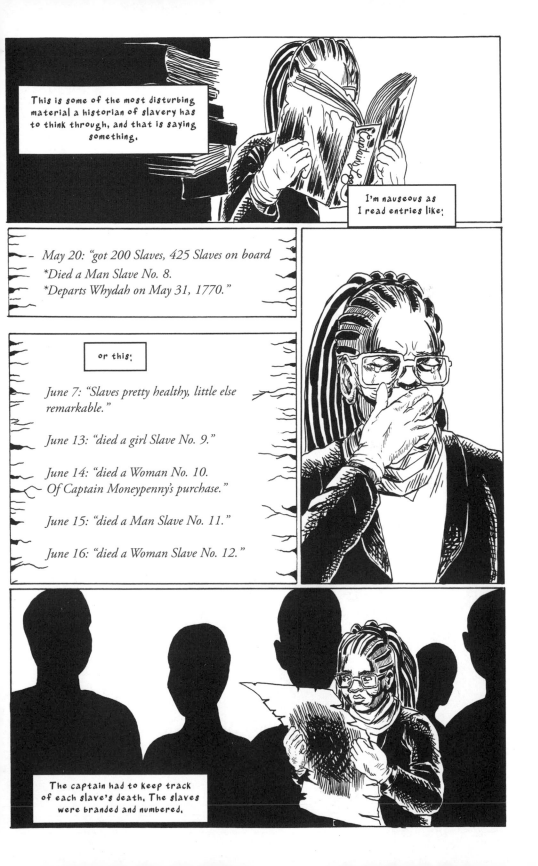

This is some of the most disturbing material a historian of slavery has to think through, and that is saying something.

I'm nauseous as I read entries like:

May 20: "got 200 Slaves, 425 Slaves on board
*Died a Man Slave No. 8.
*Departs Whydah on May 31, 1770."

or this:

June 7: "Slaves pretty healthy, little else remarkable."

June 13: "died a girl Slave No. 9."

June 14: "died a Woman No. 10. Of Captain Moneypenny's purchase."

June 15: "died a Man Slave No. 11."

June 16: "died a Woman Slave No. 12."

The captain had to keep track of each slave's death. The slaves were branded and numbered.

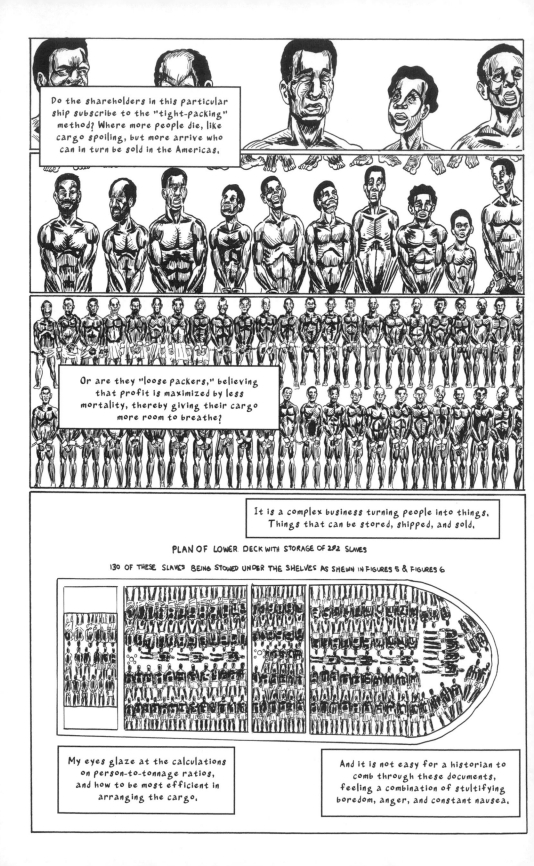

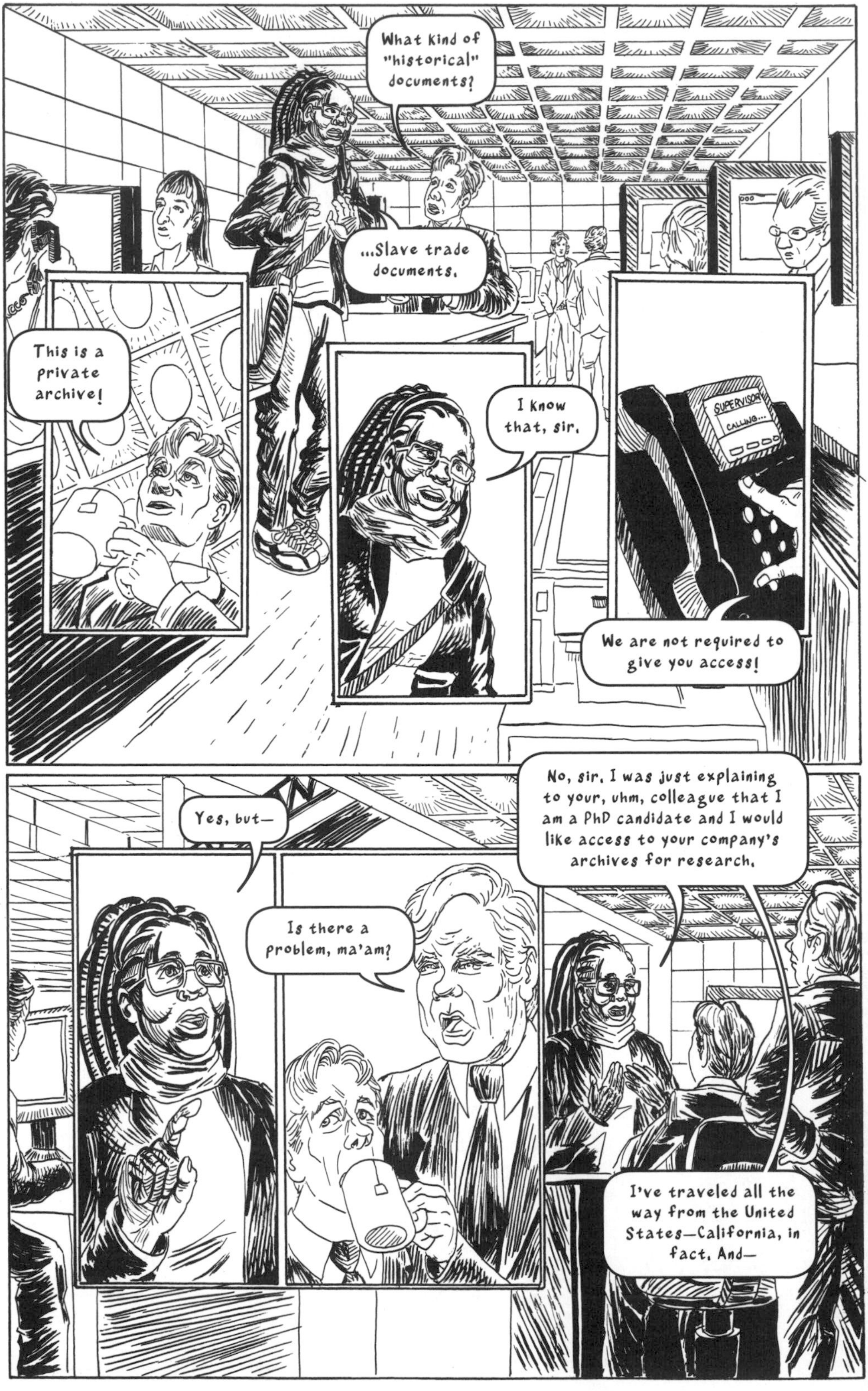
What kind of "historical" documents?
...Slave trade documents.
This is a private archive!
I know that, sir.
SUPERVISOR
CALLING...
We are not required to give you access!
Yes, but—
Is there a problem, ma'am?
No, sir. I was just explaining to your, uhm, colleague that I am a PhD candidate and I would like access to your company's archives for research.
I've traveled all the way from the United States—California, in fact. And—

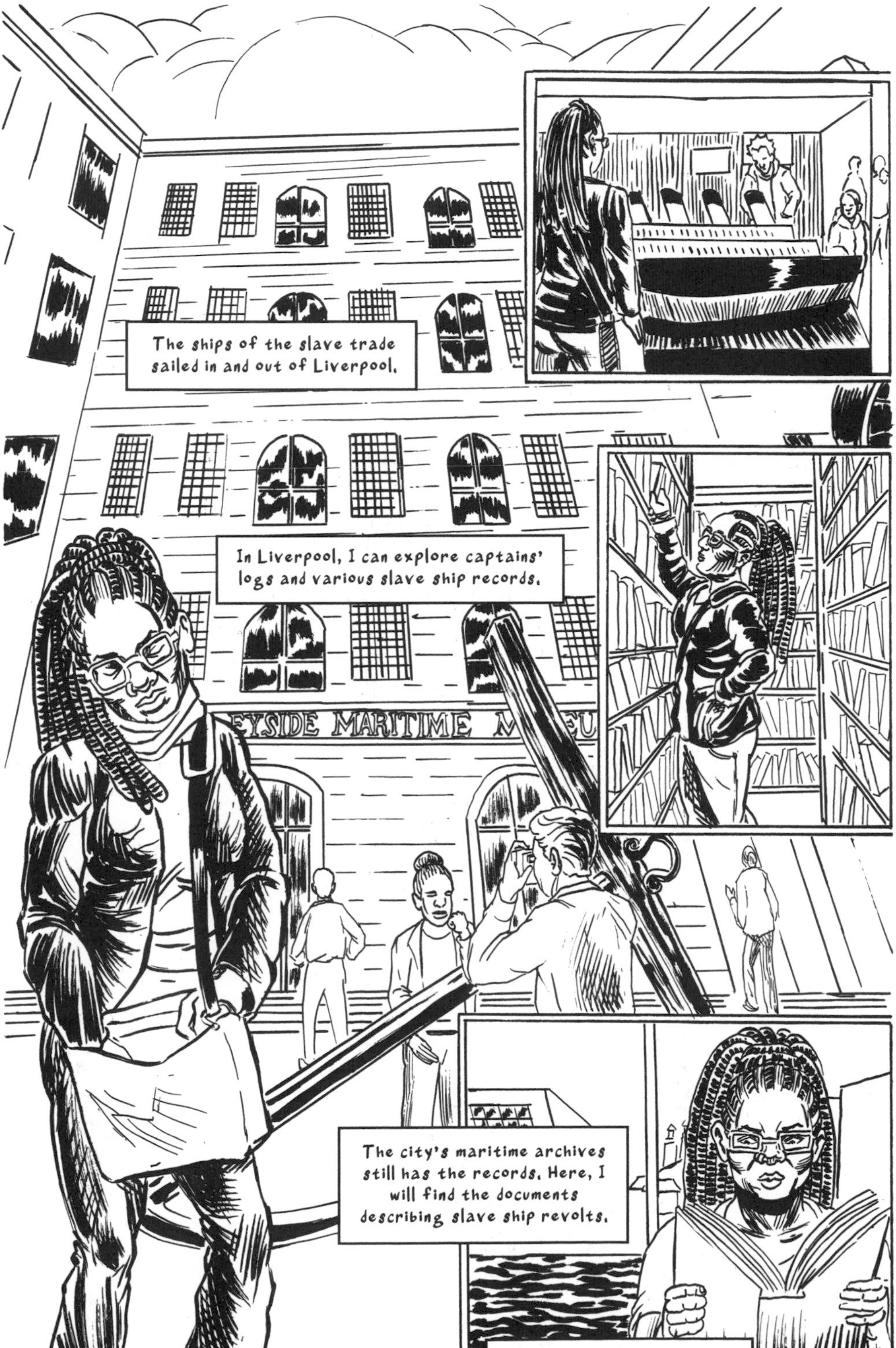
The ships of the slave trade sailed in and out of Liverpool.
In Liverpool, I can explore captains' logs and various slave ship records.
EYSIDE MARITIME M EU
The city's maritime archives still has the records. Here, I will find the documents describing slave ship revolts.
So many slave ship revolts.

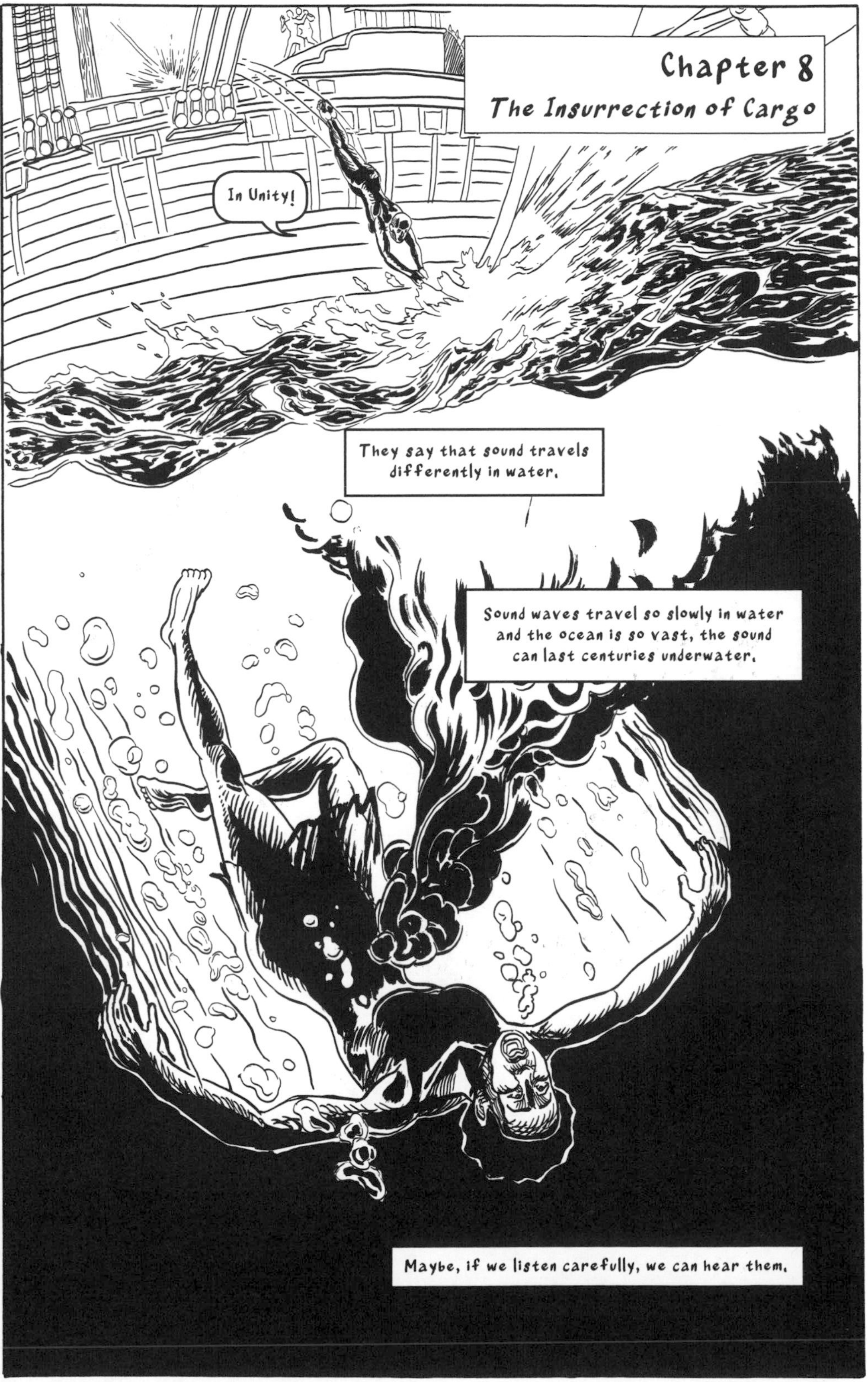
Chapter 8
The Insurrection of Cargo
In Unity!
They say that sound travels differently in water.
Sound waves travel so slowly in water and the ocean is so vast, the sound can last centuries underwater.
Maybe, if we listen carefully, we can hear them.

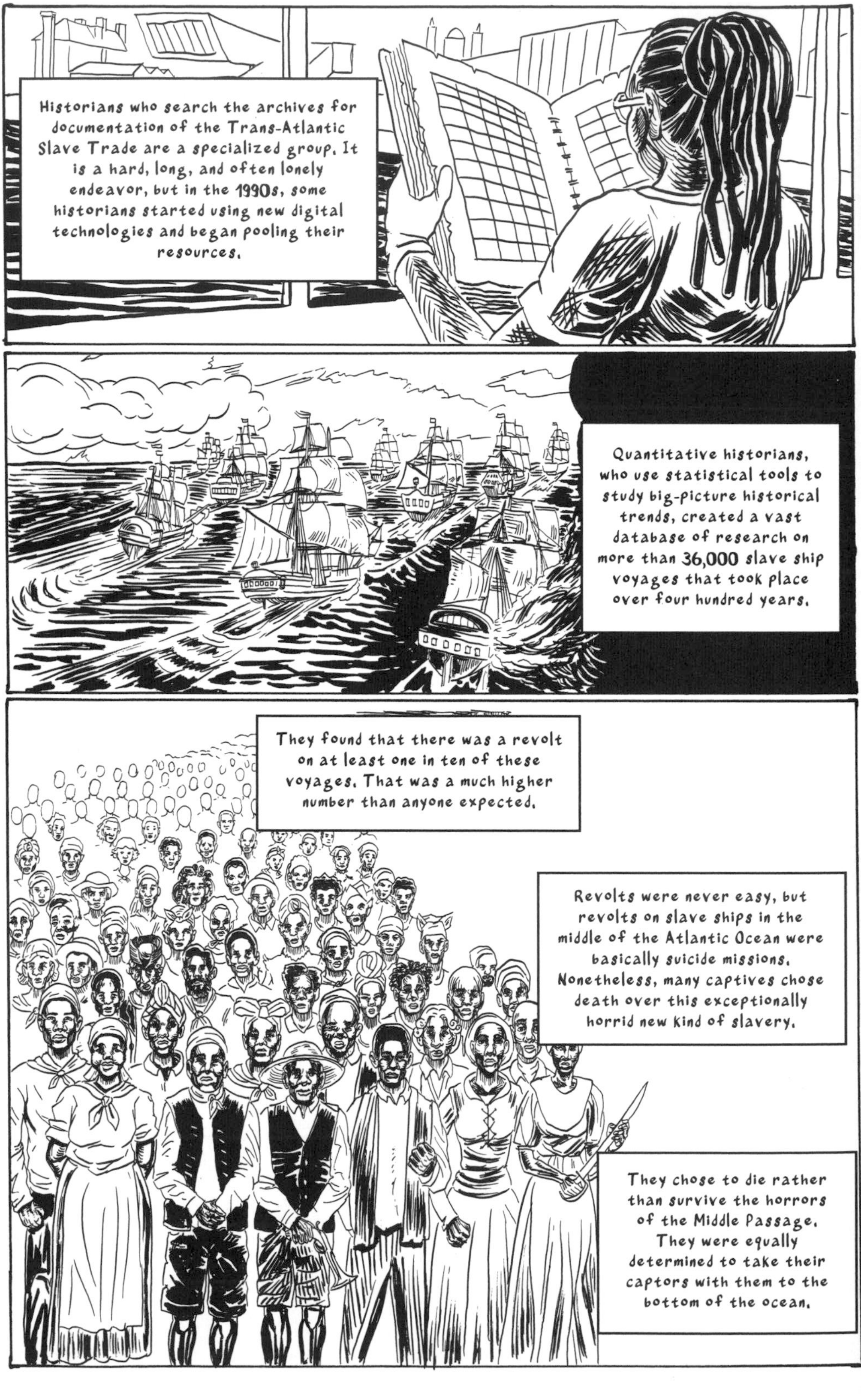
Historians who search the archives for documentation of the Trans-Atlantic Slave Trade are a specialized group. It is a hard, long, and often lonely endeavor, but in the 1990s, some historians started using new digital technologies and began pooling their resources.
Quantitative historians, who use statistical tools to study big-picture historical trends, created a vast database of research on more than 36,000 slave ship voyages that took place over four hundred years.
They found that there was a revolt on at least one in ten of these voyages. That was a much higher number than anyone expected.
Revolts were never easy, but revolts on slave ships in the middle of the Atlantic Ocean were basically suicide missions. Nonetheless, many captives chose death over this exceptionally horrid new kind of slavery.
They chose to die rather than survive the horrors of the Middle Passage. They were equally determined to take their captors with them to the bottom of the ocean.

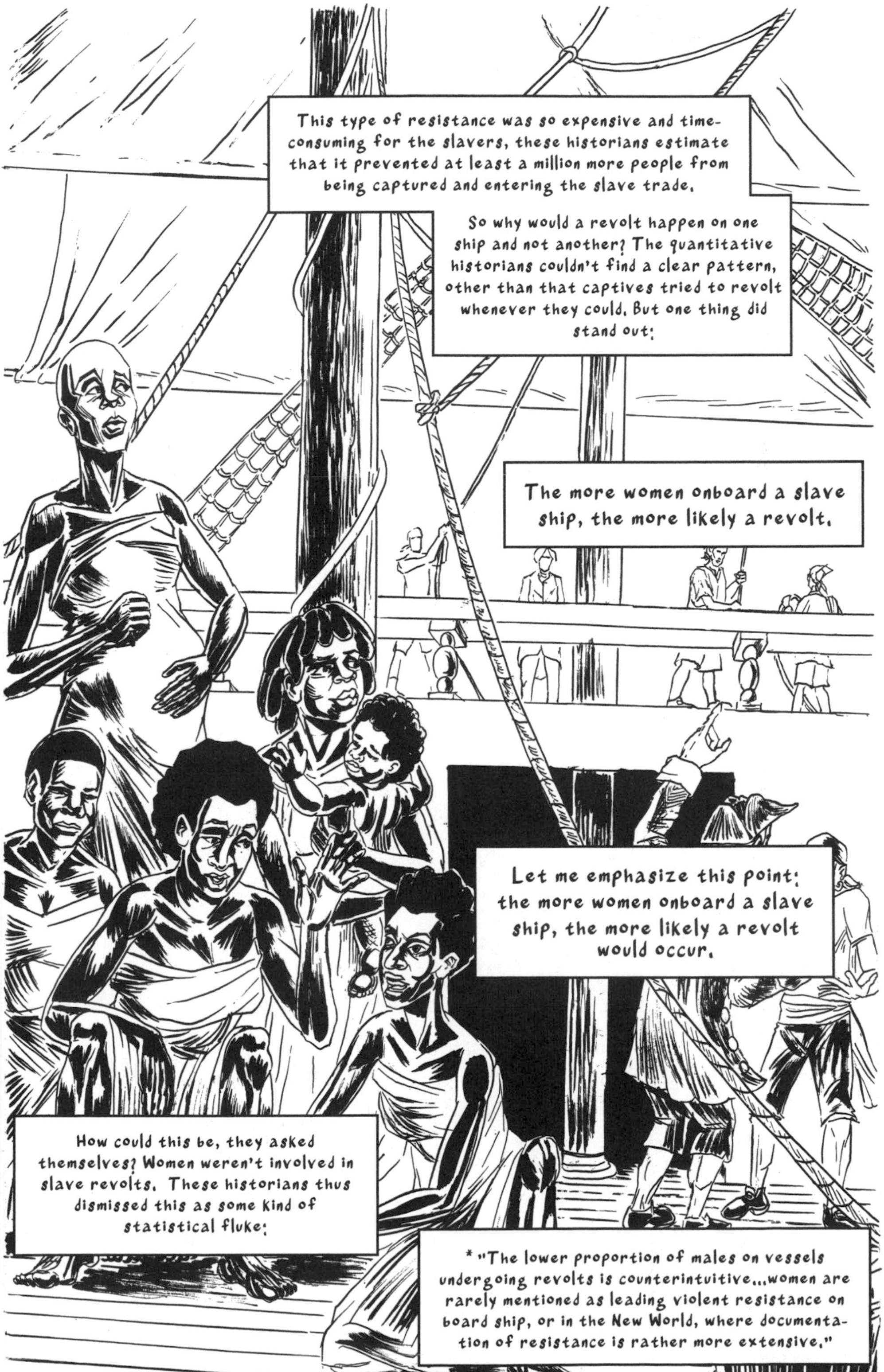
This type of resistance was so expensive and time-consuming for the slavers, these historians estimate that it prevented at least a million more people from being captured and entering the slave trade.
So why would a revolt happen on one ship and not another? The quantitative historians couldn't find a clear pattern, other than that captives tried to revolt whenever they could. But one thing did stand out:
The more women onboard a slave ship, the more likely a revolt.
Let me emphasize this point: the more women onboard a slave ship, the more likely a revolt would occur.
How could this be, they asked themselves? Women weren't involved in slave revolts. These historians thus dismissed this as some kind of statistical fluke:
* "The lower proportion of males on vessels undergoing revolts is counterintuitive...women are rarely mentioned as leading violent resistance on board ship, or in the New World, where documentation of resistance is rather more extensive."

*Behrendt et al., "The Costs of Coercion," *The Economic History Review* vol. 54, No 3 (August 2001): 460.

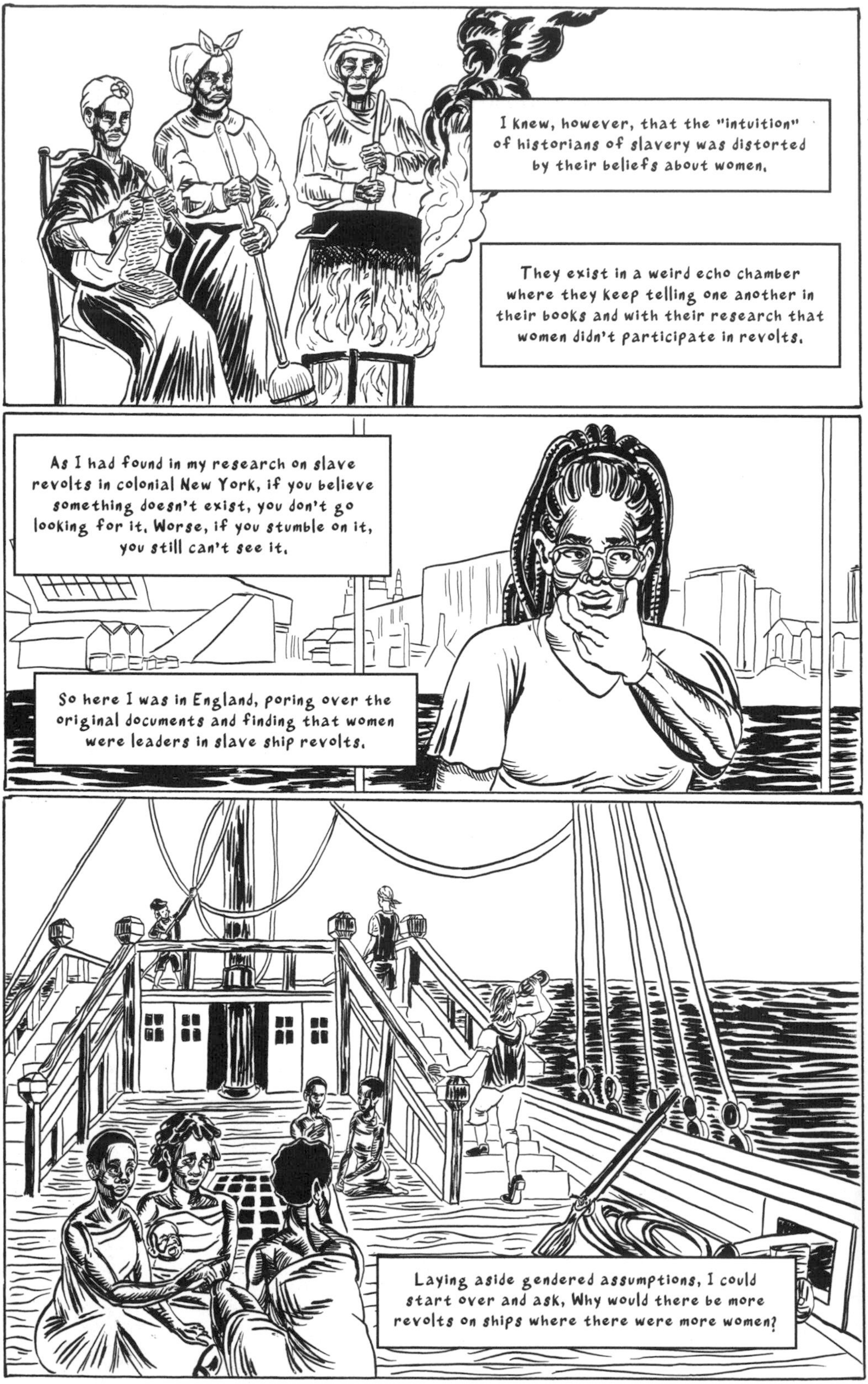

I knew, however, that the "intuition" of historians of slavery was distorted by their beliefs about women.
They exist in a weird echo chamber where they keep telling one another in their books and with their research that women didn't participate in revolts.
As I had found in my research on slave revolts in colonial New York, if you believe something doesn't exist, you don't go looking for it. Worse, if you stumble on it, you still can't see it.
So here I was in England, poring over the original documents and finding that women were leaders in slave ship revolts.
Laying aside gendered assumptions, I could start over and ask, Why would there be more revolts on ships where there were more women?

The answer was immediately obvious to me: The people who regulated this business, developed slave ship operating procedures, and actually ran the ships, kept women mostly unchained, on-deck, and near the weapons.

THE UNITY CAPTAINS LOG

THE THOMAS CAPTAINS LOG

THE EAGLE CAPTAINS LOG

THE ANNIBAL CAPTAINS LOG

THE THAMES CAPTAINS LOG

THE ROBERT CAPTAINS LOG

Report of the Lords of the Privy Council, 1789: "The Slave, if a Man, is put in Irons on the Main Deck; if a Boy, he is put on the Main Deck loose; if a Woman or Girl, they are placed without Irons on the Quarter Deck."

The women used their relative mobility and access to weapons to plan and initiate revolt after revolt after revolt.

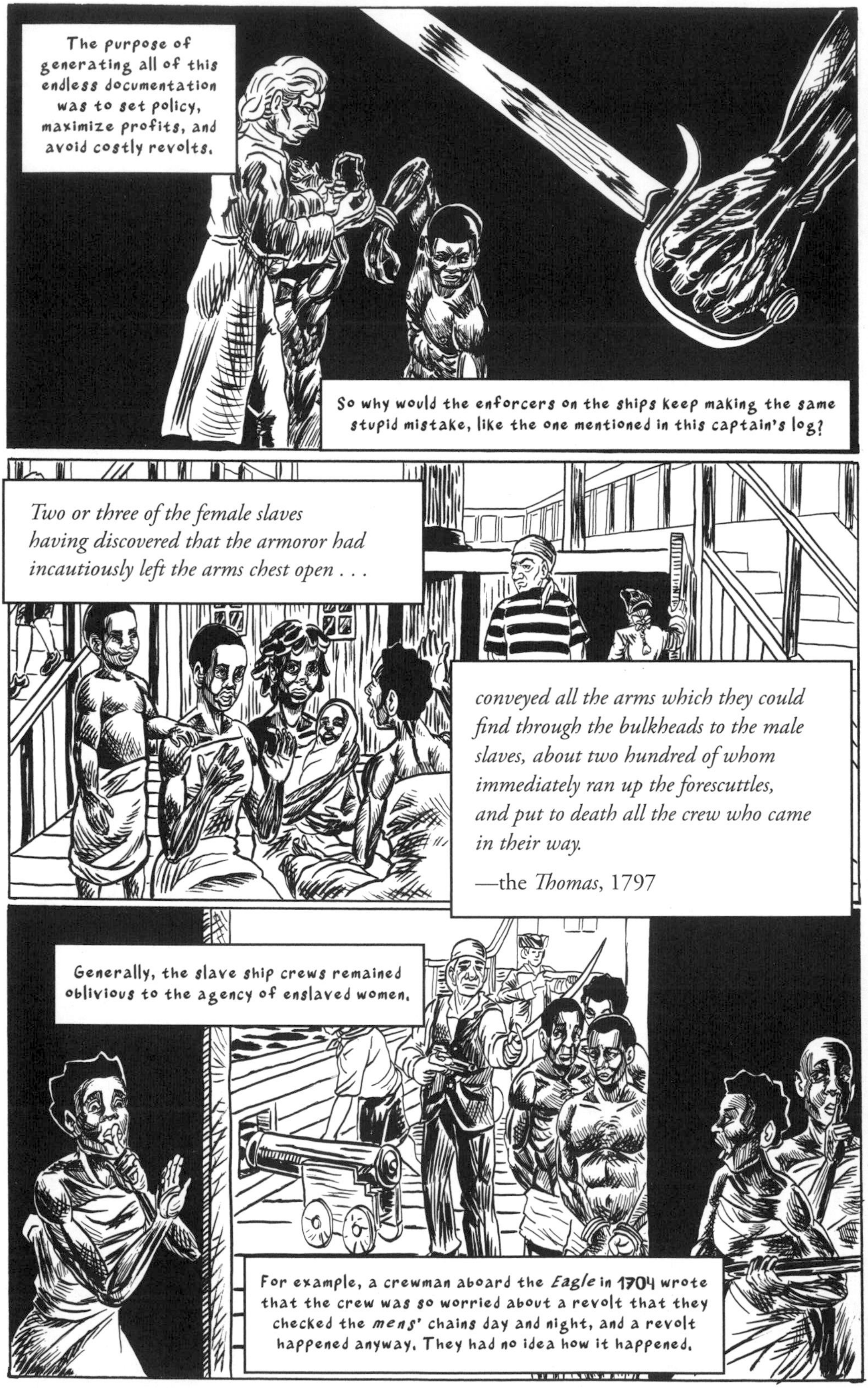
The purpose of generating all of this endless documentation was to set policy, maximize profits, and avoid costly revolts.
So why would the enforcers on the ships keep making the same stupid mistake, like the one mentioned in this captain's log?
Two or three of the female slaves having discovered that the armoror had incautiously left the arms chest open . . .
conveyed all the arms which they could find through the bulkheads to the male slaves, about two hundred of whom immediately ran up the forescuttles, and put to death all the crew who came in their way.
—the *Thomas*, 1797
Generally, the slave ship crews remained oblivious to the agency of enslaved women.
For example, a crewman aboard the *Eagle* in 1704 wrote that the crew was so worried about a revolt that they checked the *mens'* chains day and night, and a revolt happened anyway. They had no idea how it happened.

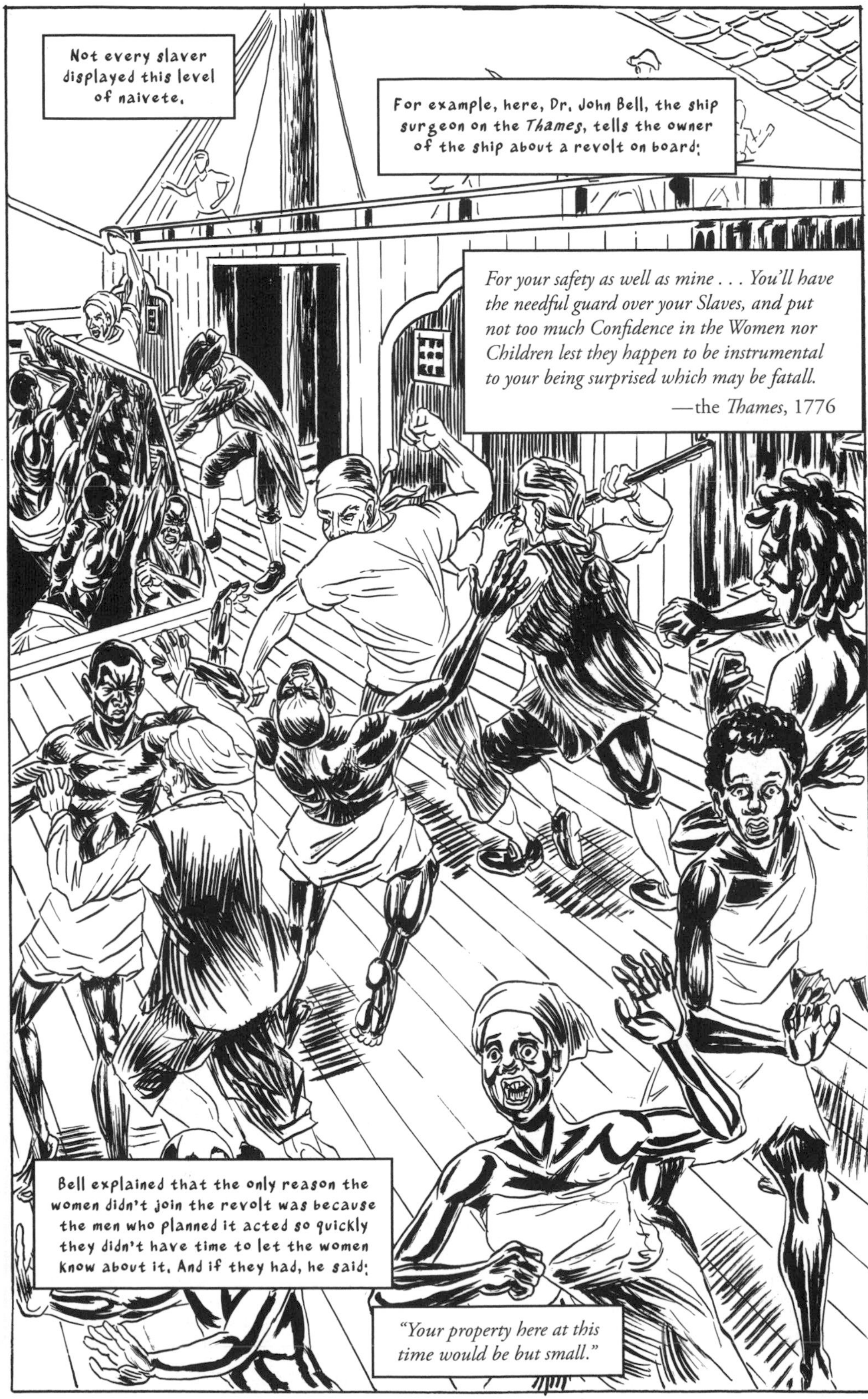

Not every slaver displayed this level of naivete.
For example, here, Dr. John Bell, the ship surgeon on the *Thames*, tells the owner of the ship about a revolt on board:
For your safety as well as mine . . . You'll have the needful guard over your Slaves, and put not too much Confidence in the Women nor Children lest they happen to be instrumental to your being surprised which may be fatall.
—the *Thames*, 1776
Bell explained that the only reason the women didn't join the revolt was because the men who planned it acted so quickly they didn't have time to let the women know about it. And if they had, he said:
"Your property here at this time would be but small."

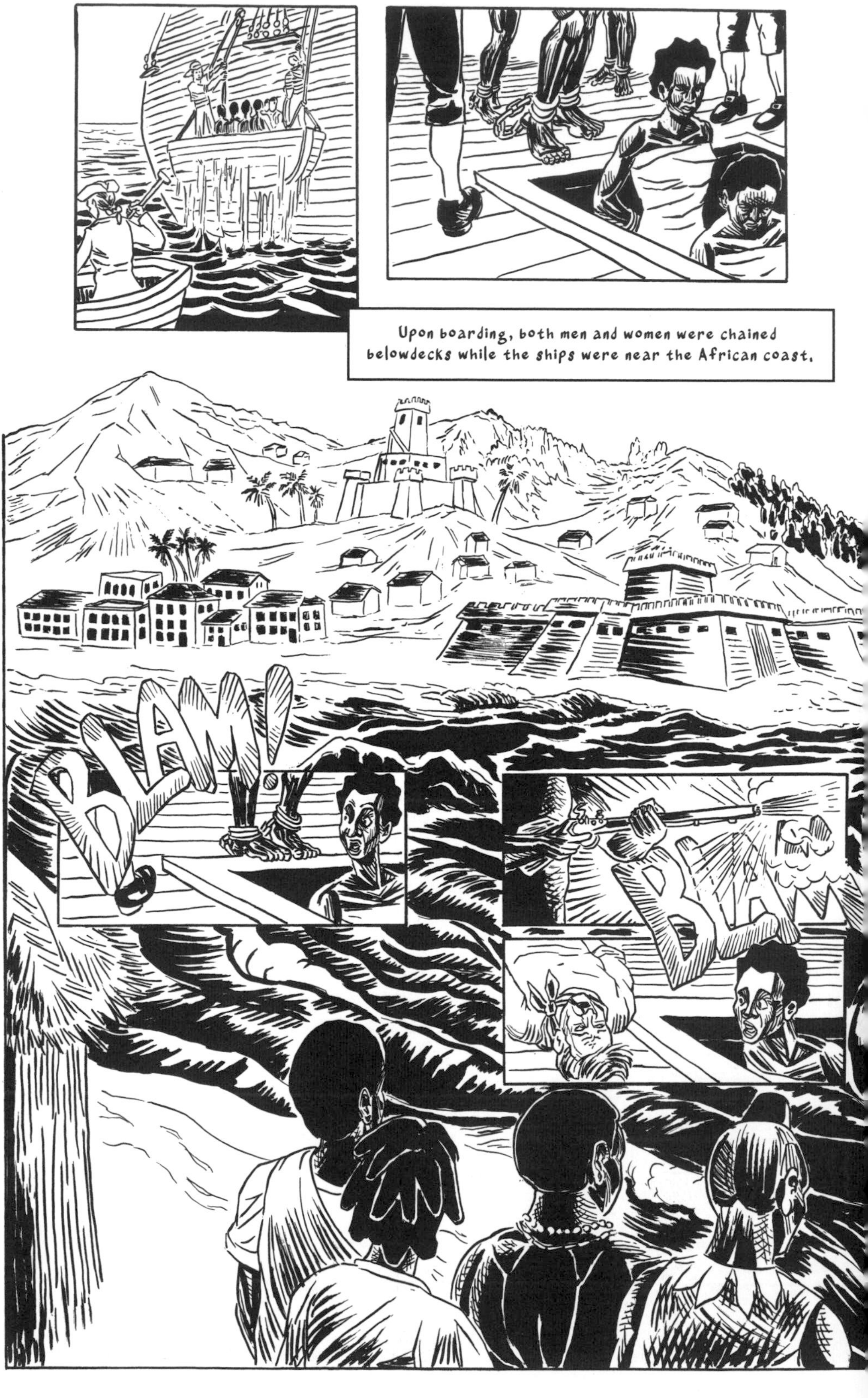
Upon boarding, both men and women were chained belowdecks while the ships were near the African coast.
BLAM!
BLAM

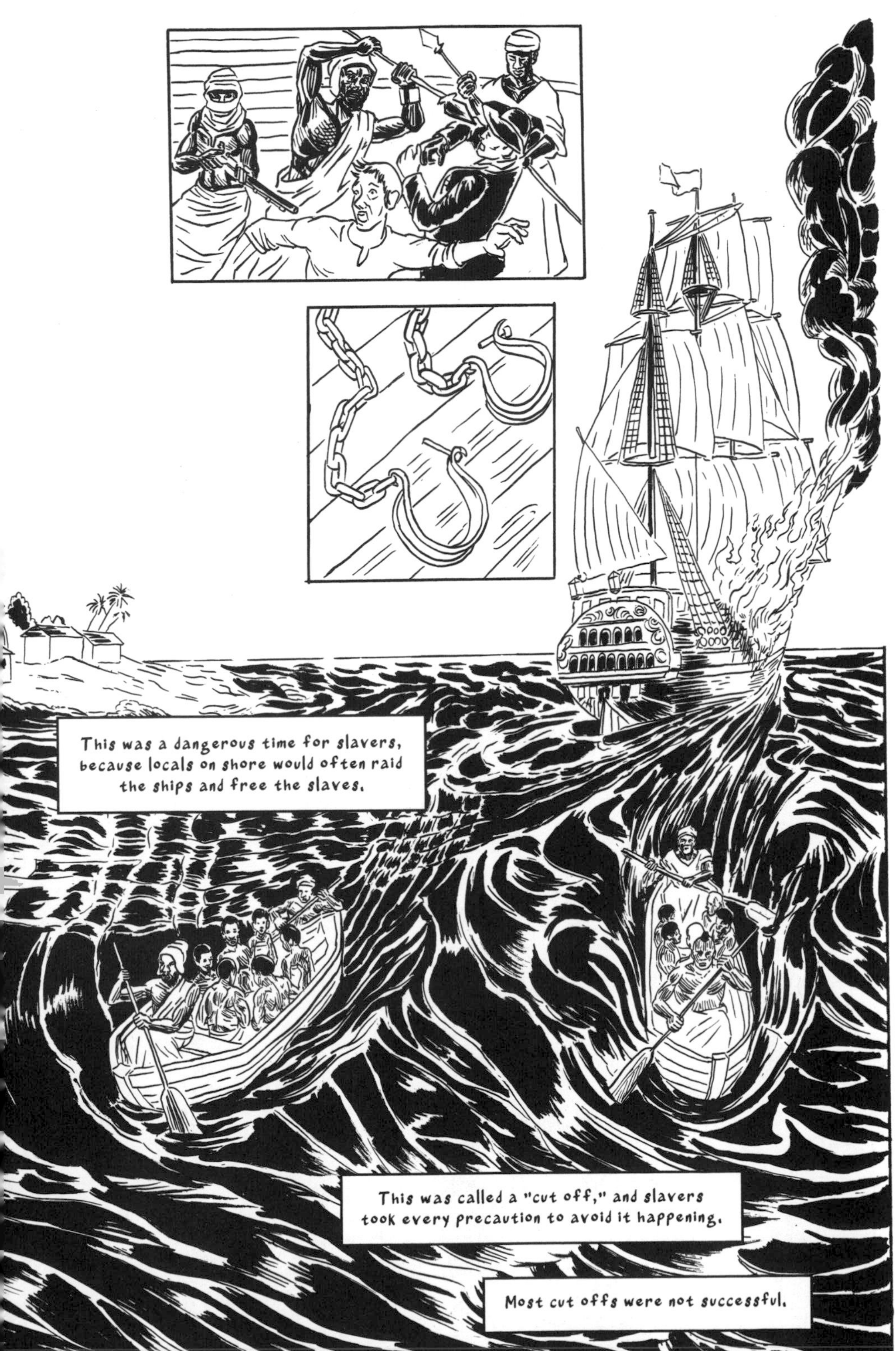
This was a dangerous time for slavers, because locals on shore would often raid the ships and free the slaves.
This was called a "cut off," and slavers took every precaution to avoid it happening.
Most cut offs were not successful.

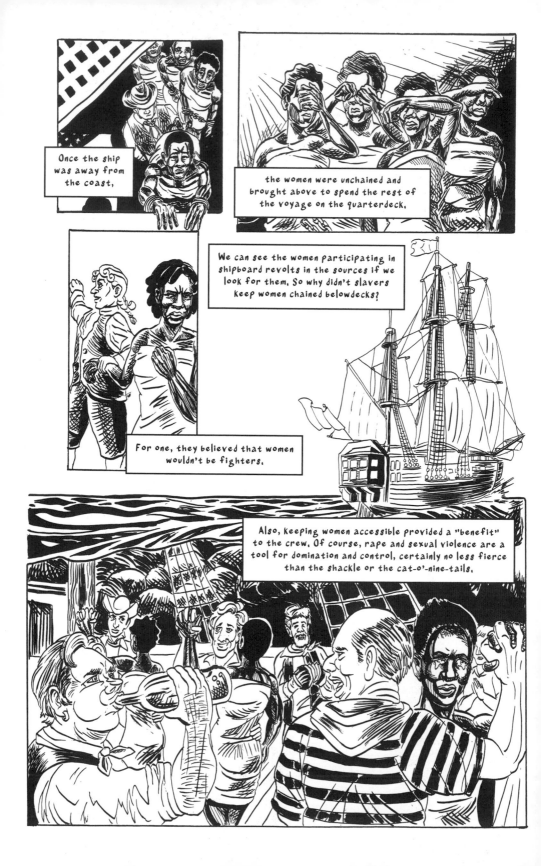

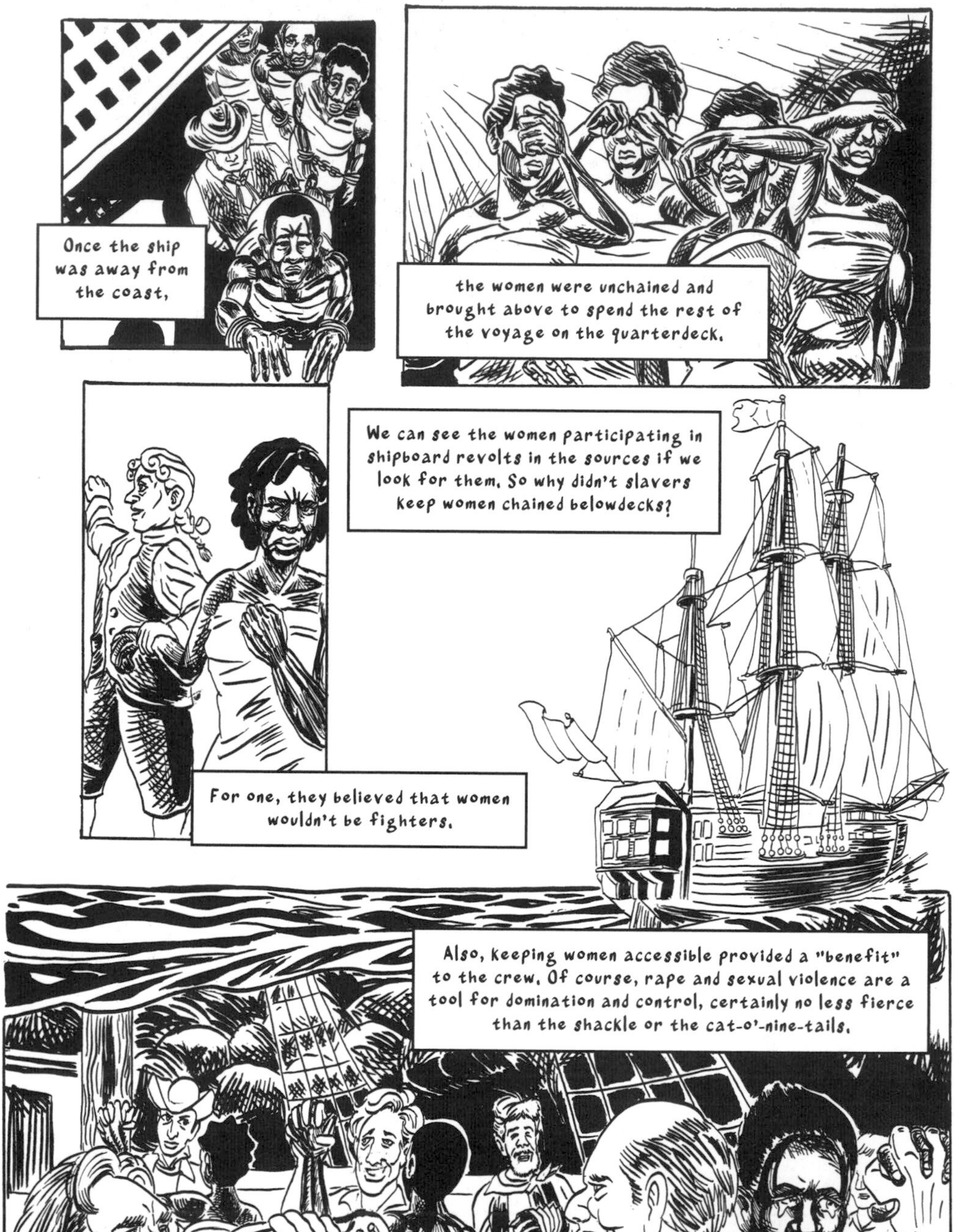
Once the ship was away from the coast,
the women were unchained and brought above to spend the rest of the voyage on the quarterdeck.
We can see the women participating in shipboard revolts in the sources if we look for them. So why didn't slavers keep women chained belowdecks?
For one, they believed that women wouldn't be fighters.
Also, keeping women accessible provided a "benefit" to the crew. Of course, rape and sexual violence are a tool for domination and control, certainly no less fierce than the shackle or the cat-o'-nine-tails.

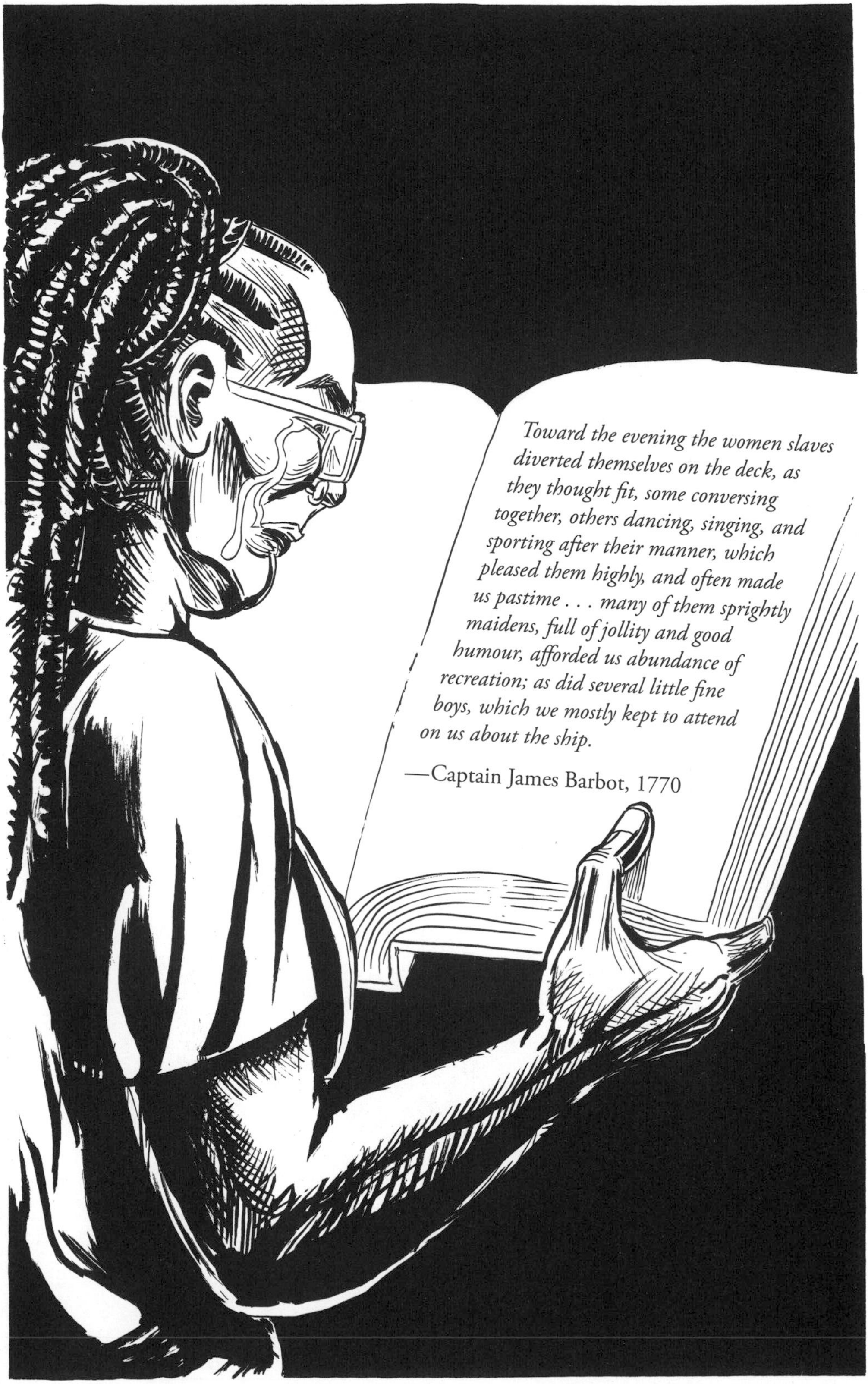
Toward the evening the women slaves diverted themselves on the deck, as they thought fit, some conversing together, others dancing, singing, and sporting after their manner, which pleased them highly, and often made us pastime . . . many of them sprightly maidens, full of jollity and good humour, afforded us abundance of recreation; as did several little fine boys, which we mostly kept to attend on us about the ship.
—Captain James Barbot, 1770

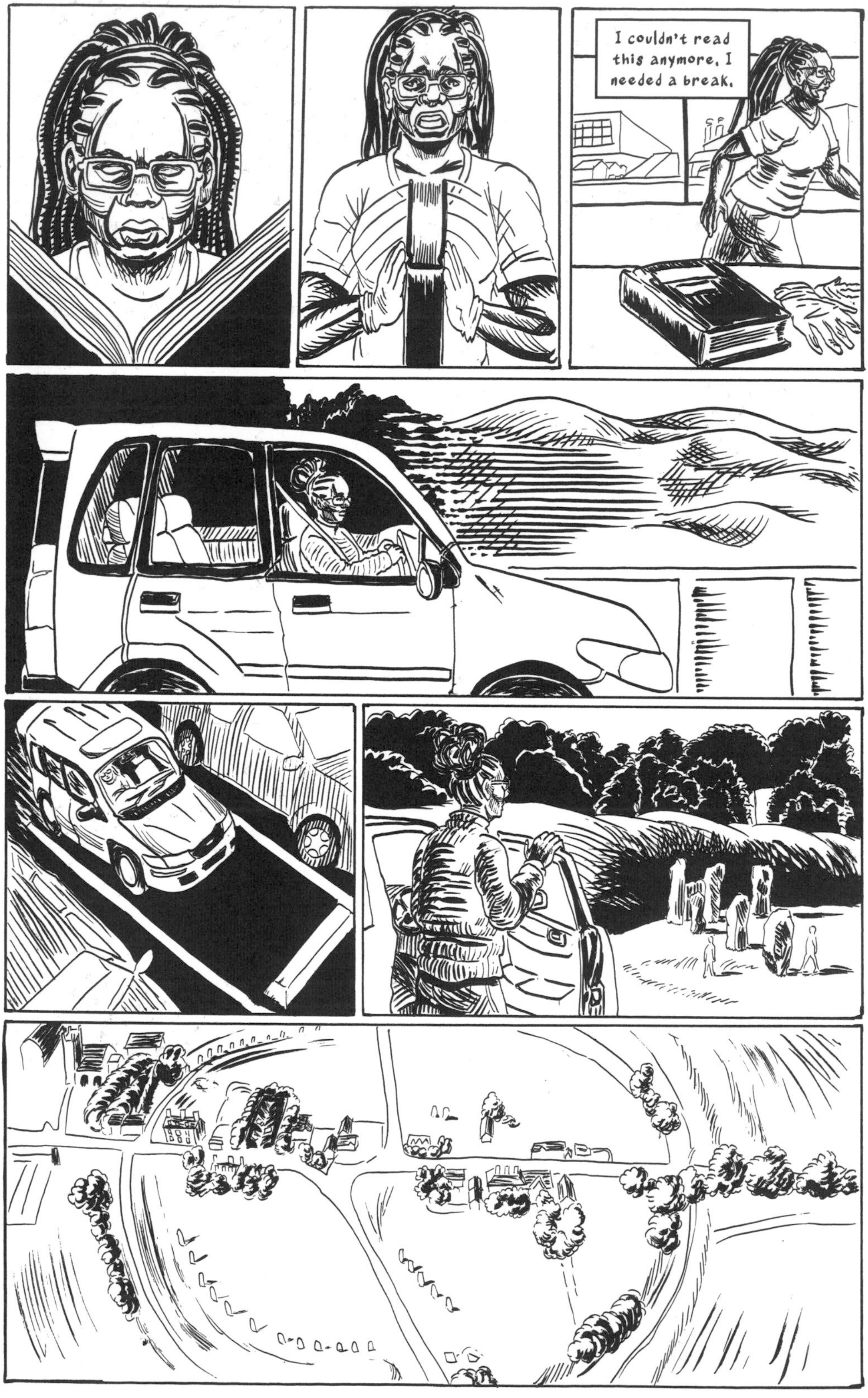
I couldn't read this anymore. I needed a break.

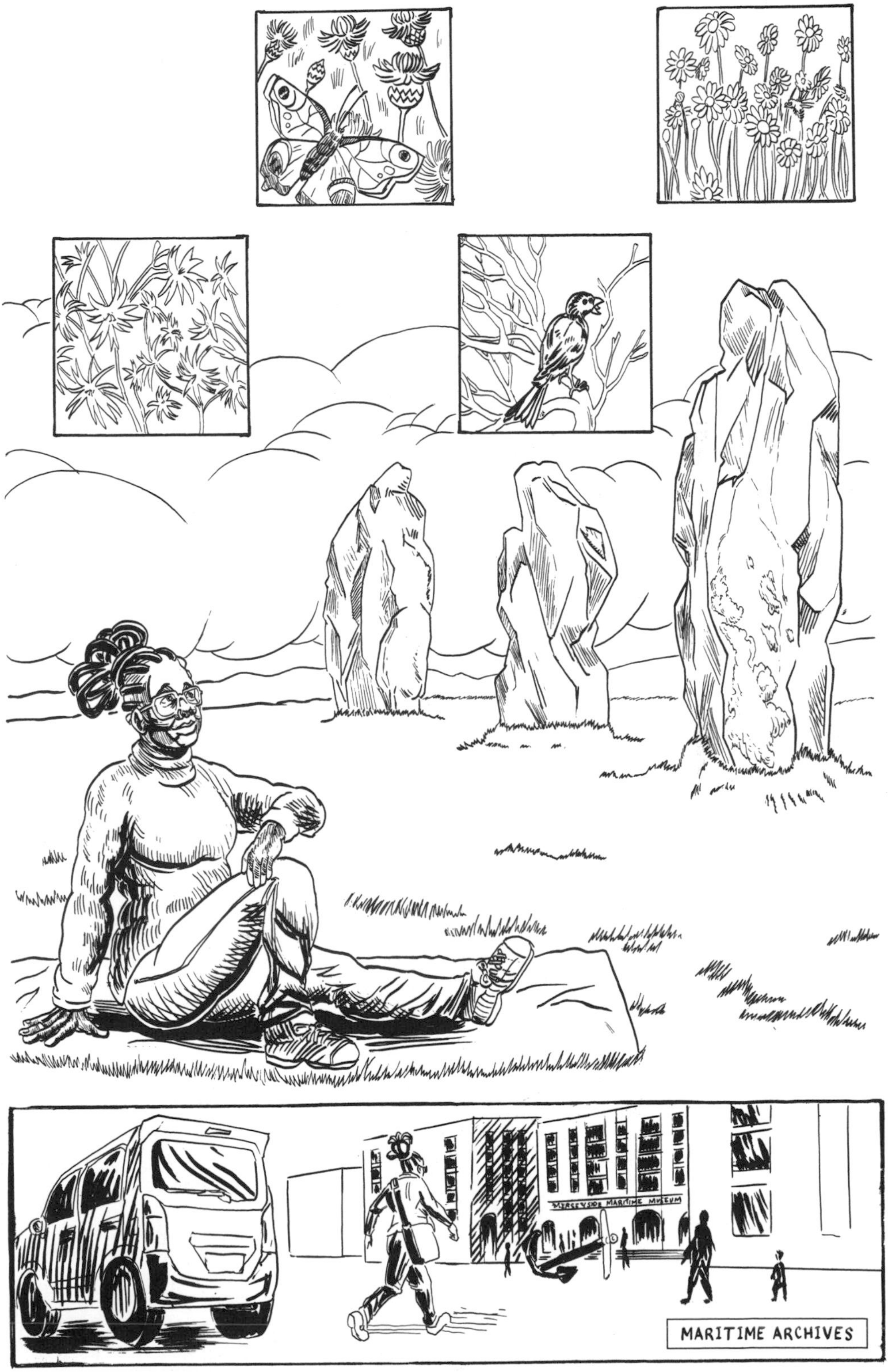
MERSEYSIDE MARITIME MUSEUM
MARITIME ARCHIVES

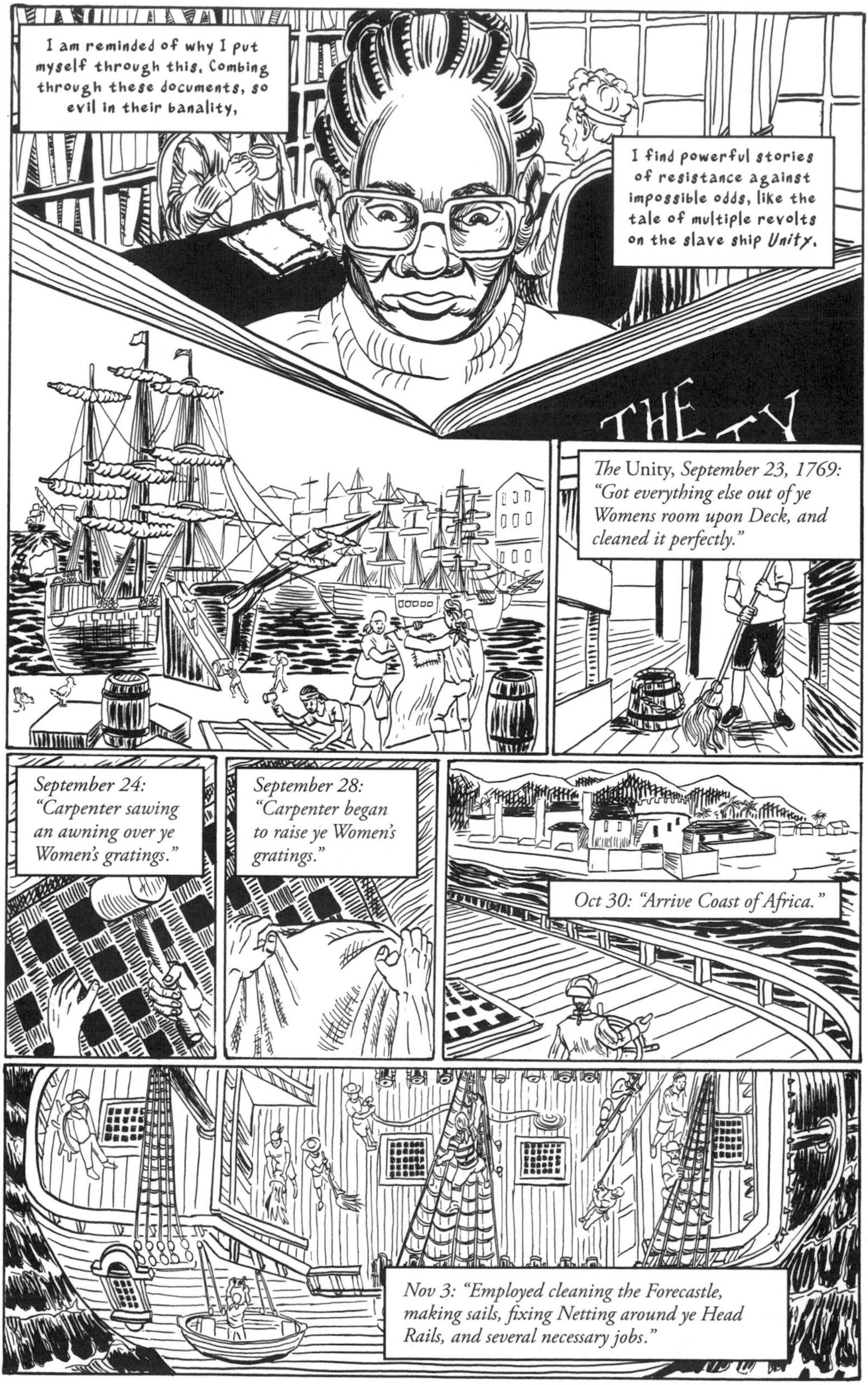
I am reminded of why I put myself through this. Combing through these documents, so evil in their banality,
I find powerful stories of resistance against impossible odds, like the tale of multiple revolts on the slave ship *Unity*.
THE
The Unity, *September 23, 1769: "Got everything else out of ye Womens room upon Deck, and cleaned it perfectly."*
September 24: "Carpenter sawing an awning over ye Women's gratings."
September 28: "Carpenter began to raise ye Women's gratings."
Oct 30: "Arrive Coast of Africa."
Nov 3: "Employed cleaning the Forecastle, making sails, fixing Netting around ye Head Rails, and several necessary jobs."

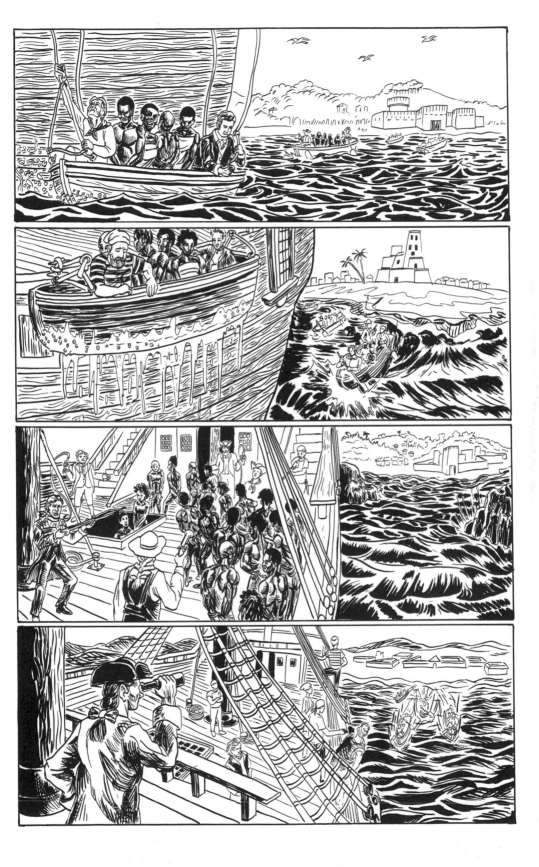

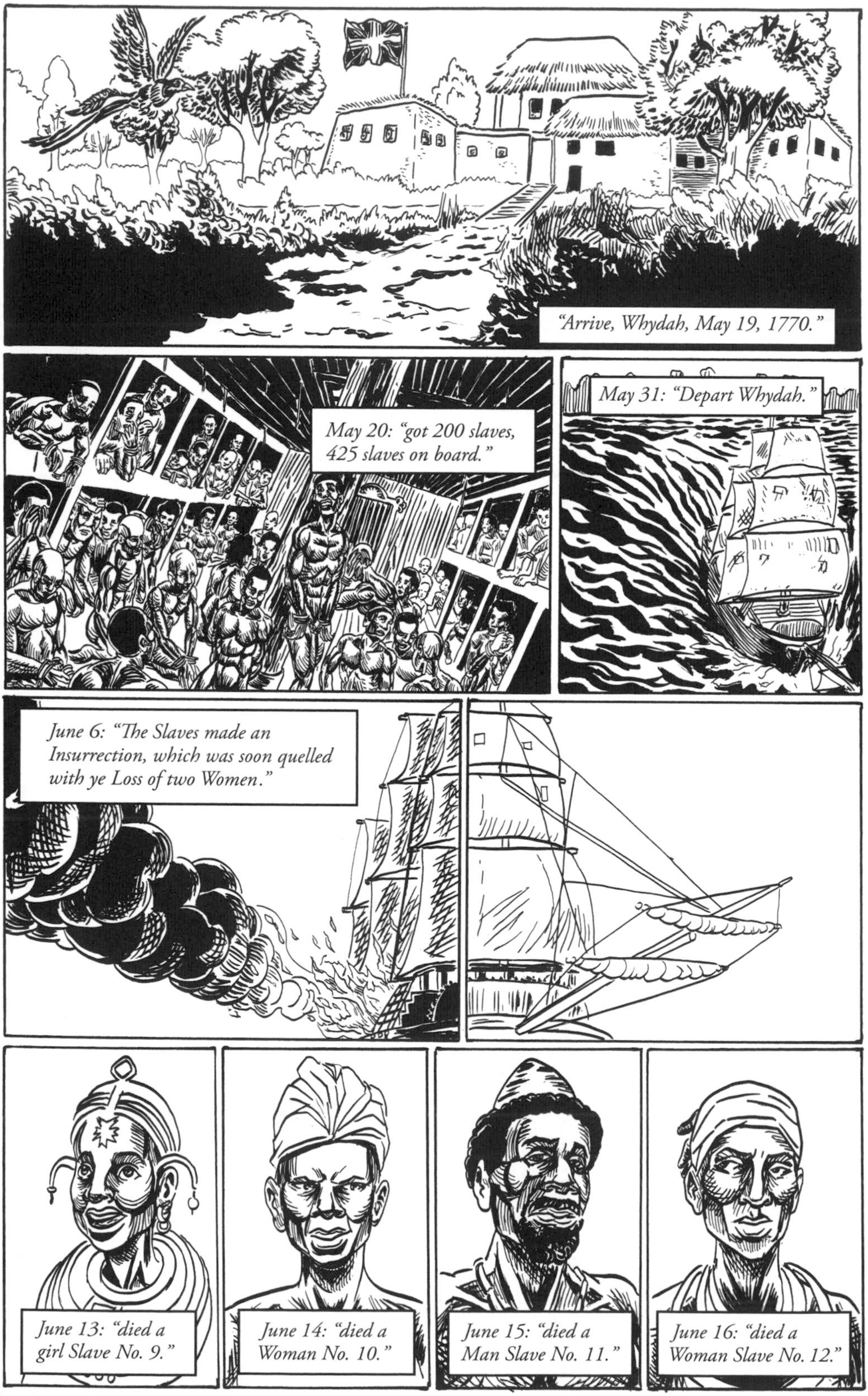
"Arrive, Whydah, May 19, 1770."
May 20: "got 200 slaves, 425 slaves on board."
May 31: "Depart Whydah."
June 6: "The Slaves made an Insurrection, which was soon quelled with ye Loss of two Women."
June 13: "died a girl Slave No. 9."
June 14: "died a Woman No. 10."
June 15: "died a Man Slave No. 11."
June 16: "died a Woman Slave No. 12."

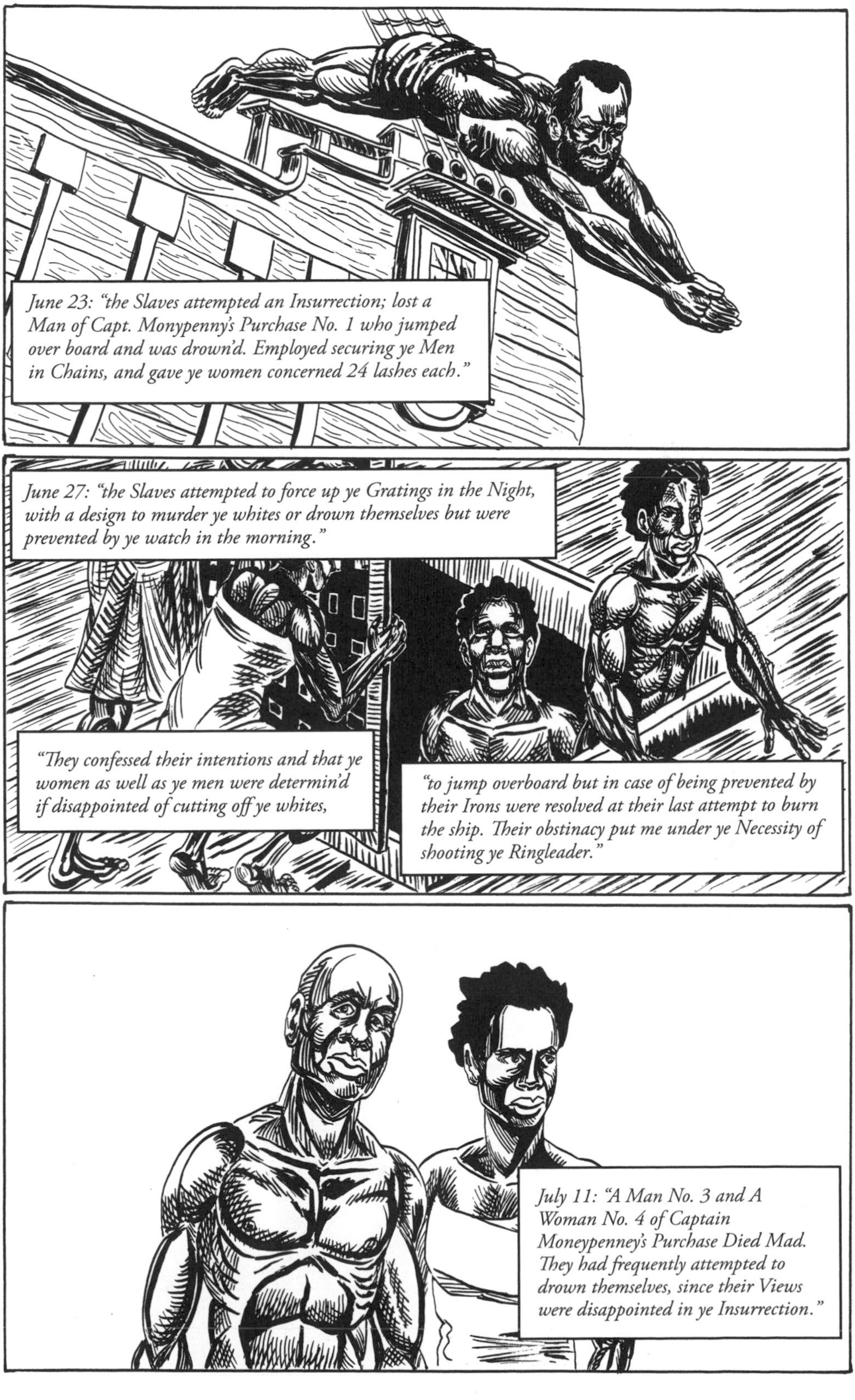
June 23: "the Slaves attempted an Insurrection; lost a Man of Capt. Monypenny's Purchase No. 1 who jumped over board and was drown'd. Employed securing ye Men in Chains, and gave ye women concerned 24 lashes each."
June 27: "the Slaves attempted to force up ye Gratings in the Night, with a design to murder ye whites or drown themselves but were prevented by ye watch in the morning."
"They confessed their intentions and that ye women as well as ye men were determin'd if disappointed of cutting off ye whites,
"to jump overboard but in case of being prevented by their Irons were resolved at their last attempt to burn the ship. Their obstinacy put me under ye Necessity of shooting ye Ringleader."
July 11: "A Man No. 3 and A Woman No. 4 of Captain Moneypenney's Purchase Died Mad. They had frequently attempted to drown themselves, since their Views were disappointed in ye Insurrection."

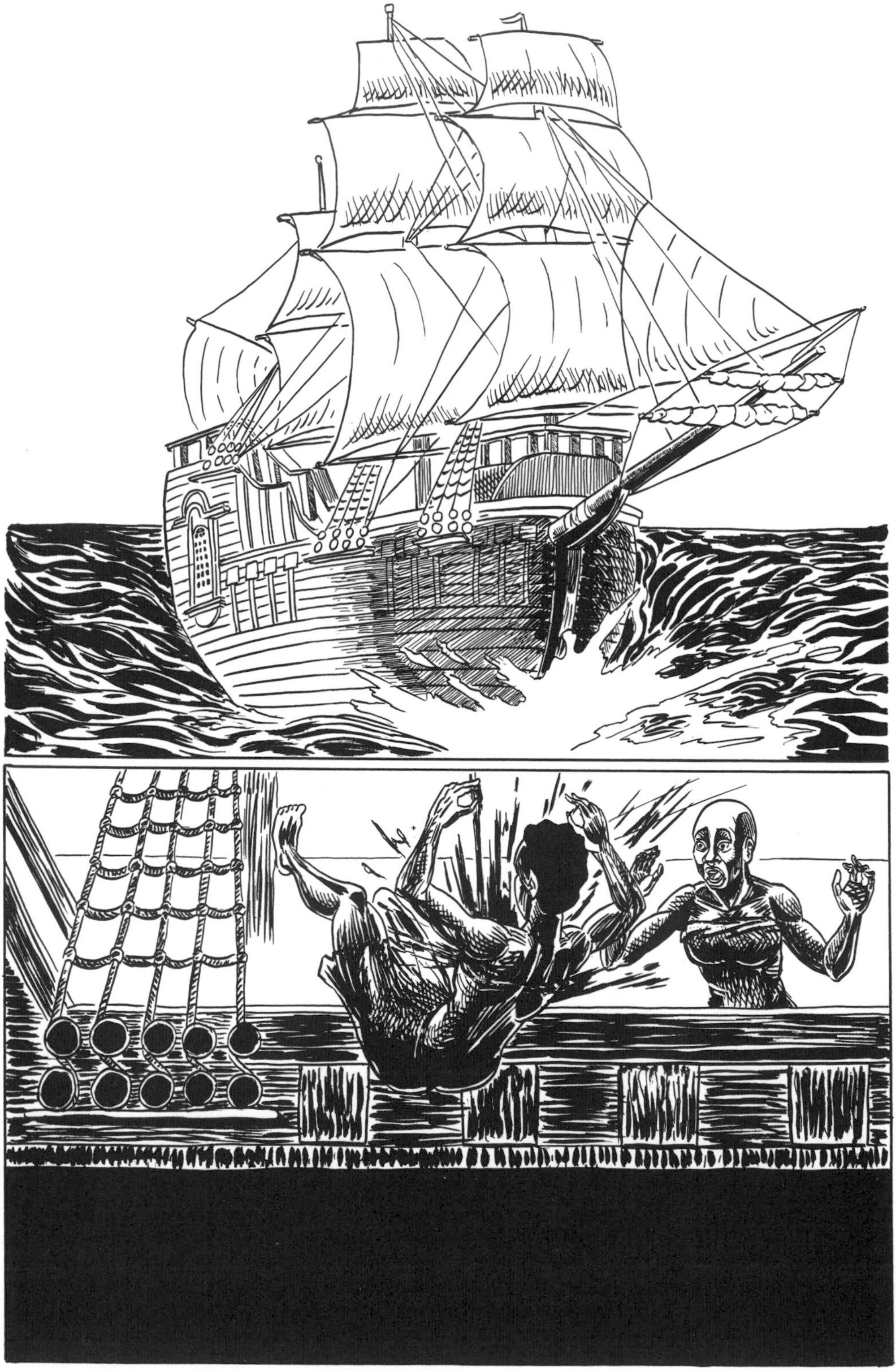

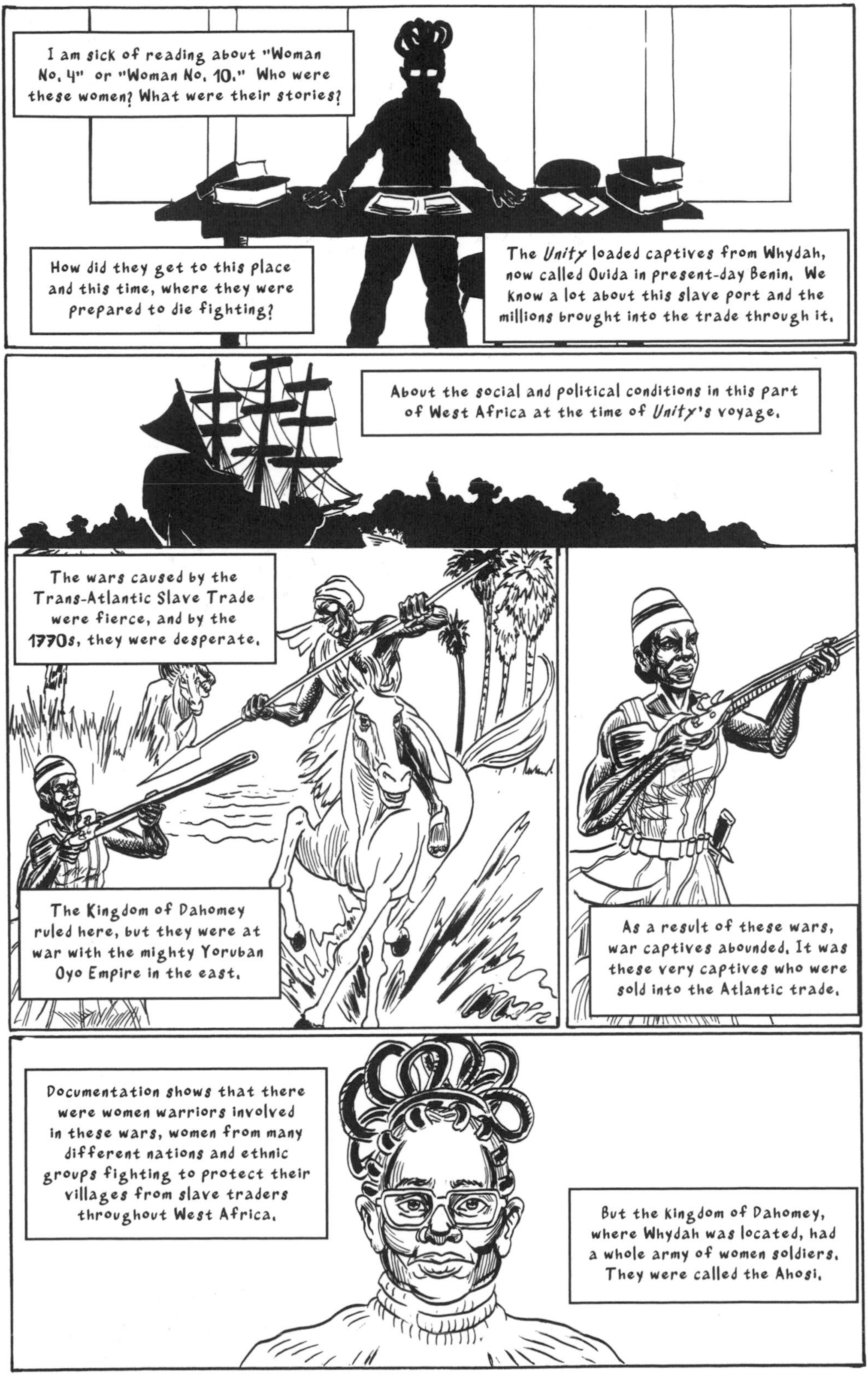

I am sick of reading about "Woman No. 4" or "Woman No. 10." Who were these women? What were their stories?
How did they get to this place and this time, where they were prepared to die fighting?
The *Unity* loaded captives from Whydah, now called Ouida in present-day Benin. We know a lot about this slave port and the millions brought into the trade through it.
About the social and political conditions in this part of West Africa at the time of *Unity*'s voyage.
The wars caused by the Trans-Atlantic Slave Trade were fierce, and by the 1770s, they were desperate.
The Kingdom of Dahomey ruled here, but they were at war with the mighty Yoruban Oyo Empire in the east.
As a result of these wars, war captives abounded. It was these very captives who were sold into the Atlantic trade.
Documentation shows that there were women warriors involved in these wars, women from many different nations and ethnic groups fighting to protect their villages from slave traders throughout West Africa.
But the kingdom of Dahomey, where Whydah was located, had a whole army of women soldiers. They were called the Ahosi.

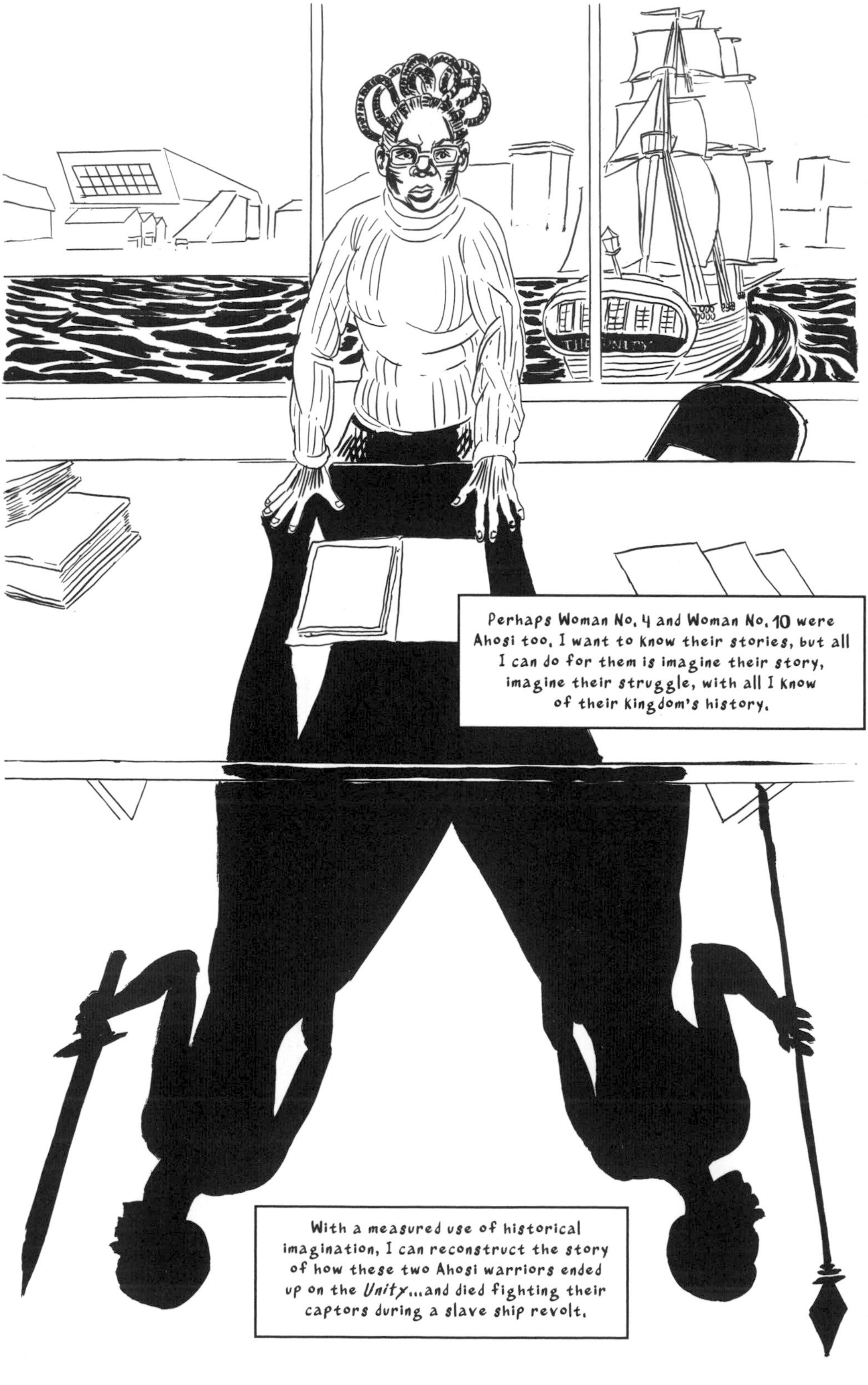
THE UNITY
Perhaps Woman No. 4 and Woman No. 10 were Ahosi too. I want to know their stories, but all I can do for them is imagine their story, imagine their struggle, with all I know of their kingdom's history.
With a measured use of historical imagination, I can reconstruct the story of how these two Ahosi warriors ended up on the *Unity*...and died fighting their captors during a slave ship revolt.

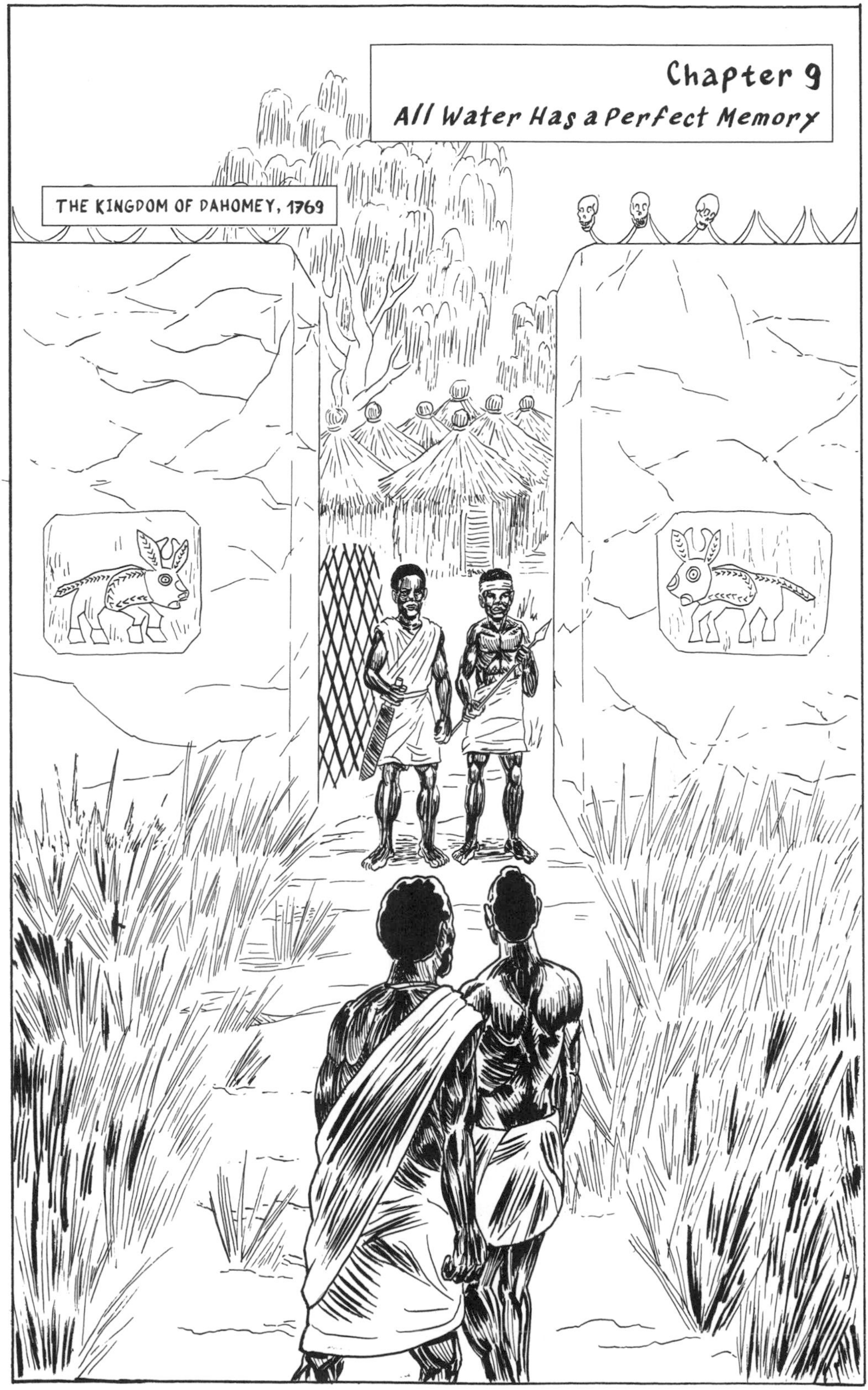
Chapter 9
All Water Has a Perfect Memory
THE KINGDOM OF DAHOMEY, 1769

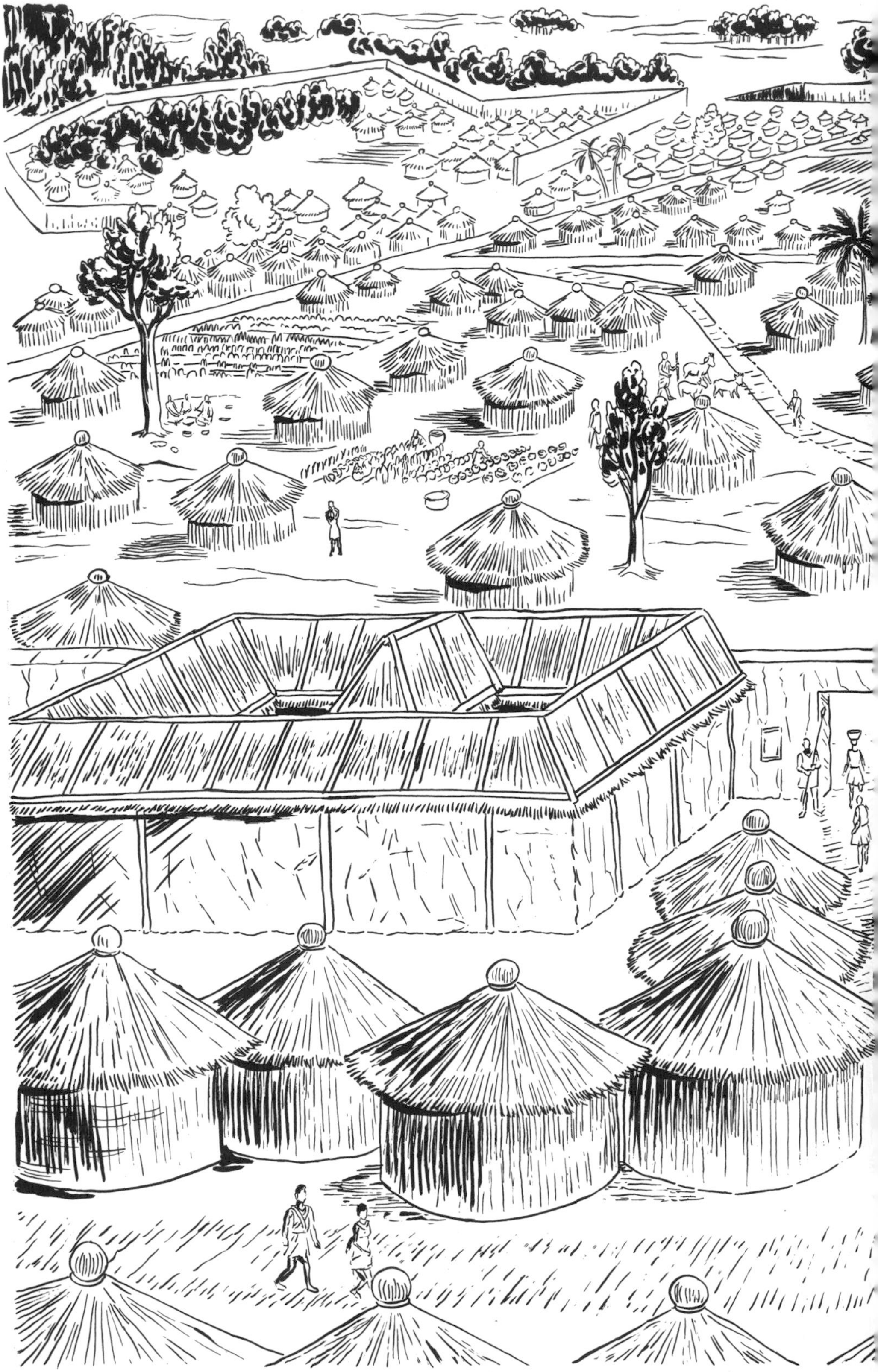

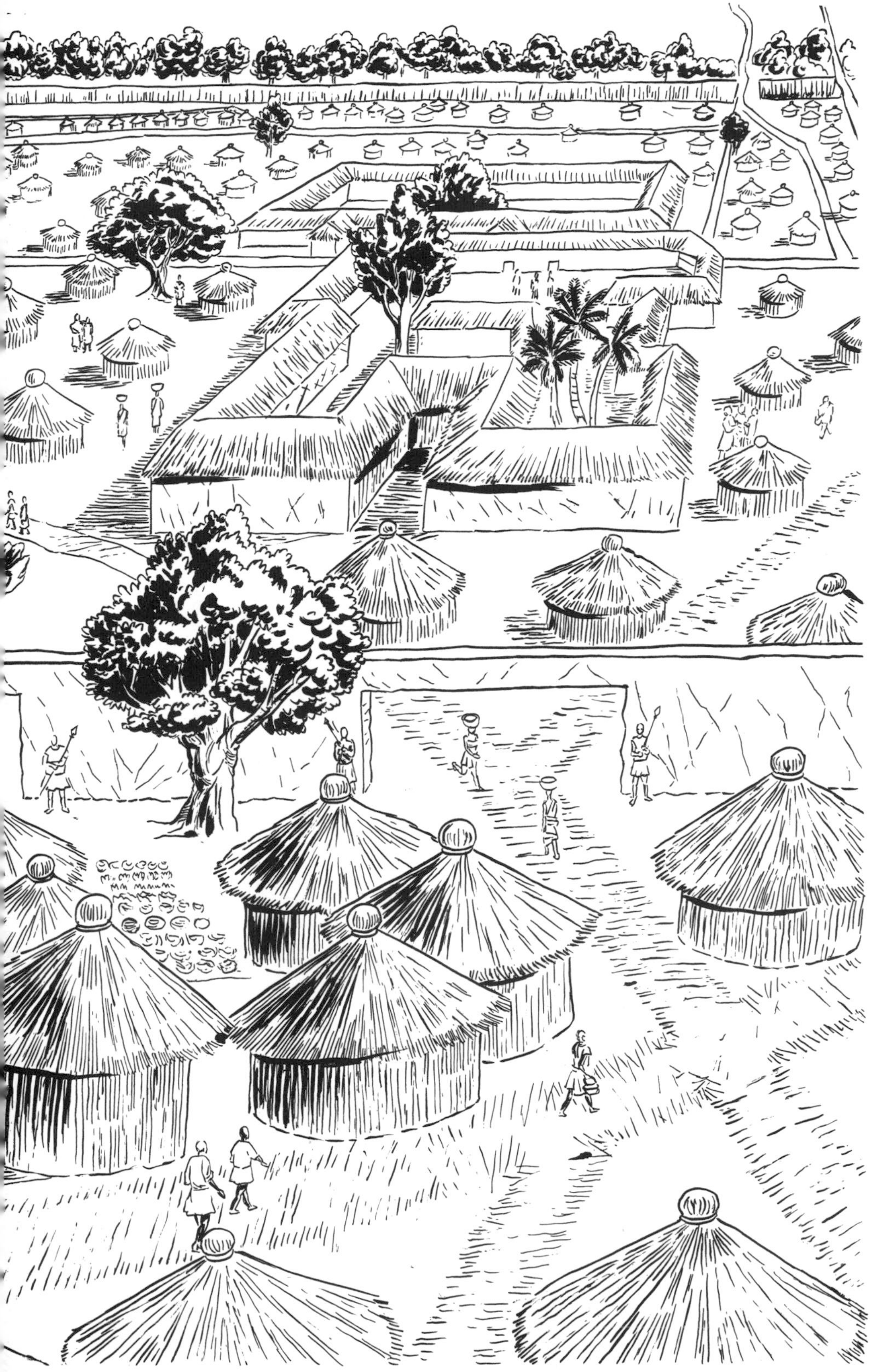

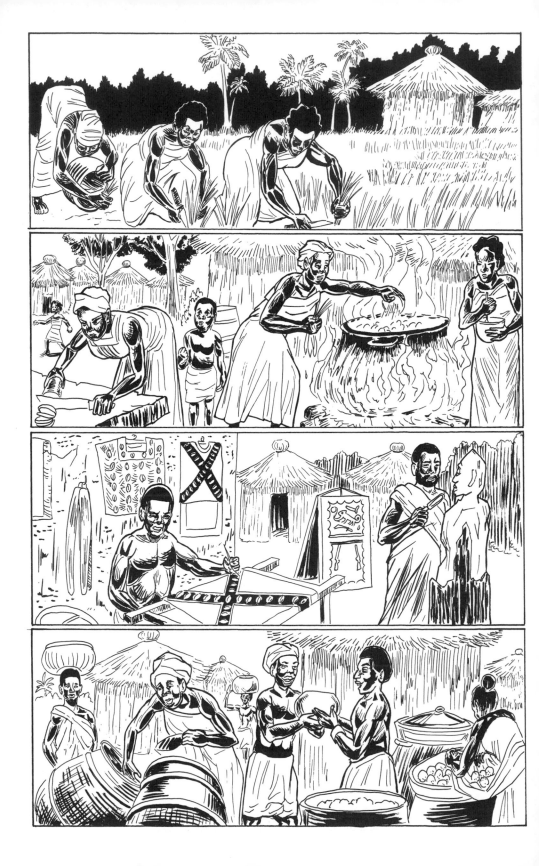

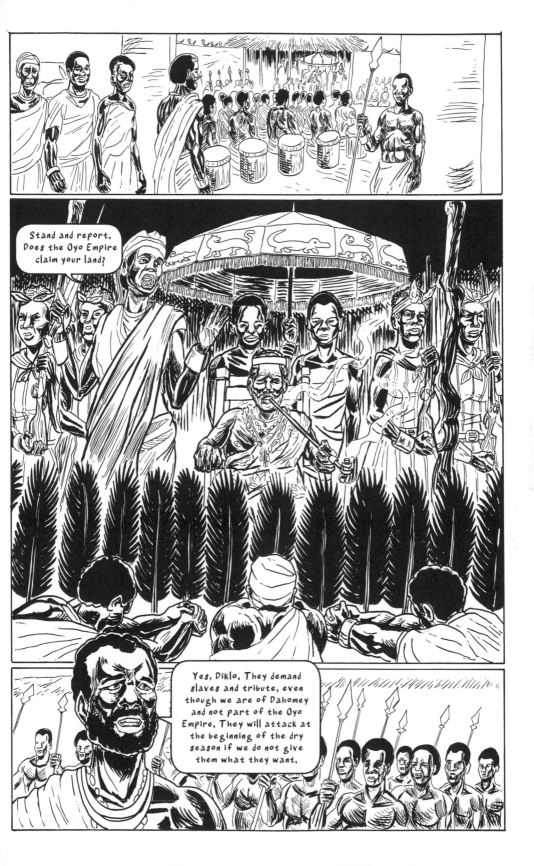

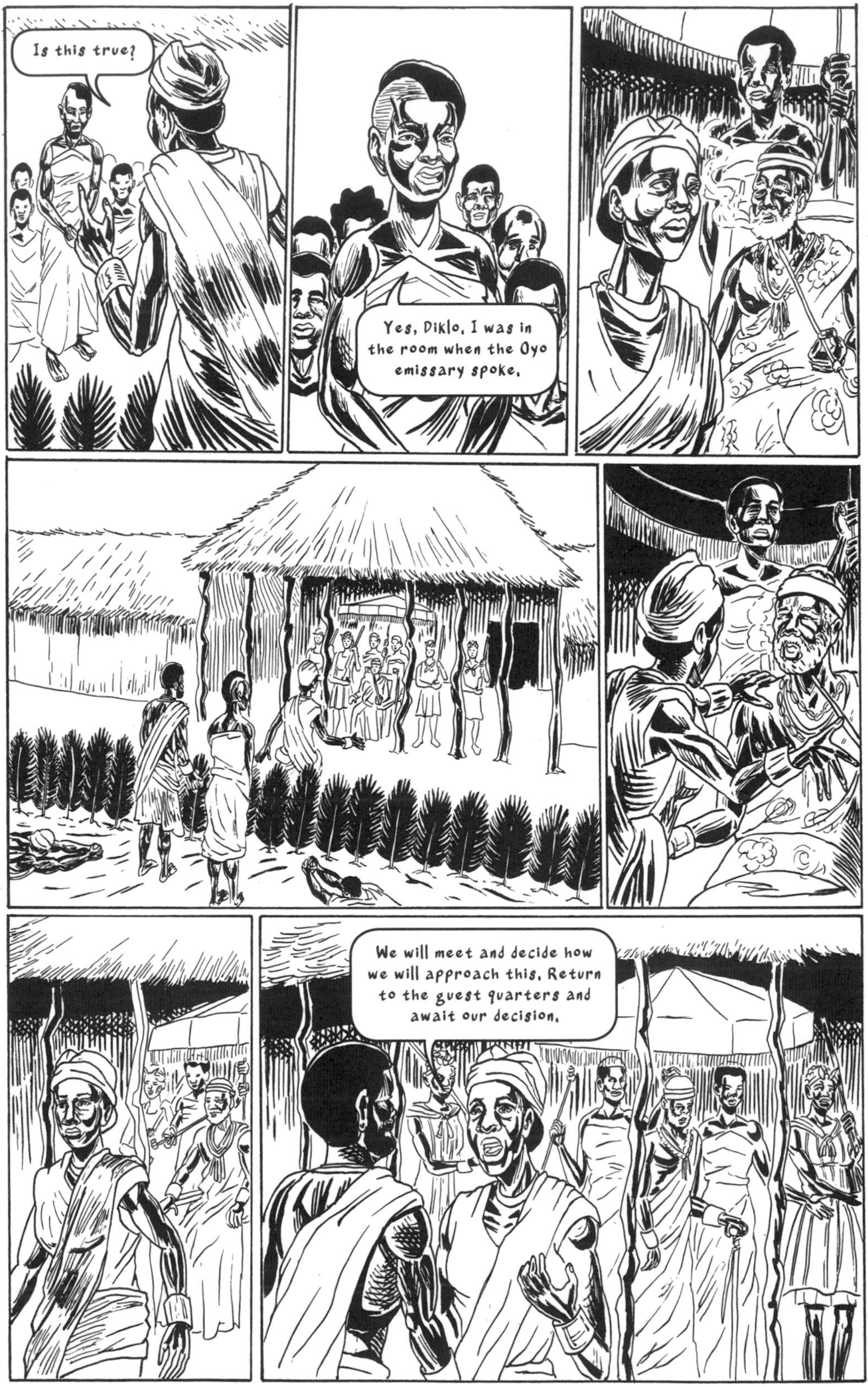
Is this true?
Yes, Diklo. I was in the room when the Oyo emissary spoke.
We will meet and decide how we will approach this. Return to the guest quarters and await our decision.

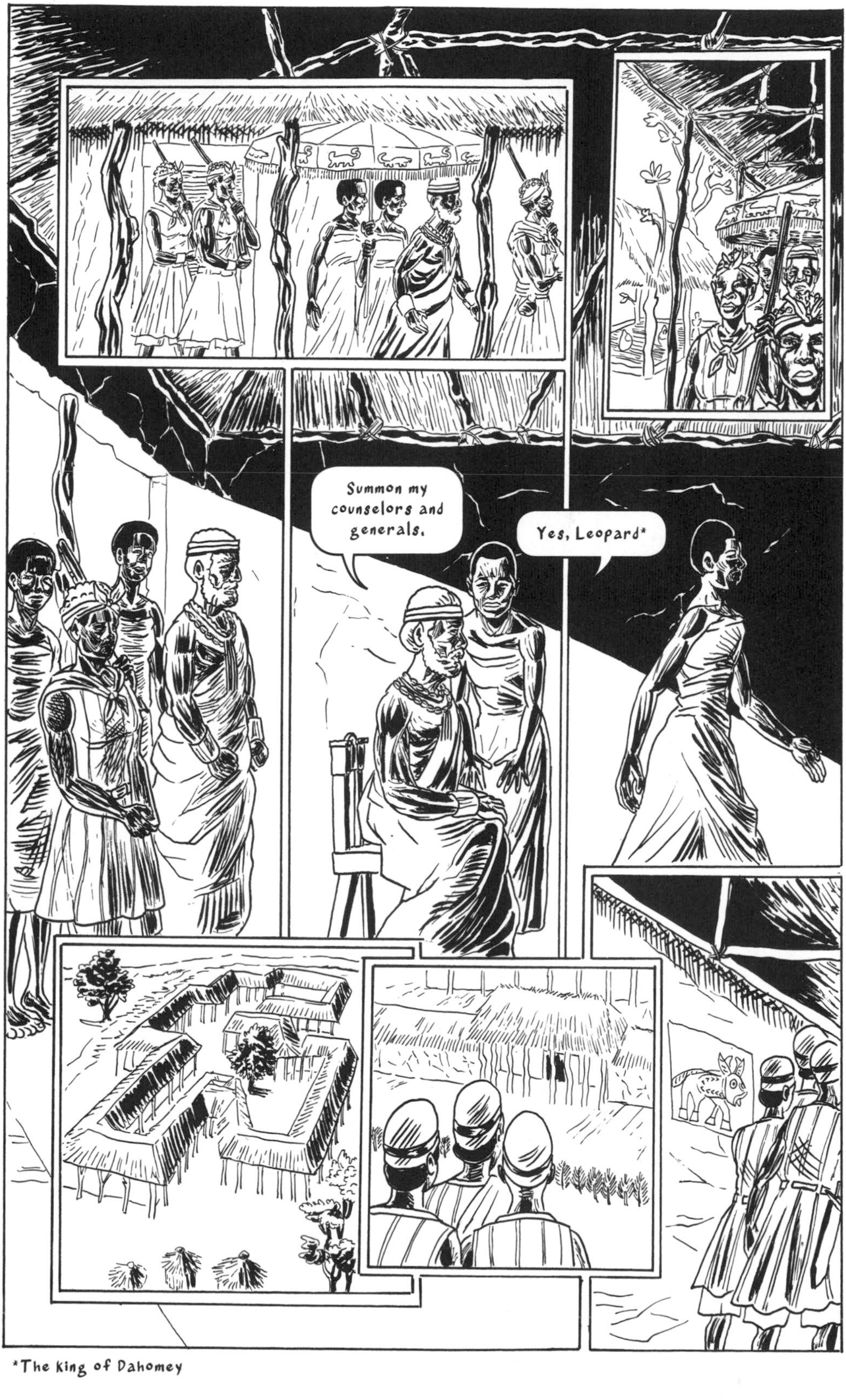
Summon my counselors and generals.
Yes, Leopard*

*The king of Dahomey

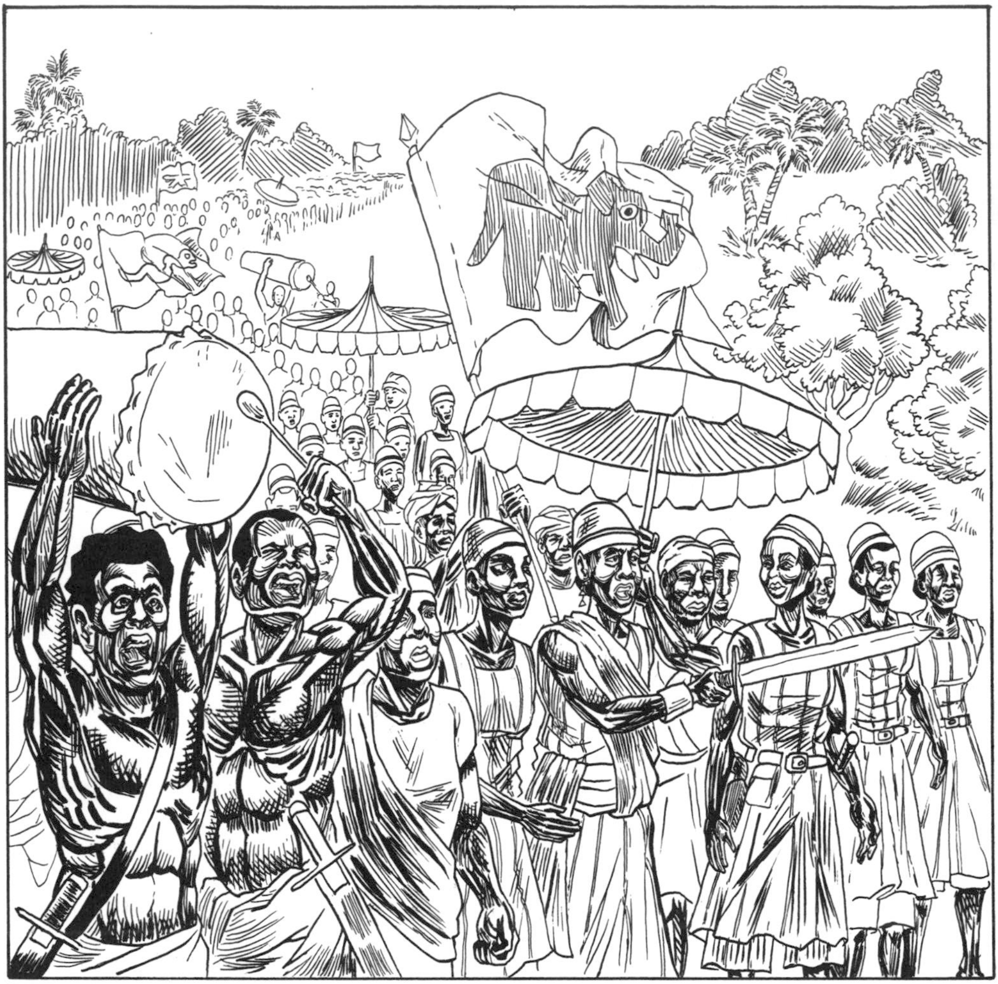

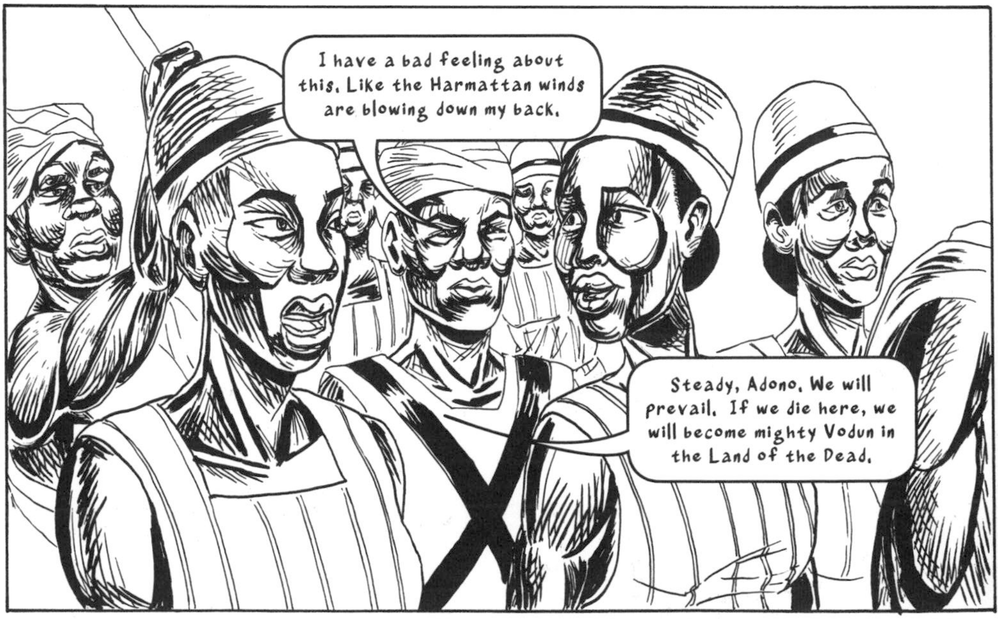
I have a bad feeling about this. Like the Harmattan winds are blowing down my back.
Steady, Adono. We will prevail. If we die here, we will become mighty Vodun in the Land of the Dead.

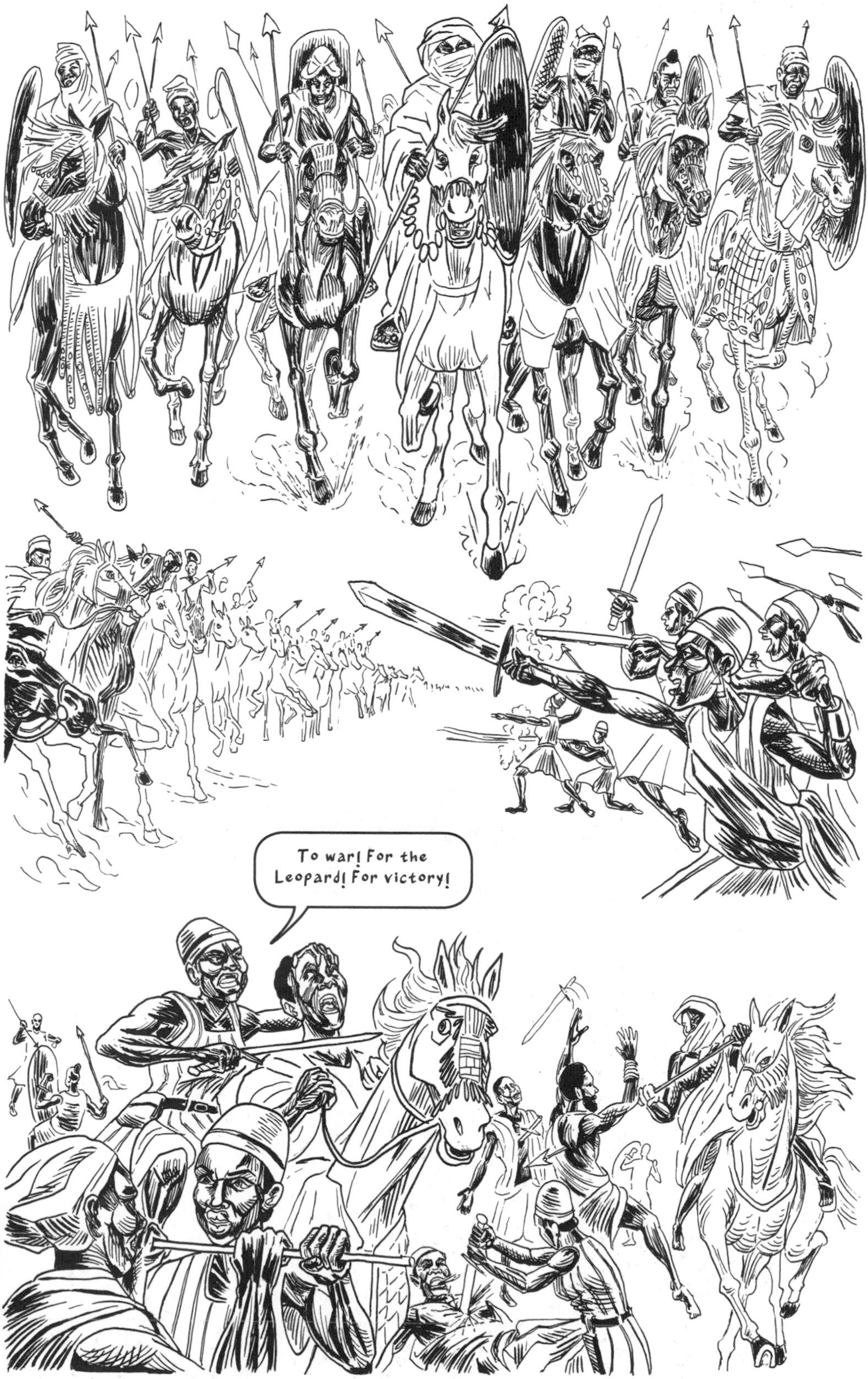
To war! For the Leopard! For victory!

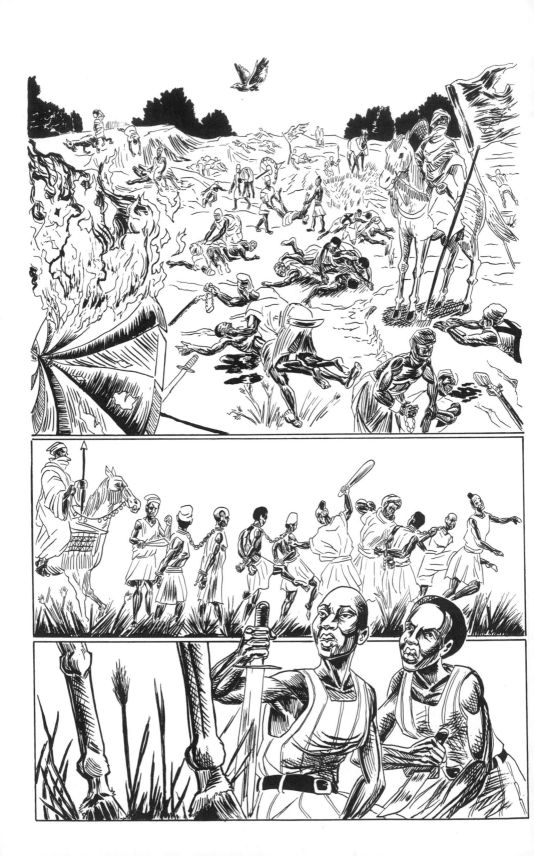

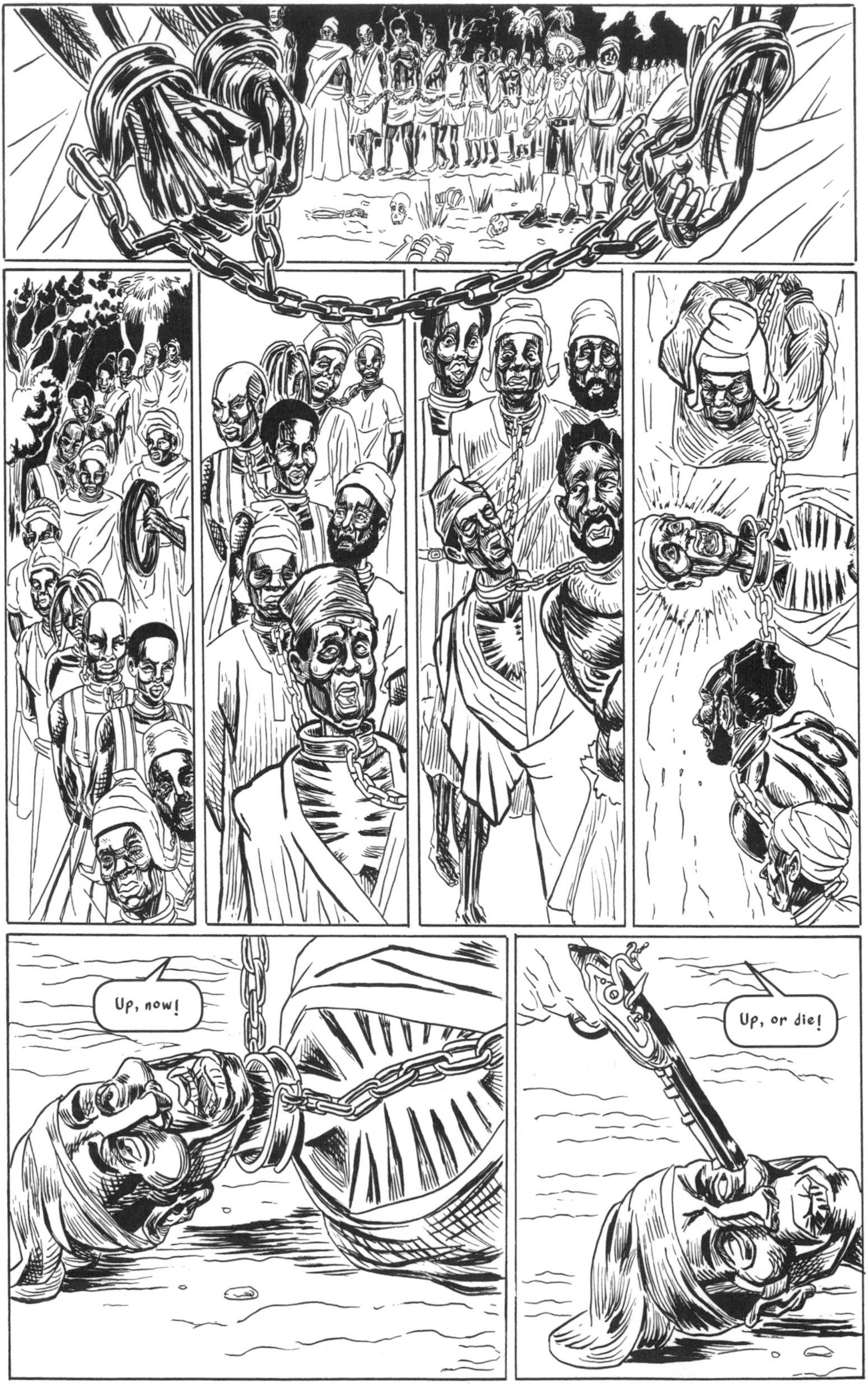
Up, now!
Up, or die!

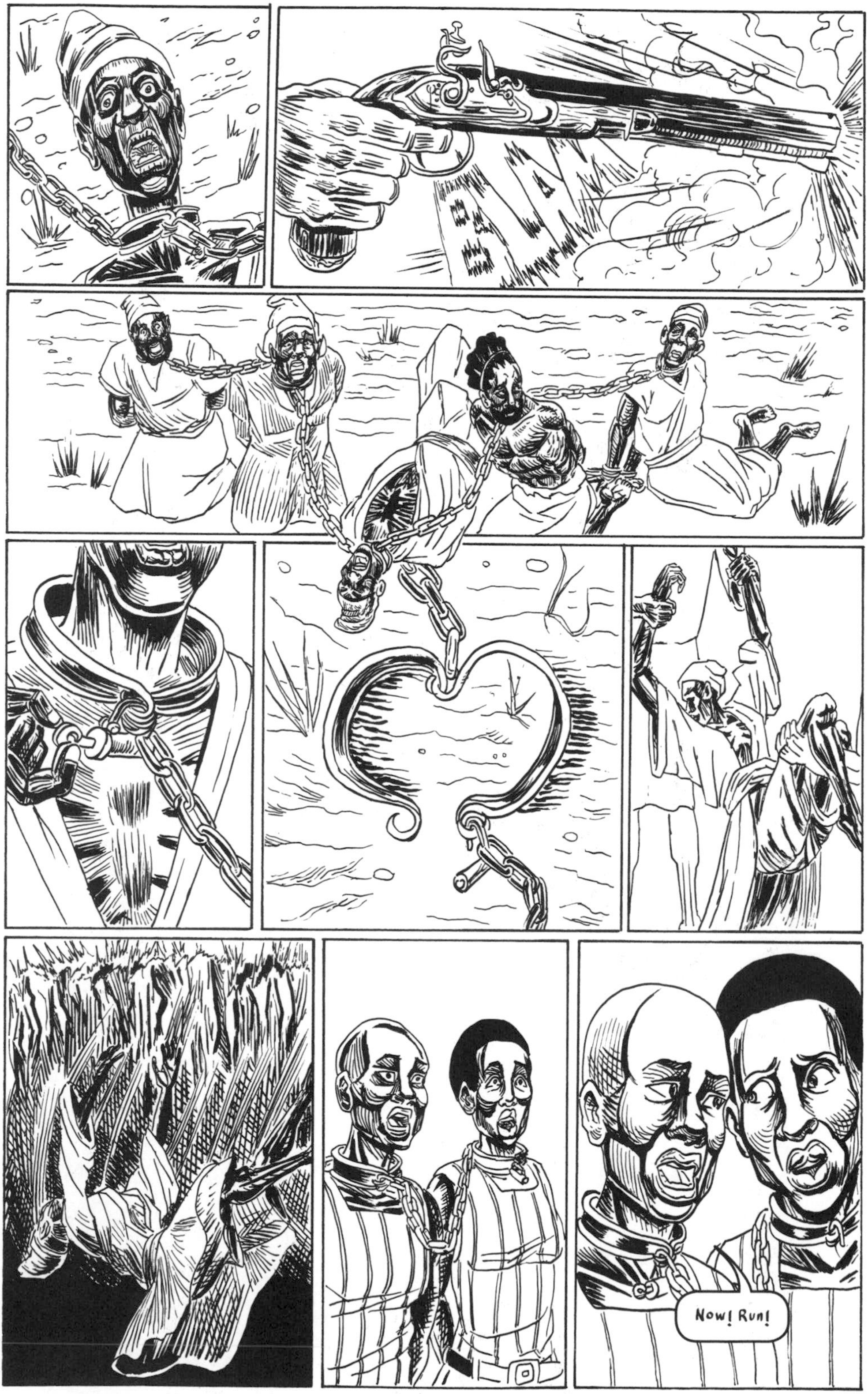
Now! Run!

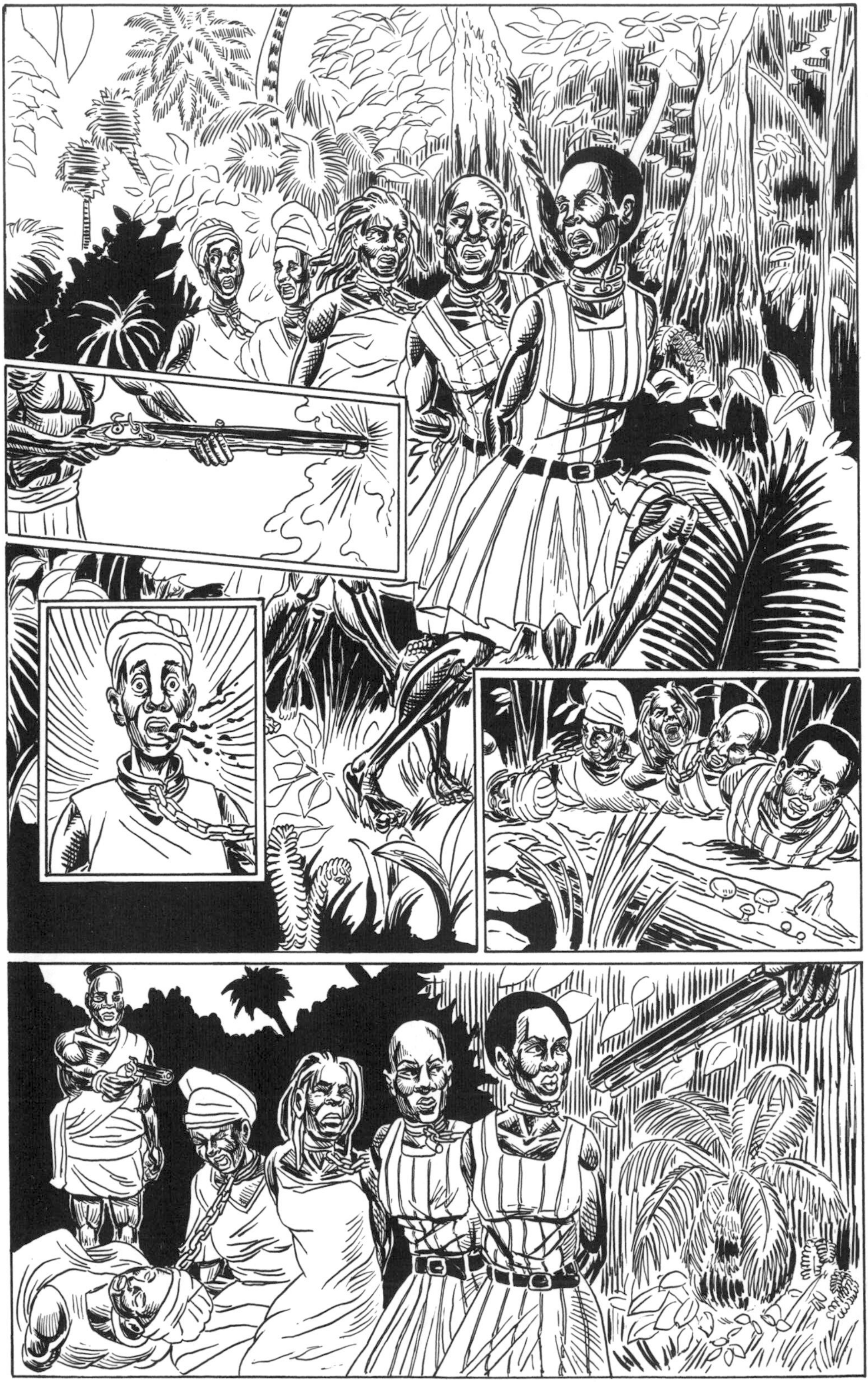

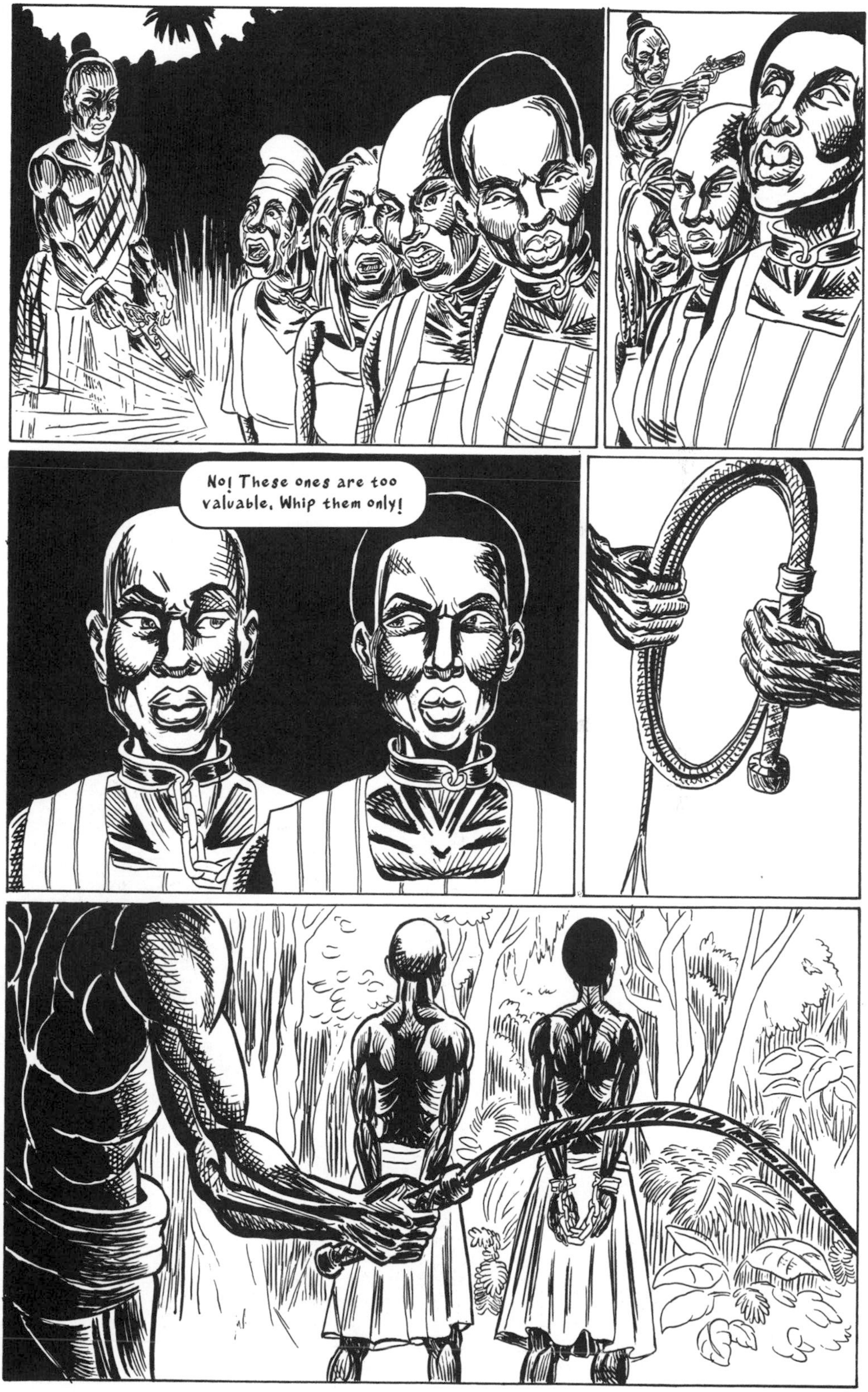
No! These ones are too valuable. Whip them only!

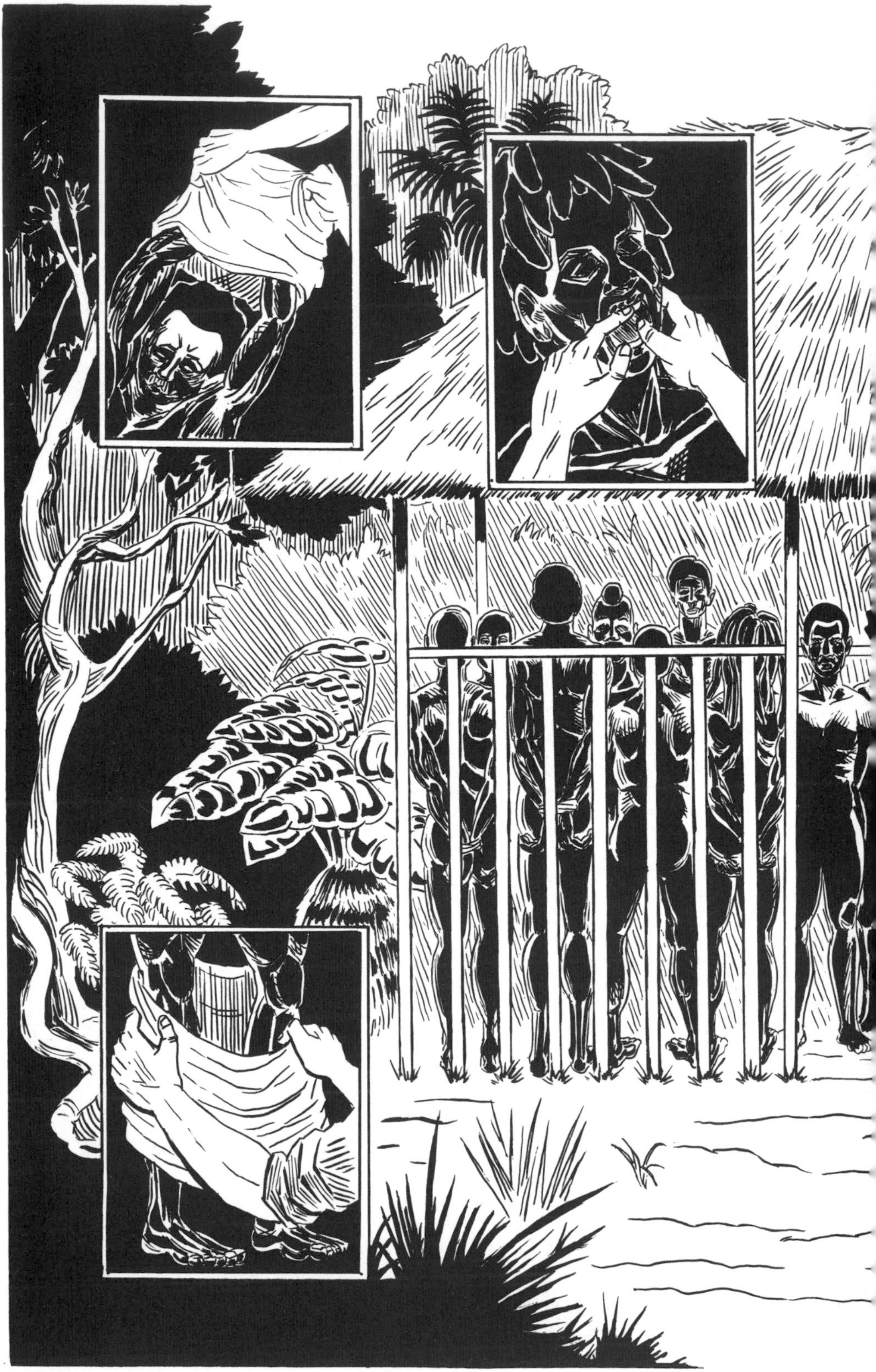

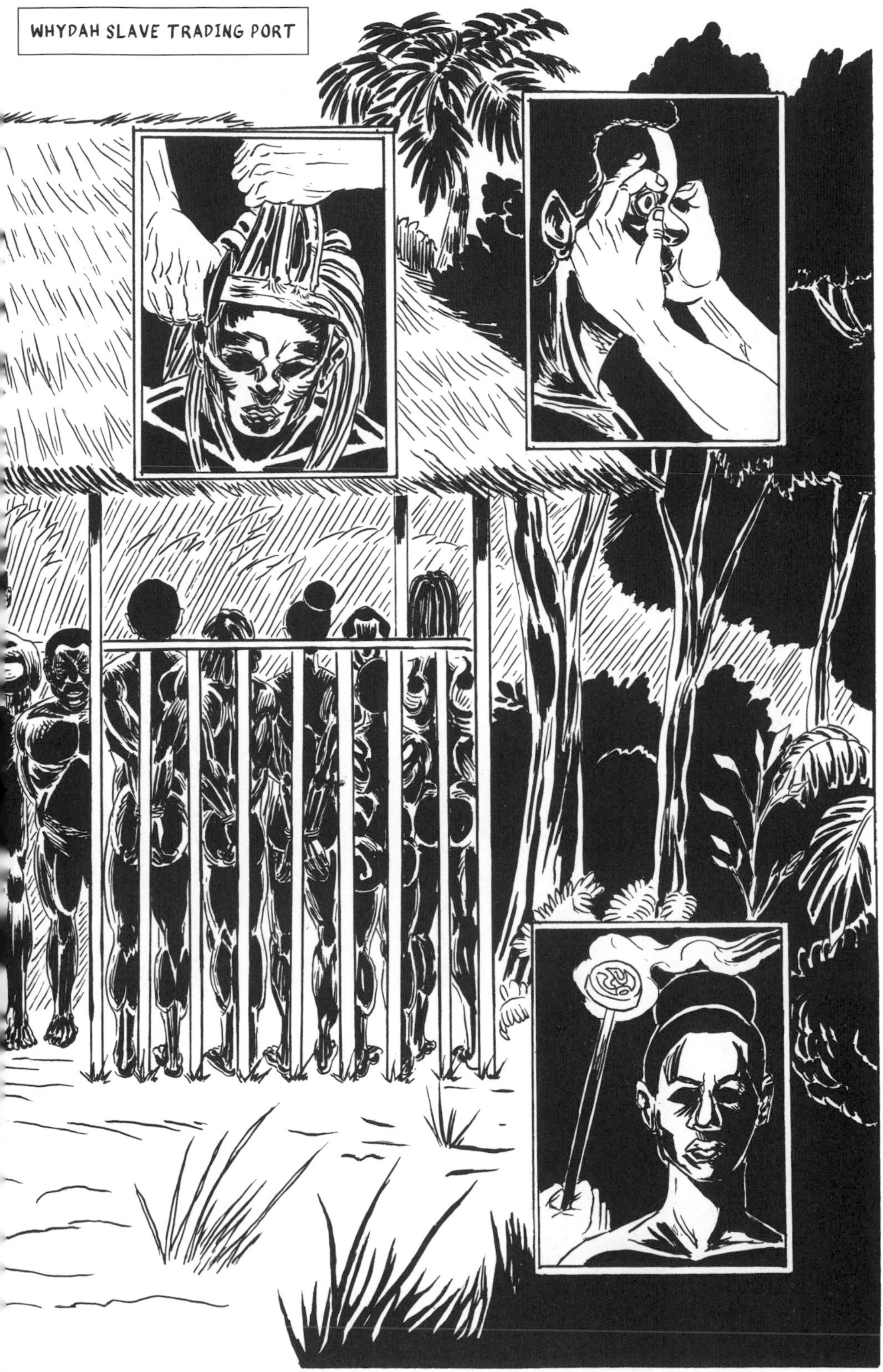
WHYDAH SLAVE TRADING PORT

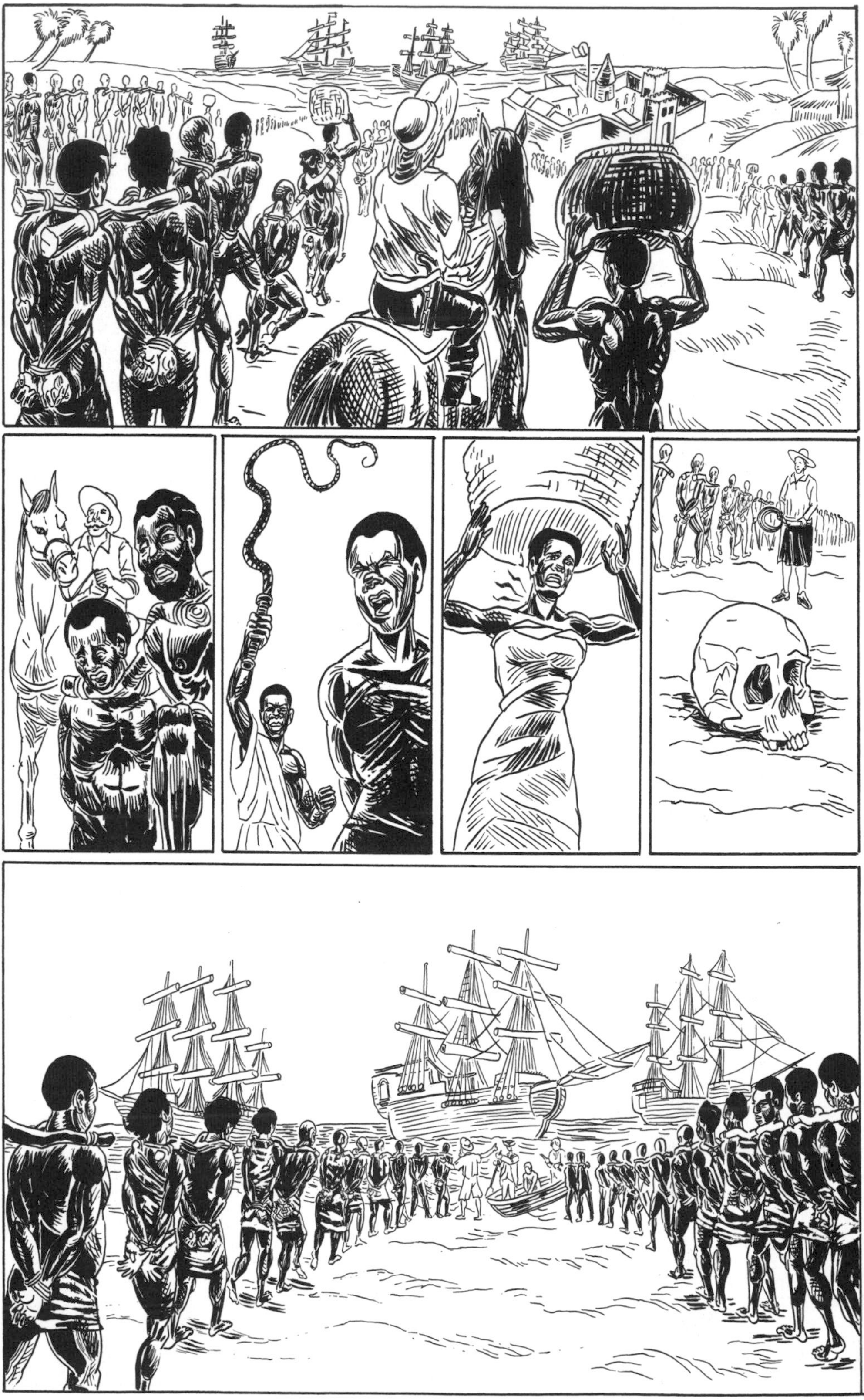

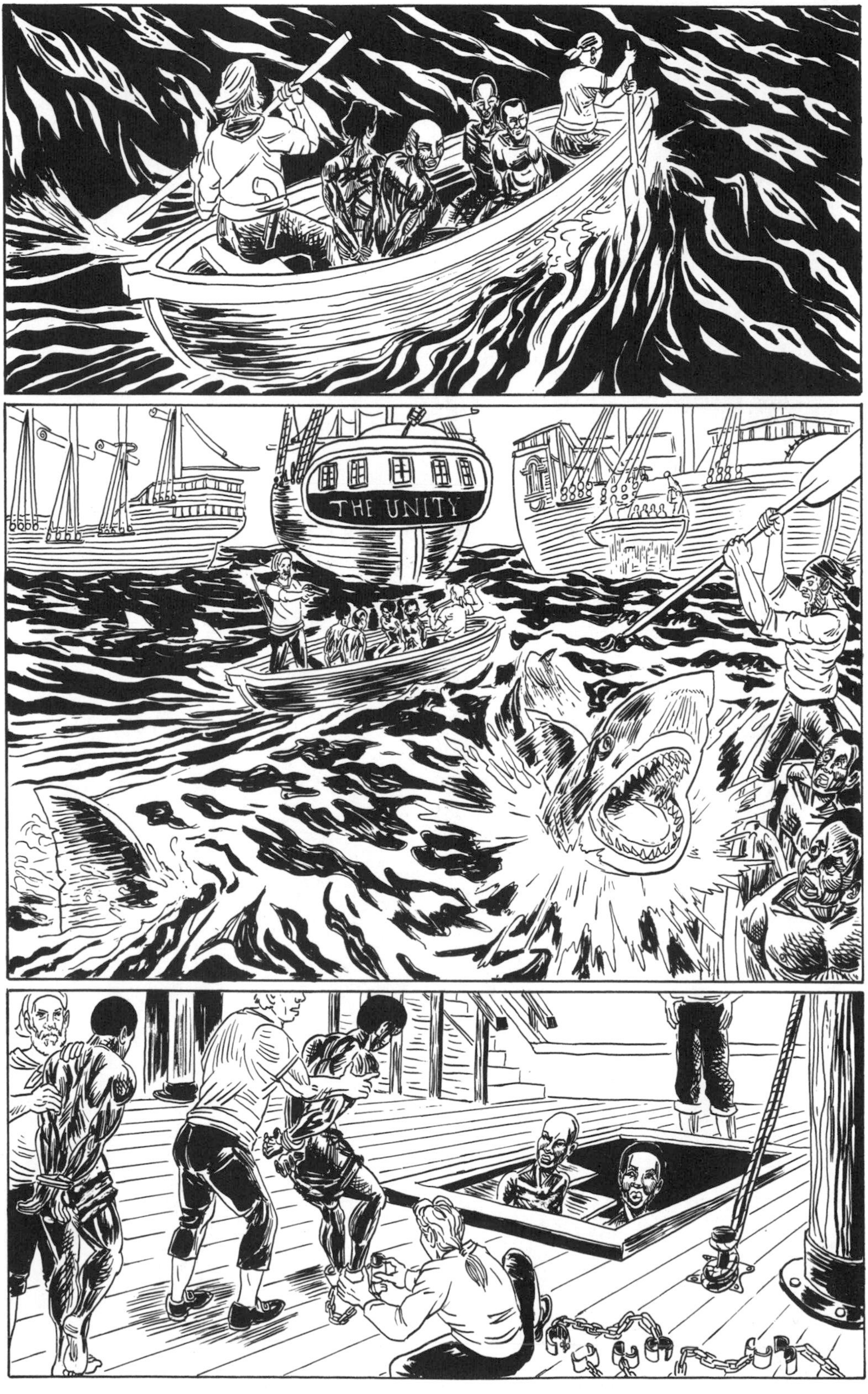
THE UNITY

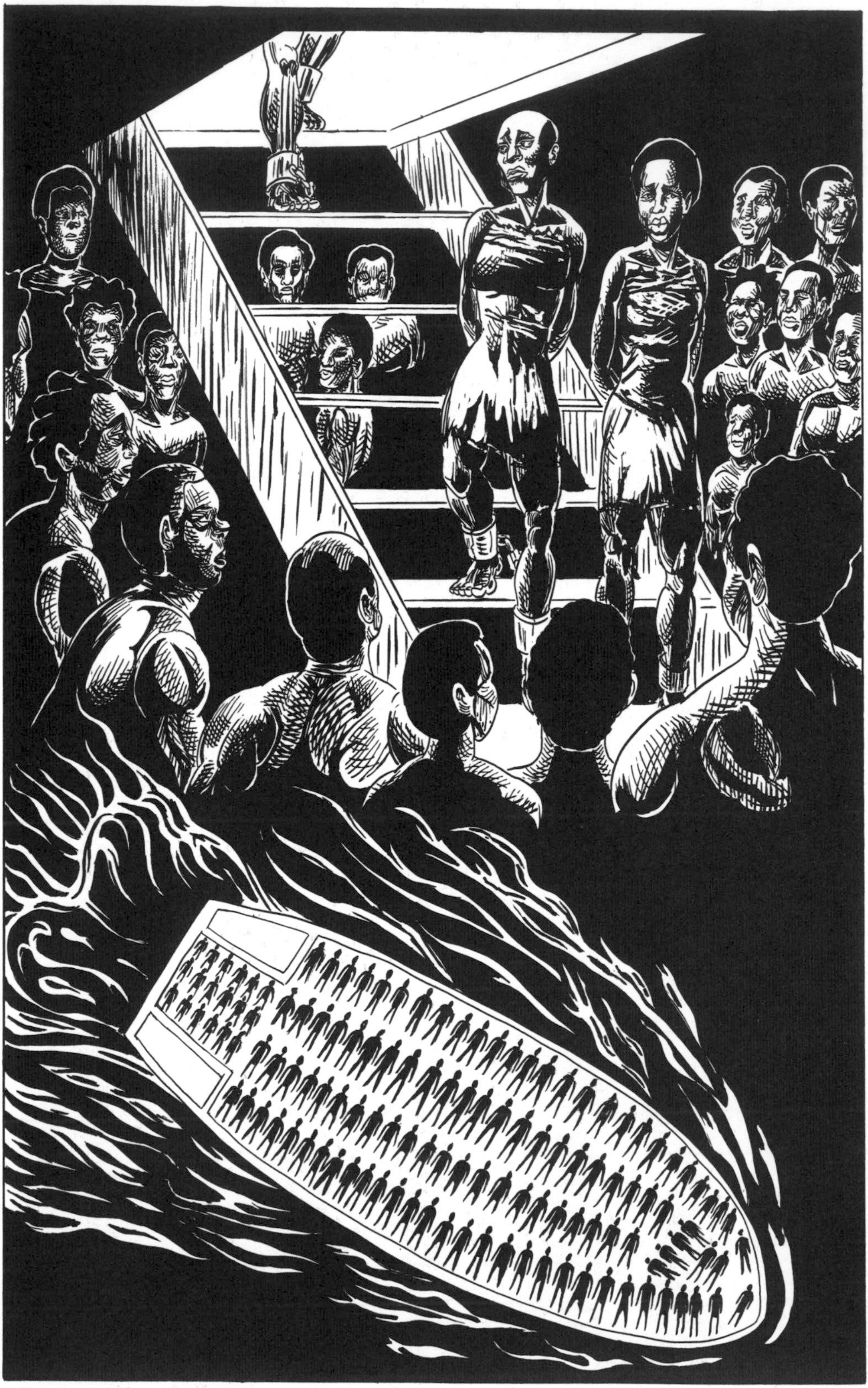

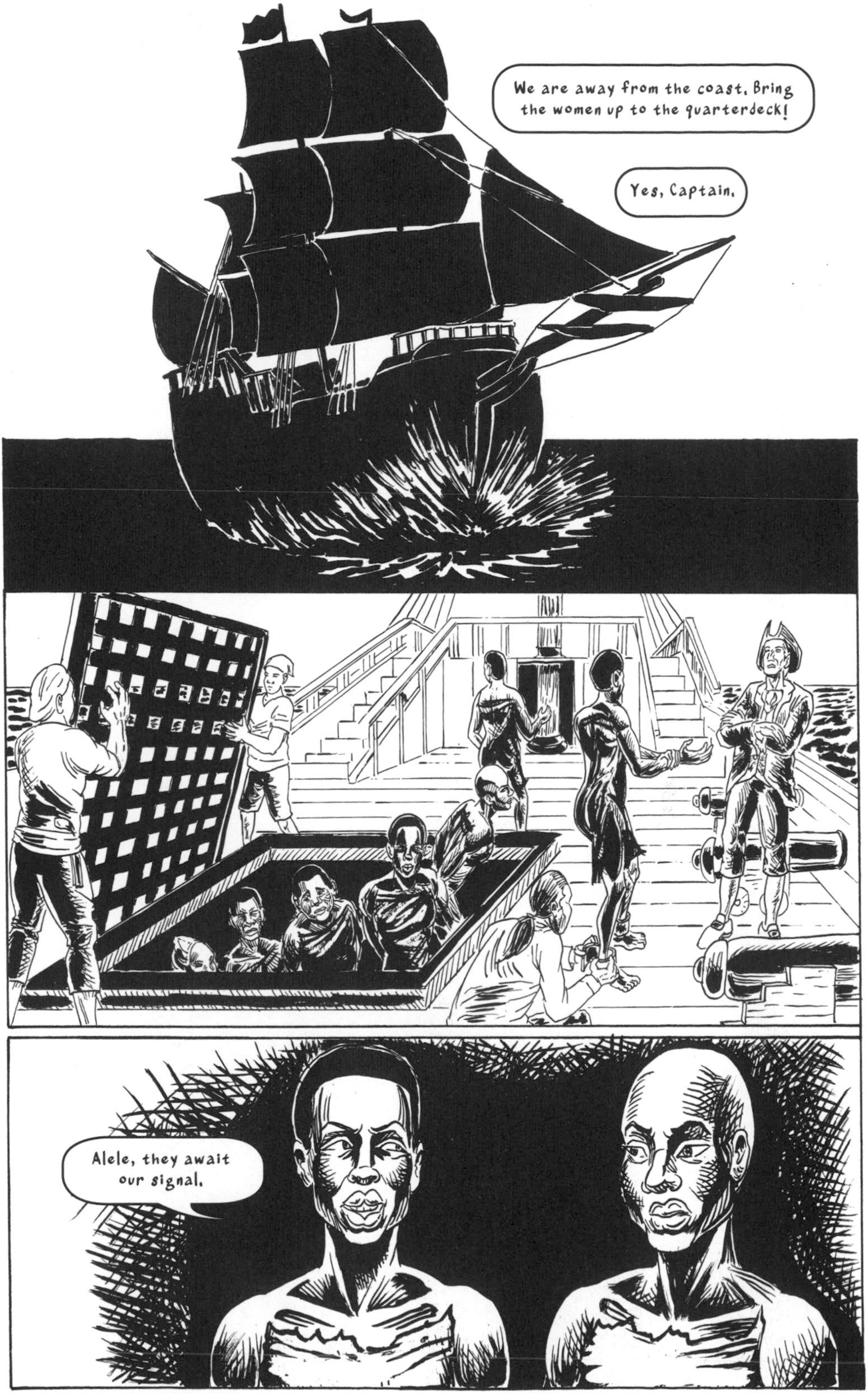
We are away from the coast. Bring the women up to the quarterdeck!
Yes, Captain.
Alele, they await our signal.

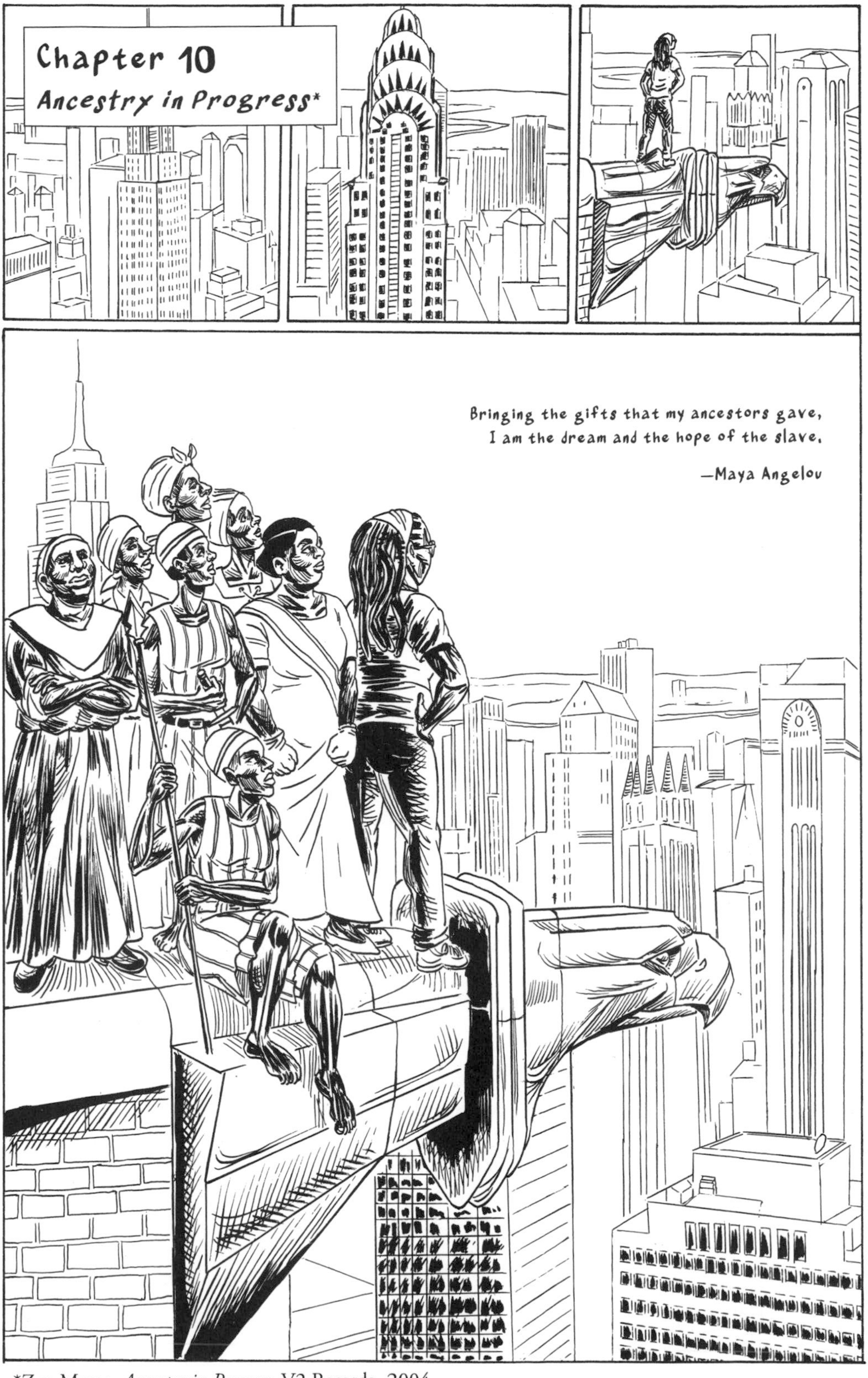
Chapter 10
Ancestry in Progress*
Bringing the gifts that my ancestors gave,
I am the dream and the hope of the slave.
—Maya Angelou

*Zap Mama, *Ancestry in Progress*, V2 Records, 2004.

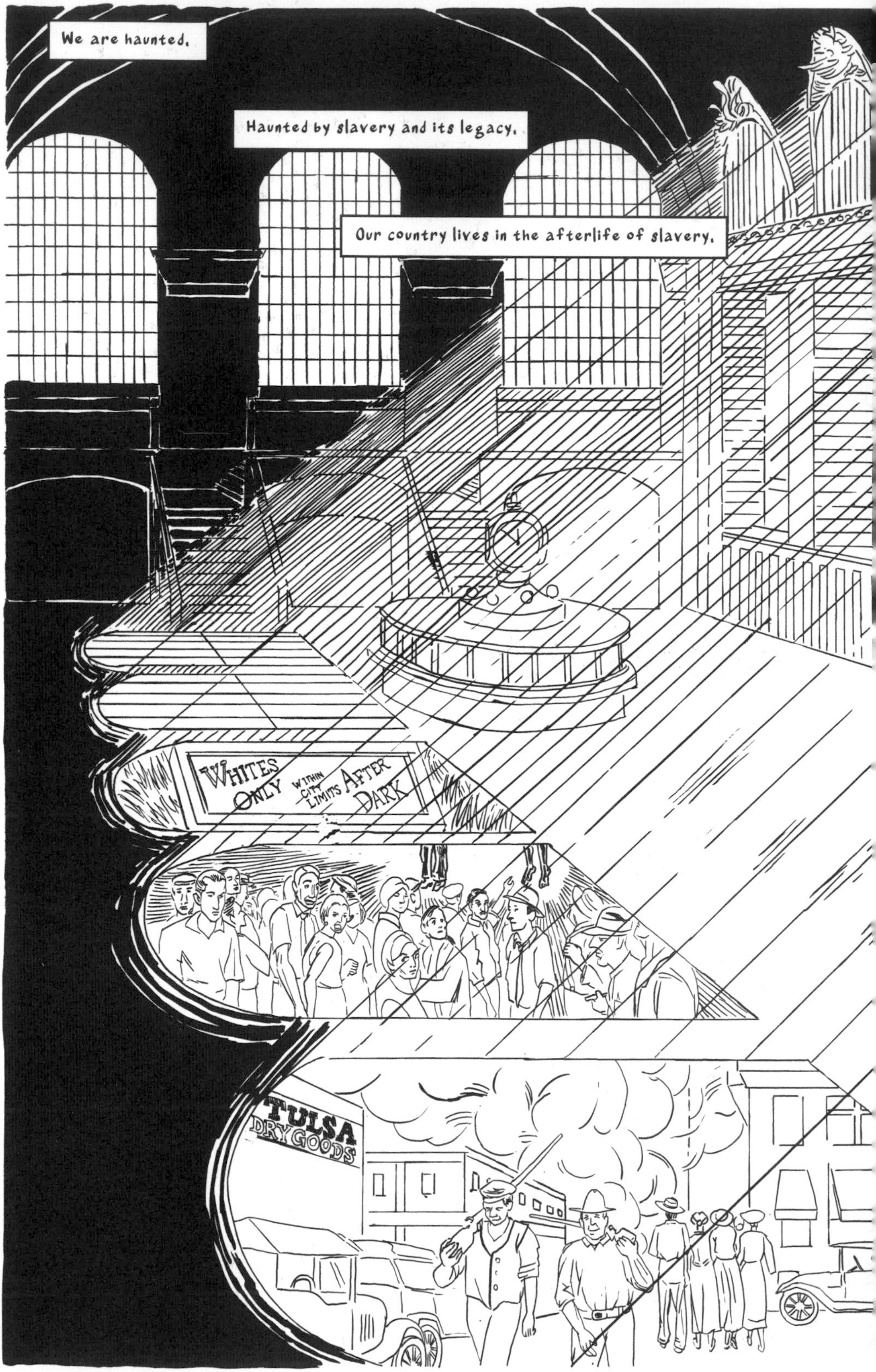
We are haunted.
Haunted by slavery and its legacy.
Our country lives in the afterlife of slavery.
WHITES ONLY WITHIN CITY LIMITS AFTER DARK
TULSA DRY GOODS

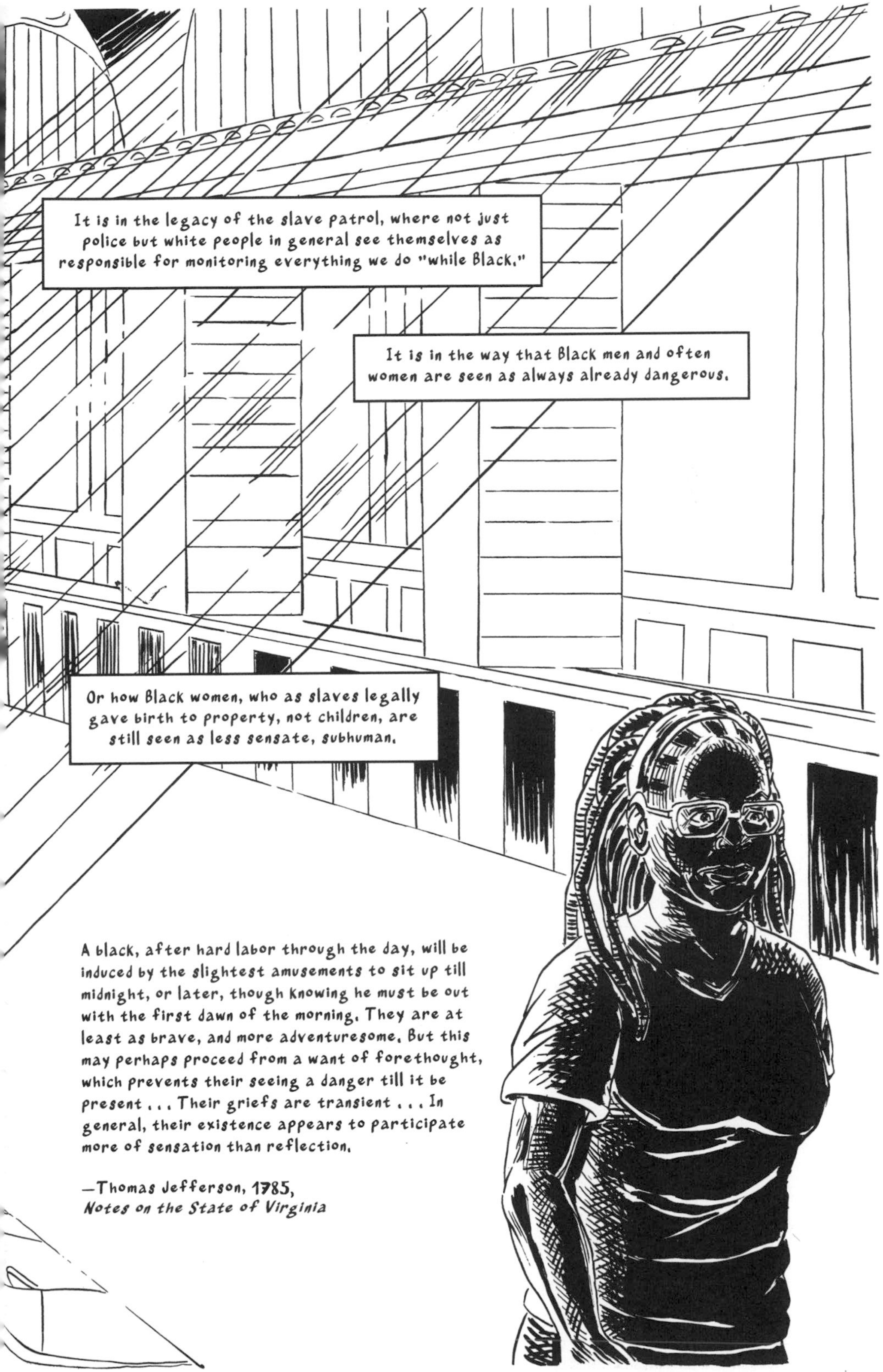

It is in the legacy of the slave patrol, where not just police but white people in general see themselves as responsible for monitoring everything we do "while Black."
It is in the way that Black men and often women are seen as always already dangerous.
Or how Black women, who as slaves legally gave birth to property, not children, are still seen as less sensate, subhuman.
A black, after hard labor through the day, will be induced by the slightest amusements to sit up till midnight, or later, though knowing he must be out with the first dawn of the morning. They are at least as brave, and more adventuresome. But this may perhaps proceed from a want of forethought, which prevents their seeing a danger till it be present . . . Their griefs are transient . . . In general, their existence appears to participate more of sensation than reflection.
—Thomas Jefferson, 1785,
Notes on the State of Virginia

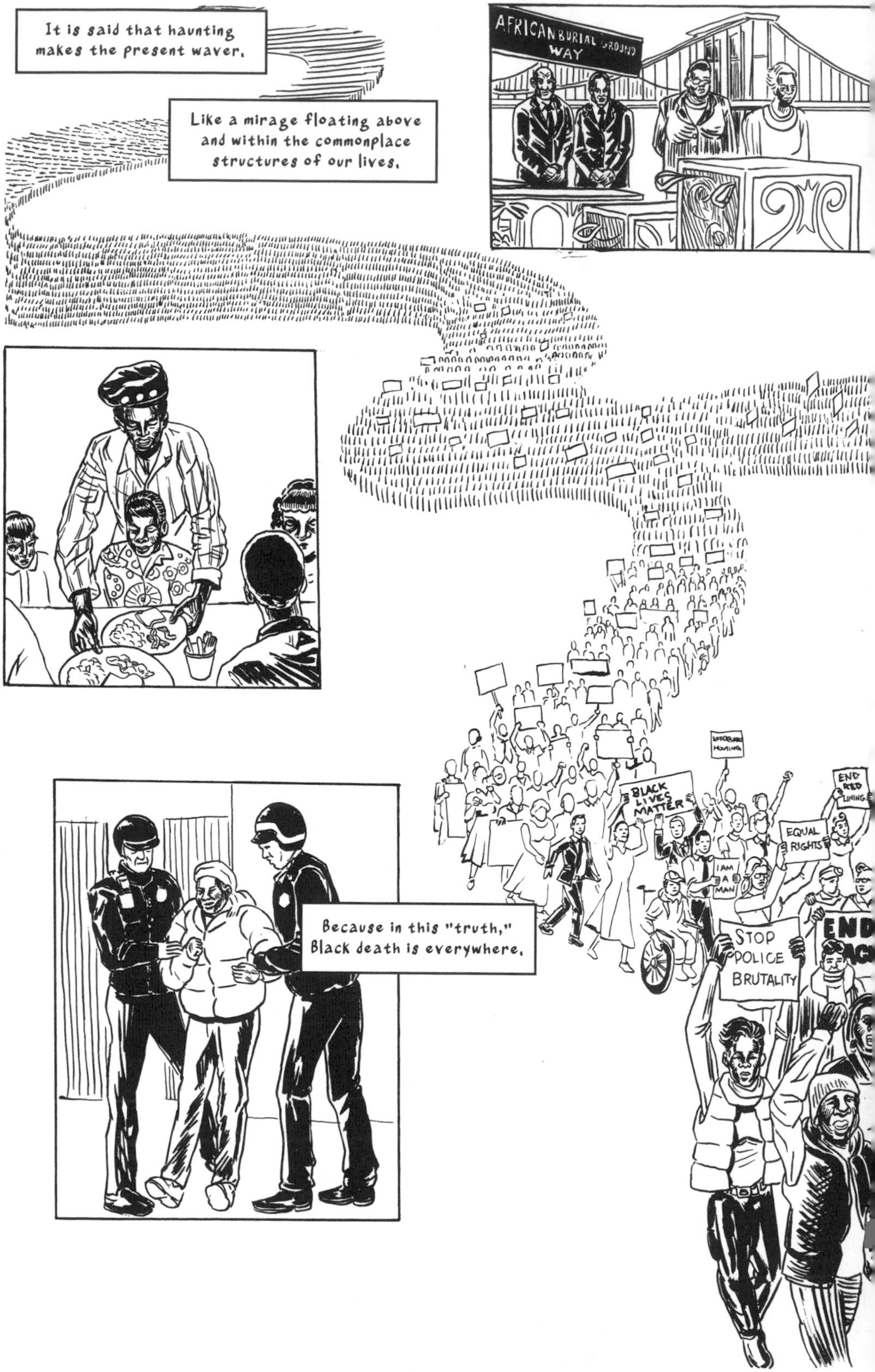
It is said that haunting makes the present waver.
Like a mirage floating above and within the commonplace structures of our lives.
AFRICAN BURIAL GROUND WAY
Because in this "truth," Black death is everywhere.
BLACK LIVES MATTER
AFFORDABLE HOUSING
END RED LINING
EQUAL RIGHTS
I AM A MAN
STOP POLICE BRUTALITY

We need to see the present waver, because the present we have been given to inhabit is impossible.

We use our haunting to question what is affirmed as the truth of our existence.

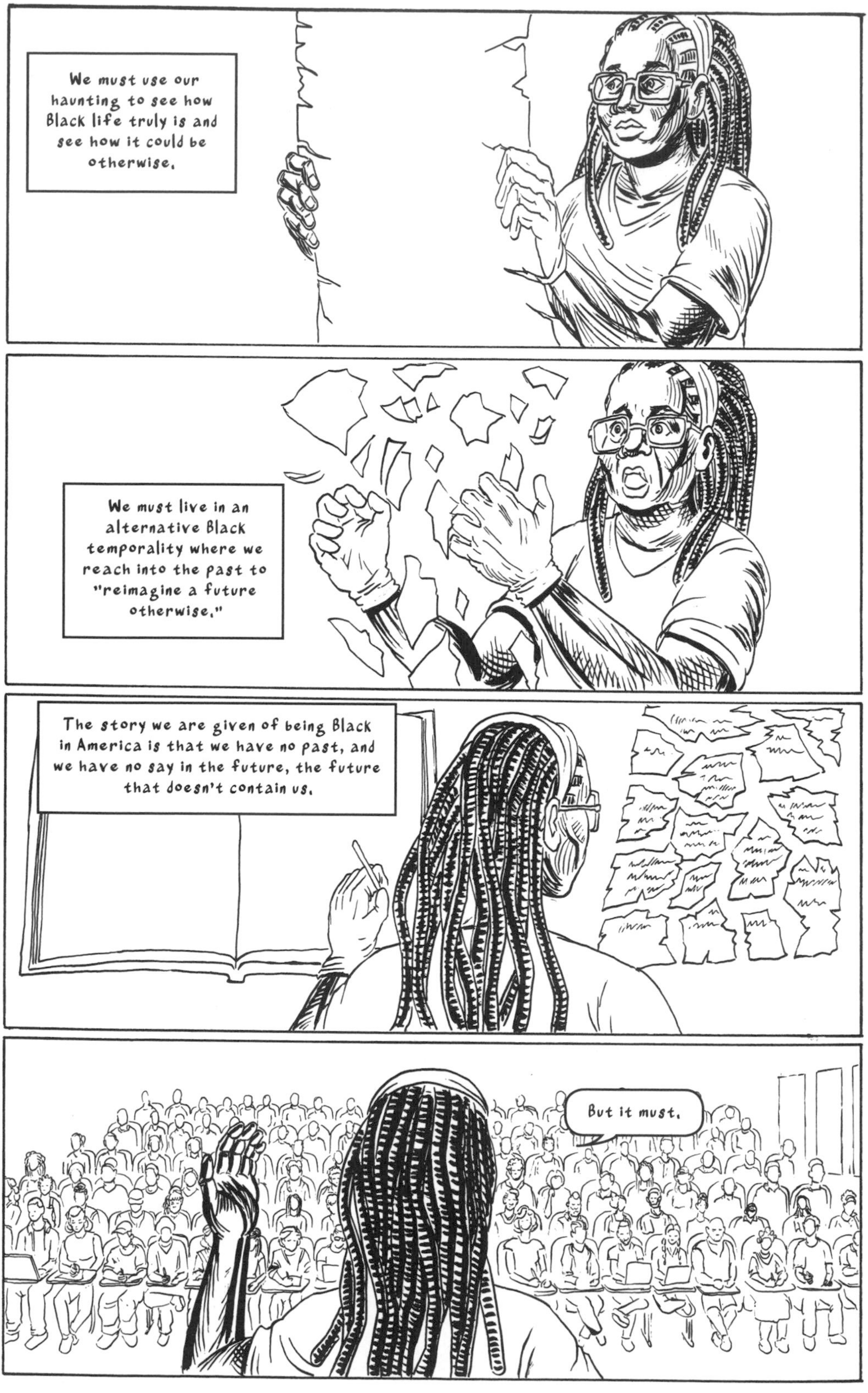
We must use our haunting to see how Black life truly is and see how it could be otherwise.
We must live in an alternative Black temporality where we reach into the past to "reimagine a future otherwise."
The story we are given of being Black in America is that we have no past, and we have no say in the future, the future that doesn't contain us.
But it must.

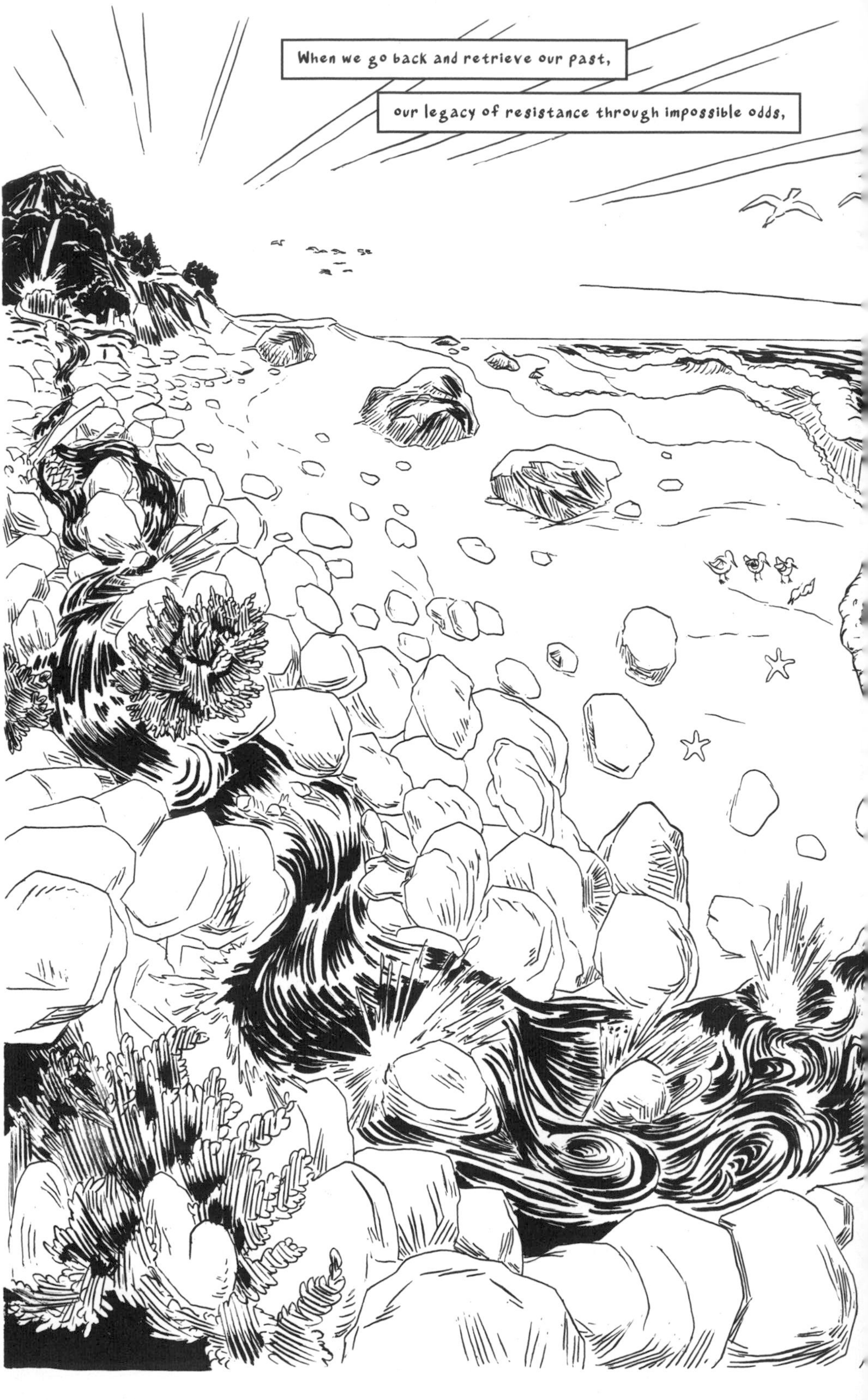
When we go back and retrieve our past,
our legacy of resistance through impossible odds,

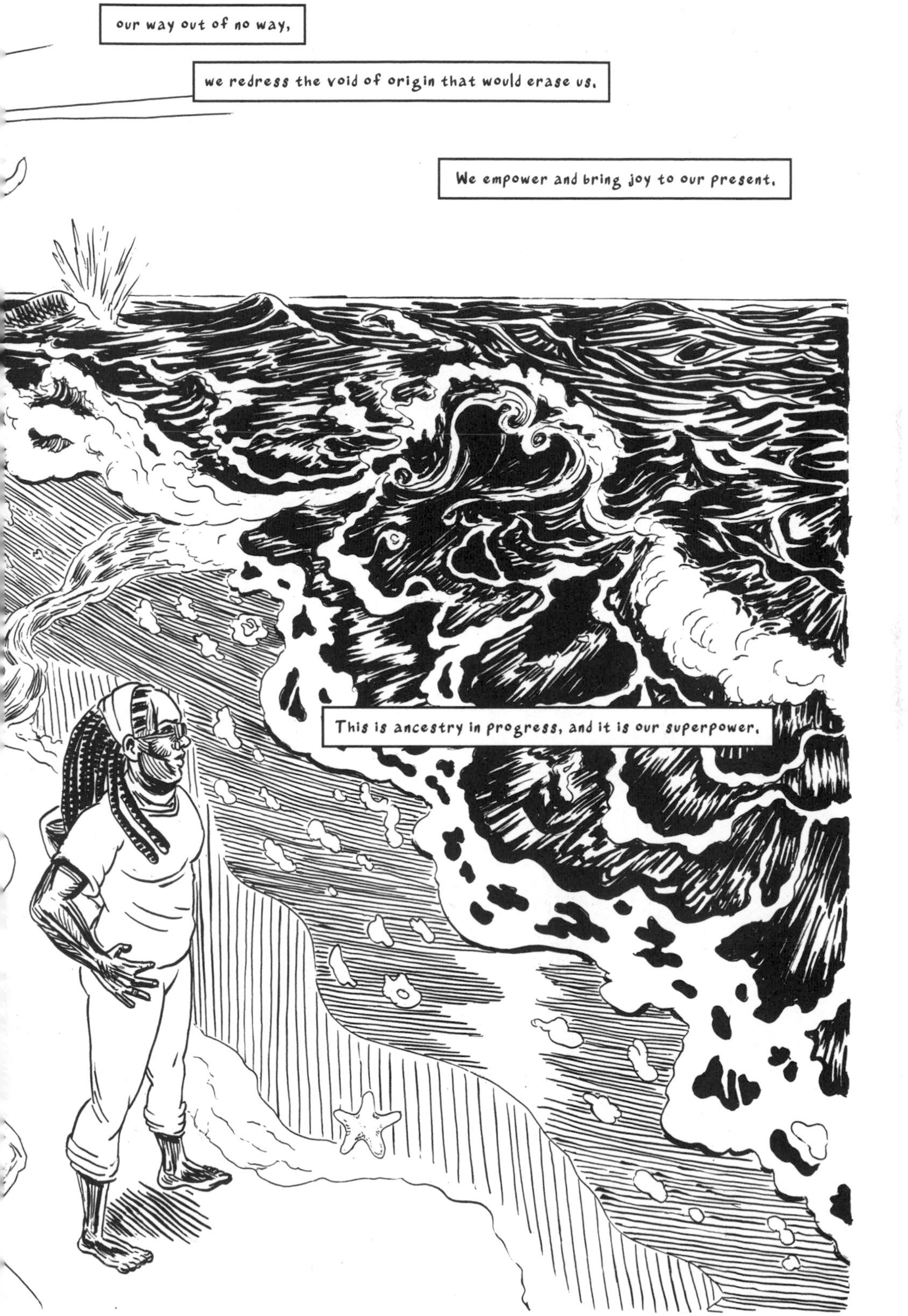
our way out of no way,
we redress the void of origin that would erase us.
We empower and bring joy to our present.
This is ancestry in progress, and it is our superpower.

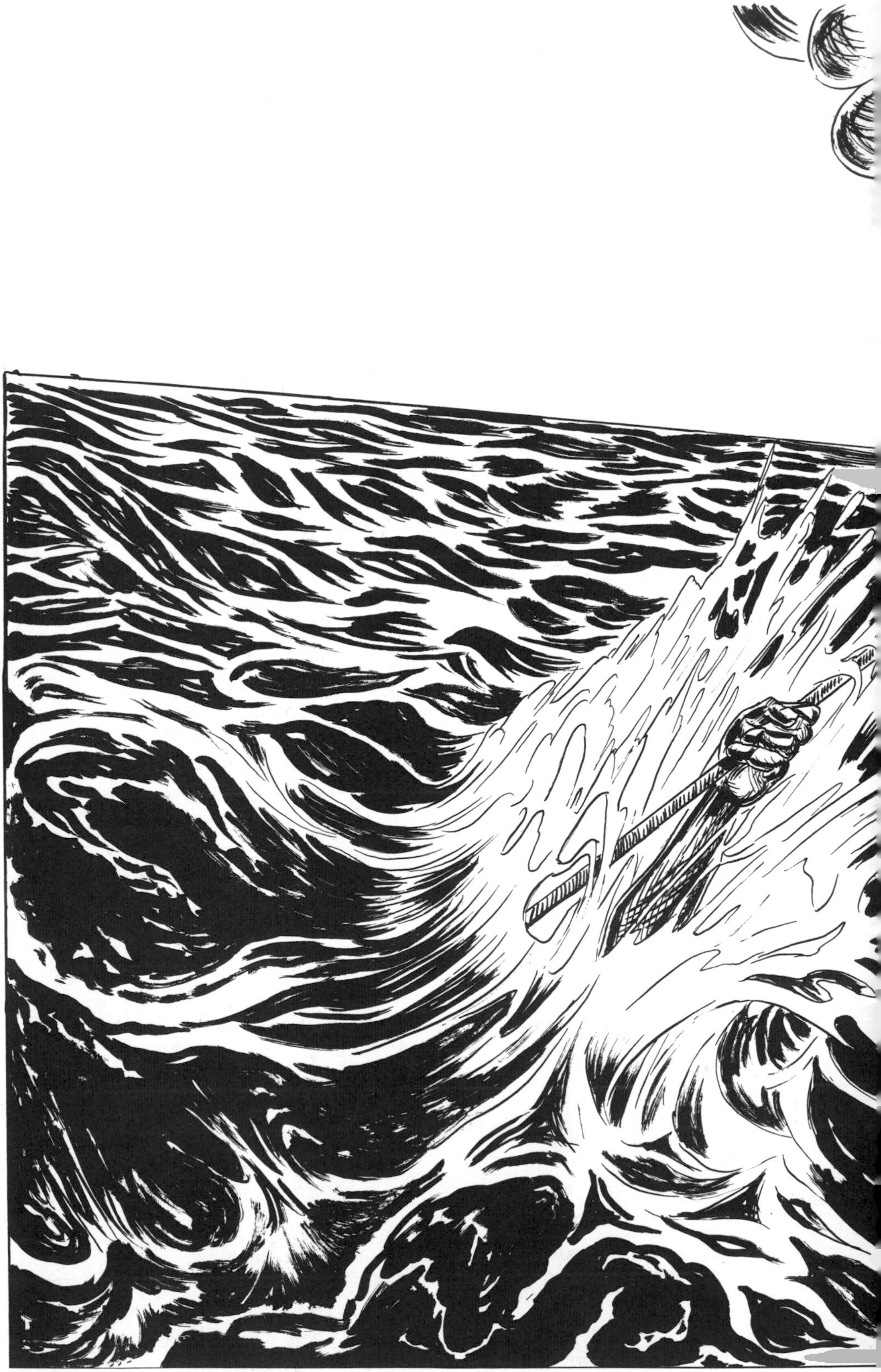

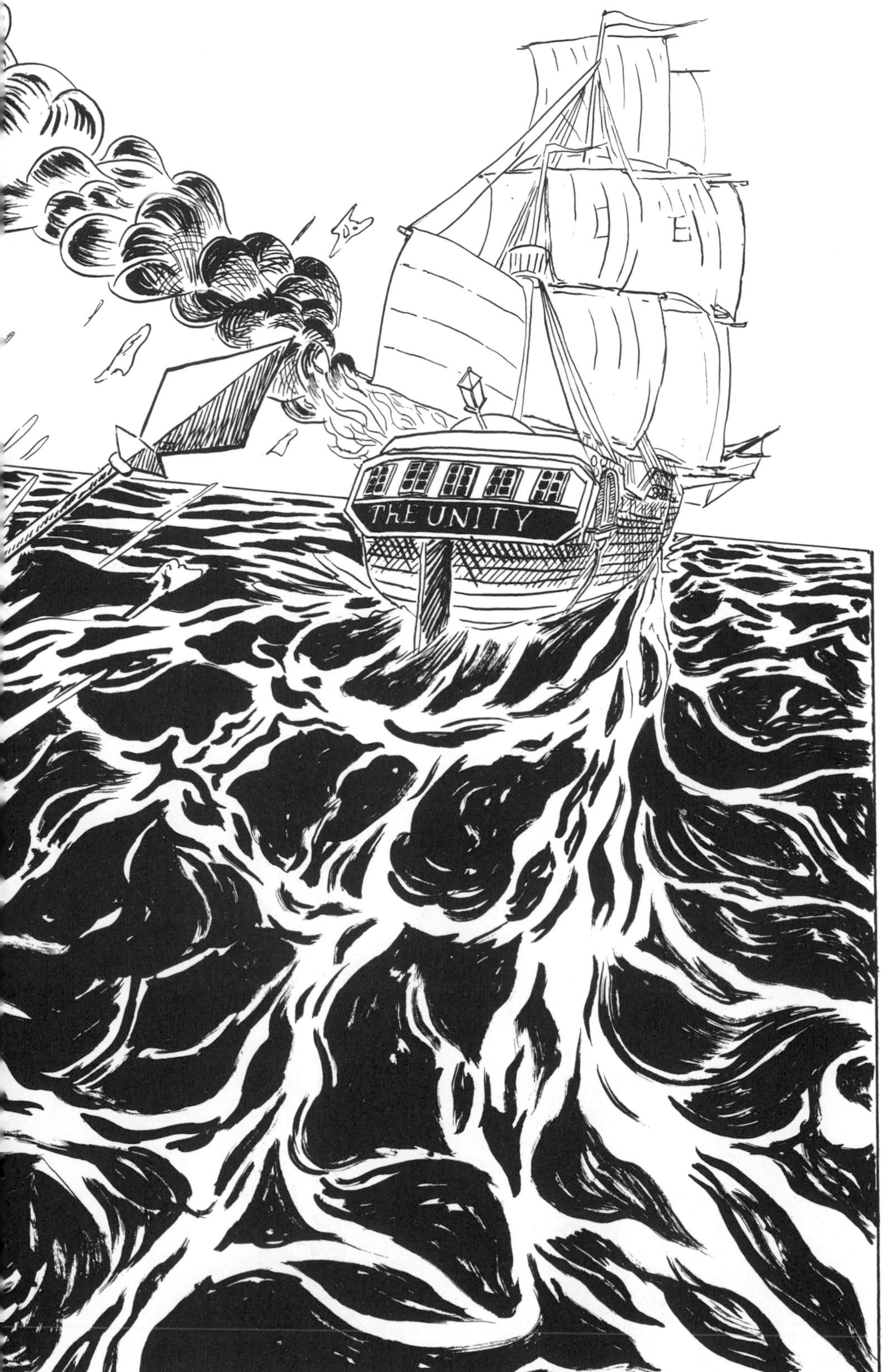
THE UNITY

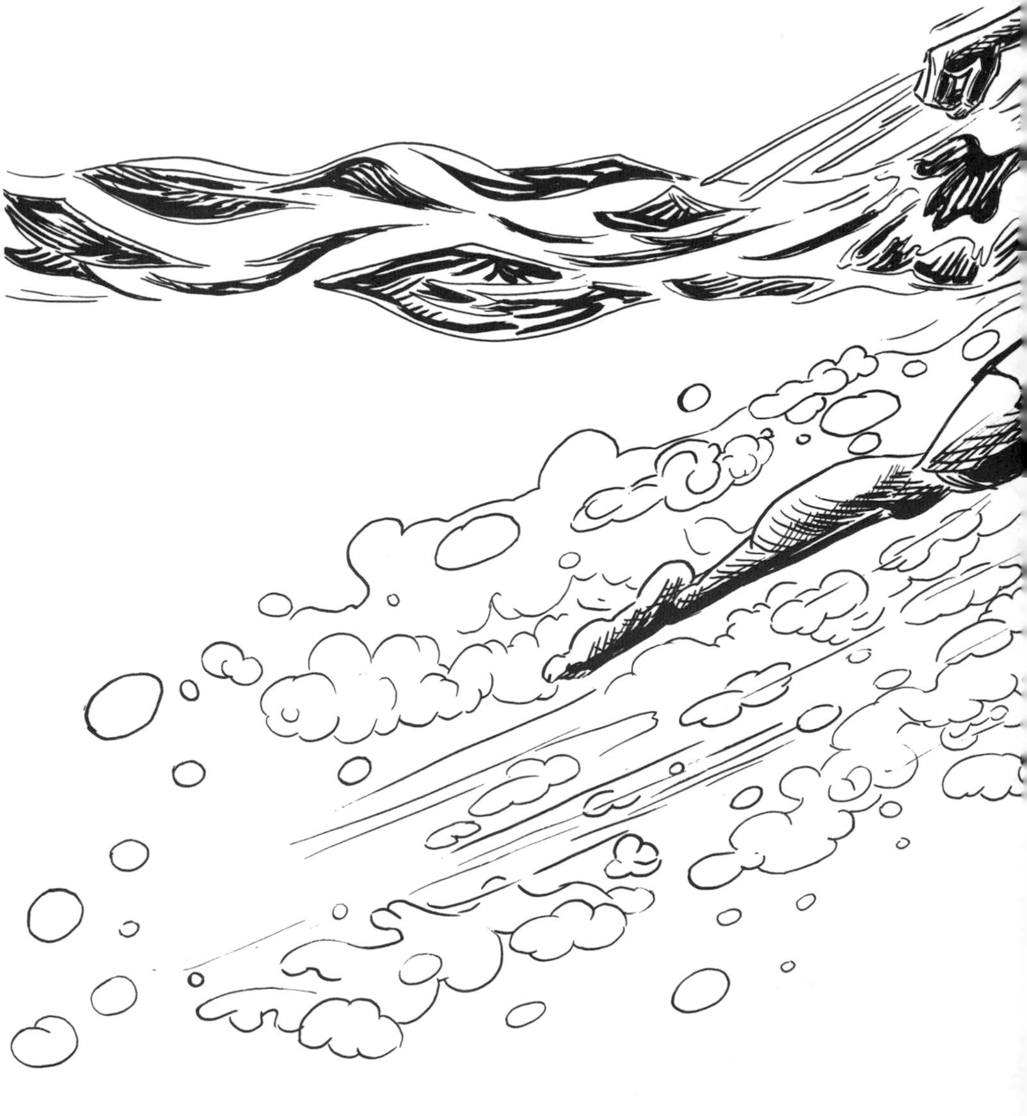

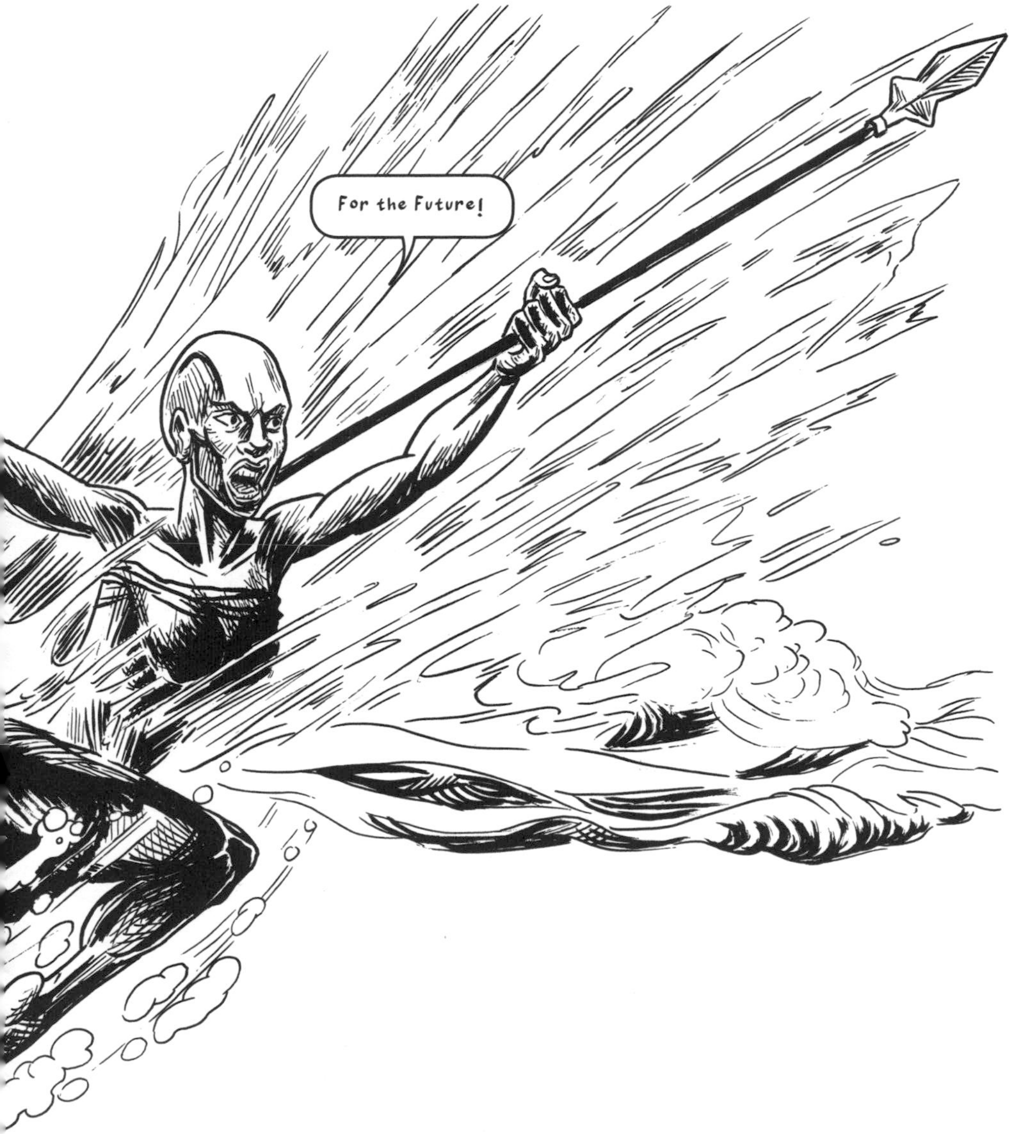
For the Future!

Acknowledgments

I wrote this book for my grandmother Harriet Thorpe Hall (1860–1927), for all the women who fought slavery, and for all of us living in its afterlife.

This book would not have happened without the support of Bea Hammond, my partner of thirty-two years. After the fourth time I was racist-fired from a professorship or teaching position, we agreed that I should step out of institutions of white supremacy, and Bea supported the family, giving me the time to figure out what was next for me. That turned out to be turning my dissertation and published articles into this graphic novel. Our son, Caleb, has helped me stay focused on what is truly important, even in the face of adversity. I also joyfully thank all of *Wake*'s supporters on Kickstarter, who gave me the resources to get a start on this book, and even more importantly, created buzz and visibility. And thanks Easton Smith for contacting the press about the Kickstarter campaign entirely on his own initiative. Special thanks here to Sara Ramirez for using their Twitter account to recommend my Kickstarter project to their gazillion followers.

Anjali Singh is my agent and my angel. Everyone thanks their agents in their acknowledgments, but Anjali picked up a somewhat abstract idea and taught me everything from how to write a book proposal to how to deal with a publishing auction. I literally knew nothing about this process and would never have thought in a million years that my passion project would be of interest to more than a handful of people. Anjali helped me see that this book was so much more than that and kept reminding me until I began to believe it. Thanks to Tananarive Due and John Jennings for connecting me to Anjali. I had the honor of Anjali calling me to say she wanted to represent me, and ever since she has fought for me and this project like a mother lion. And she even responds to my texts on weekends.

I want to thank my friend Kate Savage, who helped me think about this project in its pre-infancy, and for suggesting I be a character in this book. Kate also connected me to Hugo Martínez, who has been a diligent, thorough, and brilliant artist to work with. Hugo, your art has brought this work to life. And thanks to both Vita Ayala and Jason Little, who helped me understand how to write a graphic novel script. Deep thanks go to Sarula Bao and Caroline Brewer, who joined Team *Wake* right after it was picked up by S&S and managed pre-production. They held my hand and gave me confidence as I fumbled in the dark, trying to shift from an academic writer to a visual writer. And special thanks to Sarah Beth Hufbauer, who has been my dearest friend for over forty years, and has had my back through some very dark times. Thank you for helping me edit the final draft of this book in the midst of a pandemic over several five-hour phone calls when I had lost all sense of motivation and direction.

I also must thank Dawn Davis, the publisher and original editor of *Wake*. She believed in this project from jump and her edits made this a better book. And after Dawn left S&S, Carina Guiterman smoothly stepped in as editor, shepherding me and this book through the dizzying publishing process with the help of Chelcee Johns and Lashanda Anakwah. Thanks also to Kayley Hoffman for proofreading, Jon Evans for copyediting, and Morgan Hart, the production editor. Brianna Scharfenberg of publicity and Leila Siddiqui of marketing joined Team *Wake* with amazing enthusiasm for the work and patience with me as I kept forgetting which of them was in charge of what.

Donna Haraway, my feminist theory professor and dissertation advisor, has supported my academic work on women in slave revolts in so many ways, continuously, even fifteen years after receiving my PhD. A rare and generous advocate, her belief in the importance of this work helped me stay on course.

Finally I want to acknowledge my parents. My mother, Gwendolyn Midlo Hall, for showing me that being a historian can have a profound impact on the world. My father, Harry Haywood (1898–1985), for telling me stories of my grandmother, giving me great books to read at an early age, and showing me through lived example how to be brave and proud in the face of constant white supremacist violence—and to never give up the fight.

—Rebecca Hall

For this incredible opportunity, I thank Dr. Rebecca Hall. Also Kate Savage, our Kickstarter supporters, Leah Champagne, Jesse Moss, Dan Brawner, Gene Menerat, Brett Thompson, Luke Howard, Mike Vulpes, Bob Snead. Michael Lapinski, Sally Richardson, Kalli Padget, Erika Witt, Jonah Quinn, and Fernando Lopez.

—Hugo Martínez

Selected Primary Sources

1712 Revolt

Boston News-Letter, April 7–12, 1712.

Coroner's Inquest of William Asht, April 9, 1712. Coroner's Inquest of Augustus Grassett, April 9, 1712. Misc. MSS. NYC, Box 4, Manuscripts Collection, New-York Historical Society.

Coroner's Inquest of Adrian Hooglant, April 9, 1712. New York Public Library Manuscripts and Archives.

Governor Robert Hunter. Letters to the Lords of Trade. Public Records Office, London, CO5 1091.

Minutes of the Privy Council, 1712. Public Records Office, London, PC2/A84.

Minutes of the Common Council of the City of New York, 1675–1776. New York: Dodd, Mead, 1905.

Minutes of the Supreme Court of Judicature, 1712. Pp. 399–427. New York City Municipal Archives.

Minutes of the Quarter Sessions, 1694–1731. Pp 214–241. New York City Municipal Archives.

O'Callaghan, E. B. *The Documentary History of the State of New-York.* Albany: Weed, Parsons, 1850.

———. *Documents Relative to the Colonial History of New York.* Albany: Weed, Parsons, 1855.

———.*Calendar of New York Colonial Commissions, 1680–1770.* New York: The New-York Historical Society, 1929.

Philipse, Adolphus. Will of Adolphus Philipse. Manuscripts Division Collection, New-York Historical Society.

The Laws of His Majesties Colony of New York. London: William Bradford, 1719.

Van Dam, Rip. Inventory of the Estate of Rip Van Dam, 1749. Misc. MSS. NYC, Manuscripts Collection, New-York Historical Society.

1708 Revolt

Boston News-Letter, February 10, 1708; February 1623, 1708.

Lord Cornbury. Letter to the Board of Trade, February 10, 1708. In *Documents Relative to the Colonial History of the City of New York*, E. B. O'Callaghan, p. 39. Albany: Weed, Parsons, 1855.

Riker, James. Papers. New York Public Library, Manuscripts and Archives.

Town Minutes of Newtown. New York: Historical Records Survey, 1940.

Slave Ship Sources

Atlantic Slave Trade Database, https://www.slavevoyages.org/voyage/database.

Bandinel, James. *Some Account of the Trade in Slaves from Africa as Connected with Europe and America.* London: Longman, Brown, 1842.

Burton, Richard. *A Mission to Gelele, King of Dahomey.* New York: Praeger Publishers, 1966.

Brooke, Richard. *Liverpool as it was During the Last Quarter of the Eighteenth Century.* P. 236. Liverpool: Liverpool Publishing House, 1853.

Donnan, Elizabeth. *Documents Illustrative of the History of the Slave Trade to America.* 4 vols. New York: Octagon Books, 1965.

Hair, Paul, ed. *Barbot on Guinea: The Writings of Jean Barbot on West Africa, 1678–1712.* 2 vols. London: The Hakluyt Society, 1992.

Hastings, Hugh. *Ecclesiastical Records, State of New York, Vol. III.* Albany: J. B. Lyon Company, 1902.

House of Lords Records Office. Misc. slave ship captains' logs and surgeons' logs. London.

Snelgrave, Captain William. *A New Account of Some Parts of Guinea and the Slave-Trade, Slavery Series, No. 11.* London: James, John, and Paul Knapton, 1734.

The Unity, log of, 1769-1771, Earle Family Papers, Merseyside Maritime Museum, Liverpool, D/EARLE/1/4 (no pagination).

For a complete bibliography of sources see rebhallphd.org